MW00831565

Poetry's Touch

Poetry's Touch

On Lyric Address

WILLIAM WATERS

Cornell University Press / Ithaca and London

First published 2003 by Cornell University Press

Printed in the United States of America

Library of Congress Cataloging-in-Publication Data

Waters, William (William Addison)
   Poetry's touch : on lyric address / William Waters.
      p. cm.
Includes bibliographical references and index.
   ISBN 0-8014-4120-X (cloth : alk. paper)
   1. Lyric poetry—History and criticism.   2. Point of view (Literature)
I. Title.
   PN1361.W38 2003
   809.1'4—dc21   2003005639

Cornell University Press strives to use environmentally responsible
suppliers and materials to the fullest extent possible in the publishing
of its books. Such materials include vegetable-based, low-VOC inks
and acid-free papers that are recycled, totally chlorine-free, or partly
composed of nonwood fibers. For further information, visit our website
at www.cornellpress.cornell.edu.

Cloth printing   10 9 8 7 6 5 4 3 2 1

To Mike—

What shall we say, shall we call it by a name
As well to count the angels dancin' on a pin

and to Anne
and to my parents

Contents

Acknowledgments

MANY PEOPLE'S READINGS are folded into this book. First among these readers is Anne Nesbet. Without our seminars amid the granite of the High Sierra backcountry, to say nothing of twenty-odd years of precious fellowship, this book would not be. Other colleagues and friends who commented on the full text, improving it very much, are Christopher Ricks, Johannes Wich-Schwarz, and Mike Malone. I owe a great debt to Jonathan Culler and another reader for Cornell University Press, whose reports on the manuscript were exemplars of careful, just, and constructive criticism. To Stephen Esposito I am obliged for help with the Greek epitaph in chapter 3. The book's last chapter, concerning hands, benefited from many readers' suggestions, including especially those of Marshall Brown, George Hoffmann, Garrett Stewart, Anne Ferry, David Ferry, Jeffrey Mehlman, and Ann Keniston. The counsel of Charles Altieri, Judith Ryan, Kenneth Weisinger, Claire Kramsch, and Eric Johannesson was foundational. Bernhard Kendler and Ange Romeo-Hall, my editors at Cornell University Press, have been models of responsiveness. I thank Amanda Heller, my copyeditor, for her high standards and skill. I cannot name or count the many other colleagues, students, and friends who over the years have inspired this or that phrase or turn of thought in the book, but I know I have depended on them all.

Work on this project was supported, at different stages, by the Woodrow Wilson Fellowship Foundation, the Boston University Humanities

Foundation, and (especially) the National Endowment for the Humanities. I am deeply grateful for their funding; and I thank Boston University for granting the leaves of absence in which I could write.

To my father I owe the love of words. I can't think what profounder debt I could carry: it is the core of joy in this work. My mother has sustained me unfailingly in loving ways beyond count; to the example of her good sense, generosity, and strength I credit just about everything.

This work is dedicated to Anne and to my parents, and to the one with whom all my words blessedly run out.

Acknowledgment is made for permission to reprint the following texts:

"At North Farm," from *A Wave*, by John Ashbery. Copyright © 1981, 1982, 1983, 1984 by John Ashbery. Reprinted by permission of Georges Borchardt, Inc., for the author. World rights excluding USA/Canada granted by Carcanet Press Ltd.

Reprinted by permission of Farrar, Straus and Giroux, LLC: "Insomnia" from *The Complete Poems 1927–1979* by Elizabeth Bishop. Copyright © 1979, 1983 by Alice Helen Methfessel.

Emily Dickinson's poems F 519, F 772, F 930, and F 1268 are reprinted by permission of the publishers and the Trustees of Amherst College from *The Poems of Emily Dickinson*, Ralph W. Franklin, ed., Cambridge, Mass.: The Belknap Press of Harvard University Press, copyright © 1998 by the President and Fellows of Harvard College. Copyright © 1951, 1955, 1979 by the President and Fellows of Harvard College.

William Fitzgerald's translation of Catullus 1, "Cui dono," is reprinted by permission of the University of California Press from *Catullan Provocations: Lyric Poetry and the Drama of Position*, by William Fitzgerald. Copyright © 1995 The Regents of the University of California.

"A Message from the Emperor" from *The Transformation and Other Short Stories* by Franz Kafka, trans. Malcolm Pasley (London: Penguin, 1992), p. 175, copyright © Malcolm Pasley, 1992 is reproduced by permission of Penguin Books Ltd.

"Wait" from *Mortal Acts, Mortal Words* by Galway Kinnell. Copyright © 1980 by Galway Kinnell. Reproduced by permission of Houghton Mifflin Company. All rights reserved.

"Epitaph," from *A Mask for Janus*, by W. S. Merwin (New Haven: Yale University Press, 1952) is reprinted by permission of The Wylie Agency, Inc., for the author.

"You're" from *Ariel* by Sylvia Plath copyright © 1961, 1962, 1963, 1964,

1965 by Ted Hughes. Reprinted by permission of HarperCollins Publishers Inc. and, outside the United States, by permission of Faber and Faber.

Reprinted by permission of North Point Press, a division of Farrar, Straus and Giroux, LLC: "In a Foreign Park" from *New Poems [1907]* by Rainer Maria Rilke, a bilingual edition translated by Edward Snow. Translation copyright © 1984 by Edward Snow. "Black Cat," "Lullaby," and "Snake-Charming" from *New Poems [1908]: The Other Part* by Rainer Maria Rilke, translated by Edward Snow. Translation copyright © 1987 by Edward Snow. "But if you'd try this" and "The way that bright planet, the moon" from *Uncollected Poems* by Rainer Maria Rilke, translated by Edward Snow. Translation copyright © 1996 by Edward Snow.

Jürgen Theobaldy's "Irgend etwas," from *Zweiter Klasse: Gedichte* (Berlin: Rotbuch, 1976), is reprinted and translated by permission of the poet.

A longer version of chapter 4 appeared in volume 2, number 2 of *Literary Imagination*, © 2000. Used by permission of the Association of Literary Scholars and Critics.

"This Is Just to Say" by William Carlos Williams, from *Collected Poems: 1909–1939*, Volume 1, copyright © 1938 by New Directions Publishing Corp. Used by permission of New Directions Publishing Corporation.

Introduction

TO WHOM does a poem speak? Do poems really communicate with those they address? Is reading poems like overhearing? Like intimate conversation? Like performing a script? In this book I pursue these questions by reading closely a selection of poems that say *you* to a human being, and by trying to describe the reading process as it encounters these instances of address. In the diverse poems I discuss here—poems not just addressing different categories of fictive and real persons but written in several different eras and languages—the address itself always becomes an axis of the poem's concern. The poem persistently revolves around, or thinks about, the contact that it is (or is not) making with the person to whom it is speaking.[1]

I have wanted to study this kind of lyric address because collectively such poems suggest a way of talking about poetry as a form of contact.[2]

---

1. I leave aside, as not raising the same questions, both apostrophe to nonhuman entities—houses, tigers, the age—and most poems addressing groups of people.

Readers interested in the *you* of advertising and recruitment posters ("Uncle Sam wants YOU") should see Spitzer's 1949 essay "American Advertising" (350–51). Spitzer stresses the ambiguities permitted by the English *you*, which can correspond to five distinct forms in some other languages (singular and plural familiar and polite, as well as the impersonal pronoun). French and Russian poems frequently address a polite *vous* or *vy*, whereas the formal *Sie* is rare in German poetry. (I have no account of why this should be so.) The classic study of the *T* and *V* pronouns (as they are called) across languages is by Brown and Gilman.

2. I speak of "poetry" and "lyric" interchangeably throughout the book. This practice is

It is arguable whether, as W. R. Johnson claims (3), every human addressee in a poem is directly or indirectly a figure for you, the poem's actual reader; might the reader not find herself identifying with the poetic
speaker more than with that speaker's addressed beloved? But there is a
continuity between poems addressing the poet's friends, lovers, or missing dead and those other works—the later focus of this book—that dwell
on their own reception by a reader. When poems address their readers,
the topic of the pronoun *you* and the topic of reading (what it is like to be
a person reading a poem) become two sides of a single coin. This, then, is
the end to which my investigation of lyric address leads: the claim that
we as readers may feel in second-person poems, in a poem's touch, an in-
timation of why poetry is valuable, why it matters to us, and how we
might come to feel answerable to it.[3]

Readings that bring poetry's *you* to the fore lay before us an unusual
perspective. At least since the Romantics and Hegel, the preponderance
of attention has gone to the "lyric I" and lyric subjectivity. Poems are still
commonly thought of as sheer expression, the voice of the *I* "*over*heard,"
as John Stuart Mill put it, distinguished by "the poet's utter uncon-
sciousness of a listener" (12). Lyric is famous for calling upon things that
do not hear—the west wind, a skylark, death, one's pen, and so on—and
this could make us think that the word *you* in poetry is suspended from
doing what it usually does. All that hailing of abstractions, objects, and
people can look like so much empty rhetorical flourishing, address cut off

not new—see Preminger s.v. "lyric"—but I am aware of two possible objections: first that
the English term "lyric" should be reserved for its narrow sense of poems with a special relationship to music, and second (a different point) that "poetry" is anyway too broad a category to be critically useful. For the first, I prefer to acknowledge that "lyric" has come to
have, in English as in German, both narrow and broad senses; context makes clear the intended use (see Lamping 76–78 for a critique of the notion that lyric is related to song). For
the second objection, I hope the book will prove itself, even without being able to say what
poetry is.

   3. I do not take up the question of how reading poems (silently or aloud) is different from
reciting them or hearing them read aloud or recited. I write, and mostly think, of readers;
many points hold true for listeners as well. Also, "second-person poems," as I use the phrase,
are poems preoccupied with address, though many of them also say *I* and could therefore
be called first-person poems as well.

   Certain critical conventions hold that instead of touch we must always speak of an unbridgeable gap between the linguistic and the real, or between the ostensible act and its
meaning (as when saying *you*, for example, is taken to be an attempt to hoodwink or domi-
nate the other). What has not been clear, however, is how to square these ideas with the way
people actually read, and with what makes us care about reading.

from any possible efficacy and so gone slightly mad.[4] A consequence of this view is that address would be incidental to the real matter of a poem. Who (or what) gets addressed, when and how, will say little about the work's artistic or human concerns if all a poem's hailings are equally void of effect and therefore essentially interchangeable.

In fact, the prevailing critical approach to poetic address—when critics have attended to address at all—presumes a version of this idea. Northrop Frye followed up Mill's aperçu by proposing that "the poet . . . turns his back on his listeners" (*Anatomy* 250). Jonathan Culler responded with a seminal essay, "Apostrophe," in which he argues that the figure of poetic address *is* essential to lyric. Culler writes that apostrophe—principally calling on beings that do not hear—is "the pure embodiment of poetic pretension" (143); when he goes further and proposes that one might seek "to identify apostrophe with lyric itself" (137), he, like Frye, suggests that lyric is radically turned away from any actual hearer and is preoccupied instead with the poet's own effort to sound like a poet ("poetic pretension").[5] Numerous critics have since developed Culler's theory of apostrophe, but the arguments continue to imply that a poet turns his back not just on his listeners but also on any differentiation between the entities he addresses (listening or not).[6]

There were admittedly good reasons for the line of thinking that developed these various notions of poetry as overheard or as not genuinely communicative (bent on fictive addressees). Theorists from antiquity onward have spoken of the lyric as a monologic genre, and though that term originally meant that only one voice speaks, it is often understood as if it meant instead that a poem has no hearer beyond the poet himself, no true *you* (and so only a plethora of false ones). The ways a poem resembles ordinary communication (as a short form that can consistently be an ad-

4. The variety of unhearing addressees in lyric increased with Kenneth Koch's book of witty apostrophic poems *New Addresses* (2000), poems that speak "To Orgasms," "To My Old Addresses," "To My Fifties," "To World War Two" ("You were large . . . "), and so on.

5. Throughout this book I restrict the term "apostrophe" to mean only address to unhearing entities, whether these be abstractions, inanimate objects, animals, or dead or absent people. Some writers (Jonathan Culler and Barbara Johnson, for example) implicitly follow this same practice; other writers, by contrast, speak of "apostrophes to the reader," which in my own usage would be a contradiction in terms. In chapter 4 I discuss in detail the end of Culler's essay, where he turns to a poem that does address a person.

6. Writers who have developed or critiqued Culler's notion of apostrophe include Clymer, Engler, Findlay, Barbara Johnson, and Kneale. See also de Man, "Autobiography" and "Lyrical Voice." On invocation, see Schindler 1–10 and especially Greene, "Poetry as Invocation." See also Preminger s.v. "apostrophe."

dress from one person to another) make us especially aware of how it differs, too; and one of the chief differences is that much poetry is unconstrained by the care for an interlocutor that governs conversation or letter writing.

But key facts have been lost to view in the critical focus on address as a rhetorical trope or as a maneuver of the monologic poetic self.[7] For one thing, the implication that all poetic addresses are equally fictive distorts literary history: like J. S. Mill himself, critics in this vein have, consciously or not, been taking the Romantic lyric or ode as a prototype—"feeling confessing itself to itself, in moments of solitude" (12). But countless poems have been addressed to a patron, or "To the Reader"; more than one epoch has given pride of place to these forms. Such poems *are* mindful of their addressees and are concerned to guide their uptake, and this fact must weigh against the view just presented. Still more crucially, in many poems of every kind and era—and this topic, more than literary-historical concerns, will occupy me in this book—address is deeply bound up with what the work intends to express. Saying *you,* and the irreplaceable particularity of that addressee, can be the center of a poem's gravity. This may be true even when, as in elegy, the addressee is a person who cannot hear. For example, in Catullus's celebrated lament addressed to his dead brother, the poet says he has traveled across many peoples and seas to the funeral rites

> ut te postremo donarem munere mortis
> et mutam nequiquam alloquerer cinerem

> so that I might present you with the last gift of death
> and might address in vain the mute ash.[8]

The paradox of a difficult journey undertaken "in order to" do something "in vain"—namely address the dead, as he is now doing—touches near the heart of the poet's anguish and the poem's act. But this hopeless address to the absent is, as much as any other rite, itself the "last gift of death" that the poet brings. The address and its futility are both utterly integral to Catullus's poem. To discuss this address chiefly as an example of apostrophic trope would miss seeing that the reality of the human addressee is what this poem is about, and is why it is so affecting.

7. Sell 86–88 reviews the arguments of language theorists against the notion of monologue as "not interactive"; Preminger s.v. "monologue" makes similar points concerning literary monologue specifically.

8. Catullus 83, poem 101; trans. Fitzgerald 187.

In this book I will be especially concerned to draw attention to those poems, like Catullus's, which have been shaped to bear or transmit the specific force of the poem's direction and manner of address. But as for the countervailing arguments about the ways poetry is suspended from real communicative exchange and about the excessive array of *you*'s it has been hailing, as if compensatorily, since the earliest Greek lyrics—these arguments are (I will suggest) also present in the poems themselves. For example, doubts about the effectiveness of poetic address may become, as in Catullus's lines, integral to the quality of that address. In other poems, the lyric's removal from any set interlocutor opens new possibilities of self-invention or self-forgetfulness, which are in turn new forms of relation to the world, not given in quotidian language; these find their expression in the poem's conduct of its own specifically poetic ways of saying *you*.

One can easily imagine a literary-critical endeavor that would isolate some grammatical feature of texts—say, certain patterns of verb tense or mood—and identify a body of poetry that deploys this grammar with cunning or large effect. It is vital to see that address is not a linguistic feature of this kind. Rather it is the meridian of all discourse, the plumb line without which pragmatics, and so language, are strictly unthinkable. Every coherent utterance aligns itself to, is coherent with respect to, some conception of its intelligibility, and intelligibility means uptake, receivability. Even self-address is modeled, as the term itself shows, on address in the more general sense. So address is not in the strict sense a grammatical category at all; it is the fiber of language's use and being, inseparable from every word in every sentence.

In both speech and writing it is context, rather than a vocative form or the pronoun *you*, which shows us that a stretch of language is addressed to someone.[9] Most of the sentences I say to people, or write in a letter, contain no formal marker of address at all, because context has sufficed to make it clear to all interlocutors who is speaking to whom, in what situation. Short written poems, however, usually lack the cues that would play this role. Appearing without disambiguating context, such works

---

9. Sperber and Wilson's principle of "loose talk" (233–37), which governs human communication strategies in general, is one way of accounting for the context-determination of addressedness. Vocatives are noun phrases that refer to the addressee but are "not syntactically or semantically incorporated as the arguments of a predicate" (Levinson, *Pragmatics* 71), like "Ah, sunflower" or "grave Sir." (Vocatives also may include, or be closely akin to, greetings, partings, and ritual formulae, like "Gesundheit" said after a sneeze. I discuss the character of greetings in chapter 2.)

feel not so much unaddressed as underspecified for address, a crucial observation that accounts, in turn, both for the great importance of those markers of address that do appear in poetry and, as I will argue later, for a pattern of critical anxiety about *whom* poems are addressing which has left its mark on poetry criticism.

The second person and the vocative do not exhaust the ways in which poems can signal their addressees. Third-person phrases like "the reader" or "the listener"—as in the title of John Ashbery's poem "But What Is the Reader to Make of This?"—touch actual readers without addressing (saying *you* to) them. Questions, too, may find a place on the spectrum of ways an interlocutor's presence is felt; but the profusion of rhetorical questions produced by apparently solitary poetic speakers ("O how shall summer's honey breath hold out / Against the wreckful siege of battering days?") makes it a vexed issue to what extent interrogatives in general convey an explicit direction of address.[10] It would be wrong to think that every question in poetry marks the presence of a hearer. Finally, Ashbery's title "But What Is the Reader to Make of This?" illustrates also how the demonstrative *this* in a poem can designate the poem itself and so foreground the situation of reading in a way that resembles direct address to the reader.[11] These indirect allusions to the addressee lie on the periphery of my scope here; I come to self-referential lyric deixis ("this") briefly in the penultimate chapter, "The Continuance of Poems." For the most part, this book is given over to the rich variations on explicit second-person address that run through lyric poetry from antiquity forward.

The topic of poetry's addressees, to say nothing of the larger questions it raises, has attracted modest scholarly attention. John Stuart Mill opened and shut the case for most later critics with his apothegm that "poetry is *over*heard," since by these lights all poetic *you*'s must be apostrophic in the rhetorician Quintilian's sense: they turn aside (ἀπο-στρέφειν) to someone, or something, that is not the principal listener. Since Culler's essay

---

10. Shakespeare, sonnet 65. On questions in poetry, see Wolfson.

11. See Shakespeare's sonnet 18 or 55, for example. Compare the various forms of third-person phrases that gesture toward the moment of reading, each with a slightly different effect, like "my book" (Jonson), "the poem" (Ashbery), "this verse" (Shelley, "West Wind" l. 65), or "black ink" (Shakespeare, sonnet 65); there are many more. Smith (*Poetic Closure* 150) claims that reflexive reference of these kinds "is possible only in a poetic tradition in which the concept of the poem as literary artifact is acceptable. As we would expect, it is rare in the Romantic lyric or wherever the illusion of the poem as a direct unartful utterance must not be jeopardized." (Shelley's "Ode to the West Wind" would be a famous exception.)

"Apostrophe" (1977), modern criticism on the topic of poetic address has taken this type of addressee ("O wild West Wind") as its chief object.[12]

But a comparative study of address must also register multiple addressees within a single poem (rather the rule than the exception), and must concede uncertainty in the plentiful cases where a *you* eludes simple categorization. This is difficult ground. Theorists of narrative have developed a substantial body of work which at first seems to be pertinent here, focused at one very productive end on the reader and the operations of reading, and at the other on a taxonomy of the functions that the word *you* can fulfill in narrative fiction: designating narratee, protagonist, "mock" reader, inscribed or implied readers, and so on. (We have come some distance from the first puzzled critical responses to Michel Butor's 1957 novel in the second person, *La modification* [A change of heart]). But the pronouns and other deictics of the lyric poem are, as Käte Hamburger showed, epistemologically different from those of narrative fiction. And without diegesis (a "story"), lyric poems have no protagonist and thus cannot address him or her in the second person—which is the technique of so-called true second-person narrative, the chief object of recent narratological interest in the *you*-form.[13] Finally, narrative typologies, which are based on the concept of embedded levels, are helpless before poetry's freedom to move between communicative frameworks with a suddenness, or disregard, rare in any other use of language. The awkward fact is

---

12. Quintilian, *Institutio oratoria* 4.1.63–70.

There are exceptions to the emphasis on apostrophe, and I cite some of them in the pages that follow. In overview: T. S. Eliot in "The Three Voices of Poetry"—in part an answer to Gottfried Benn's reflections on "monologic lyric"—had considered various aspects of poetic address but emphasized the "third voice," poetic drama. Erich Auerbach and Leo Spitzer ("Addresses") held an exchange regarding Dante's addresses to the reader in the *Commedia*. Holden criticized excessive use of an ambiguous *you* in 1970s American poetry. Grabher studies the use of *you* in Plath, Levertov, and Ammons in a philosophical matrix (Husserl, Heidegger, Buber, Sartre). Criticism of Ashbery and Celan, special cases, is hard to apply more generally, though Costello's fine essay on Ashbery is a notable exception. See also Holloway, and Masel. Shapiro and Shapiro venture to bring Bakhtinian dialogism to the study of the lyric. The fullest studies of reader address in poetry concern Whitman, that most insistent of all poets when it comes to hailing the reader: see Larson's excellent book, as well as Nathanson and Hollis (88–123). Hollander takes up poetic imperatives, and Jackson and Rosenthal provide valuable insights into the figure of address in Dickinson and in sixteenth-century French lyric, respectively. Anne Ferry sheds light on the history and interpretive implications of those dimensions of address relating to how poems are titled (see esp. chap. 4, 105–36).

13. The collection of essays and the bibliography edited by Fludernik provide good orientation to the *you* of narrative fiction.

that poetry, from the brash parlando of Archilochus to the pronominal la-
bility of John Ashbery, enacts—for us, as readers, now—not so much a
stable communicative situation as a chronic hesitation, a faltering, between monologue and dialogue, between "talking about" and "talking
to," third and second person, indifference to interlocutors and the yearning to have one.

Part of the reason for this instability lies in the complex historical and
cognitive shift between oral delivery and writing as modes of poetic
transmission.[14] This shift (or tension: its still active forces can be felt in the
difficulty of discussing poetry without metaphors of voice or speech) is
lastingly implicated in what we readers experience as poetry's *désancrage*,
or "uprootedness," from any specified communicative situation.[15] Who
is speaking (or writing), to whom, in what context? It is difficult to answer these very basic pragmatic questions with respect to a poem. The resulting kinds of ambiguity have become integral to modern written
poetry, so that to read a poem is, again, to enter an underspecified communicative act.[16]

It was not always this way. Lyric compositions were once embedded in
a context of use to a degree that would be exceptional today. But they were
dislodged very early, with developments in ancient Greek lyric around
the fourth century BCE.[17] As Gordon Williams explains:

14. The accumulated scholarship on the relationship between literature's forms and oral-
ity-and-literacy is vast. To mention a handful of starting places: the classic works are by
Havelock (*Preface to Plato*), Derrida, and Ong (*Orality and Literacy*). See also Svenbro and
Thomas on ancient Greek literacy. Concerning medieval Europe, see Zumthor and also
Doane and Pasternack. Coulmas takes up various aspects including ideographic versus al-
phabetic cultures; Ehlich discusses deixis; and Tedlock provides an anthropological perspective. Berry and Griffiths treat the question of voice and writing in poetry, as does
Schmitz-Emans (*Schrift*). On contemporary poetry, see Bernstein. A good book on the literary meaning of "physical aspects of texts" is Levenston's *Stuff of Literature*.

15. It will be evident that for my part I have chosen not to restrain metaphors of voice in
the way I describe poetry. Certain critics contend that it is imperative to distinguish cate-
gorically between writing and orality in lyric. As I have just suggested, though, the overlap
is so pervasive in how we talk and write about poetry that such strenuous distinctions force
critical language into labored circumlocutions. For a contrasting treatment of the "nostalgia" of lyrical voice as "deluded," see de Man's essay "Anthropomorphism" (262).

16. I mean "integral" seriously, which is why I cannot go along with scholars in stylistics
who maintain, for example, that "to understand a poem is to construct for it an appropriate
context of utterance" or that "an interpretation of a poem is a completion of a speech act"
(Kasher and Kasher 79). The context always remains half-constructed, the speech act incomplete.

17. Other historical junctures have been nominated as bringing about the lyric's detachment from context. Some say the early twentieth or late nineteenth century marked the turn-

The [Greek] lyric poets wrote their poems for performance on specific social occasions like drinking-parties, celebrations of various sorts such as
that held for a returning victor at the games, hymns to be sung at temples
during religious festivals, and many more. . . . In all this, an account could
be given of poetic activity which related the poet directly to the society in
which he lived. But gradually, during the fourth and third centuries, the
social occasions which, by their very nature, instigated poetic activity, died
away and a new phenomenon appeared: the scholar-poet who worked as
a literary expert in a great library like that at Alexandria and wrote poetry
as a mere part of his activity. These poets took a step which was decisive
for later poetry: they continued to write the same sort of poetry as earlier
poets had done, but, instead of having real social occasions for which their
poems were designed, they treated the occasions as part of the imaginative
structure of their poems. So they wrote hymns without any thought of a religious performance; they wrote drinking-songs without parties in pros-
pect; they wrote epitaphs without any idea of having them inscribed on a
tombstone.

Everything we now know as lyric—including the ways we (mis)read the
poetry that was composed *before* the fourth century—has been decisively
defined by this turn of Hellenistic poetry.[18] What we call lyric poetry is
literature, something whose detachment from context is, in a manner of
speaking, its foundation. Contextlessness is different from detachment
from context, and our poems live in the latter mode, finding their "occasions," as Williams writes, "as part of the imaginative structure" of the
works themselves. This detachment from context, then, has become con-
stitutive of the modern lyric, which is also the inheritor of many other
such detachments, like the separation of lyric from music, and from voice

ing point (Paz, Trotter); some would point to the spread of or, earlier, the invention of printed
texts; others propose that poems lost their context once and for all when, after the trouba-
dours and certain poets in the Petrarchan tradition, poetry and music parted ways for good.
I am persuaded that the most significant of these points where poetry came unstuck from
context was in fourth-century Greece (see also W. R. Johnson 5), but it is possible that things
would look different if we knew more about archaic and classical Greek lyric performance
than the little we do know. In any case, I do not mean to encourage nostalgia as for an un-
fallen moment; on the contrary, everything I say in this book is happily enabled by the ar-
tistically fruitful uncertainties and ambiguities made possible by poetry's detachment from
context (whether we regard that detachment historically or structurally).

18. The sustained and passionate argument about our misreading of earlier Greek poetry
by taking it as "poetry," instead of as an utterance that *was* deeply embedded in a specific
context of use, is Dupont's book *The Invention of Literature*. Dupont also urges a renewed emphasis on performance in contemporary poetry as a means of reconnecting poetry to music
and to a social (communal) situation of utterance.

altogether, and the distances that print publication introduced between handwriting and the book held by a reader.[19]

The strange result of this history of repeated, accumulating dislocations is that poetry is, of all the ways we use language, the one with the most tenuous relation to a context of use.[20] Since any language communicates only by more or less explicit reliance on its context of use, poetry, to the extent that it is decontextualized language, is at risk of not being able to communicate its intended meaning, or, in extreme cases, anything at all. With this risk, however, is purchased a wild charge. Poetry can flame out, unexpectedly.

Pragmatics, the branch of linguistics that studies how language and its context of use interpenetrate, is for these reasons limited in its ability to characterize the lyric. For example, a pragmatic analysis of any utterance will want to know first who is speaking to whom, in what situation, with what bystanders present: these elements have shaped the form of the utterance itself, rather than being concerns outside the linguistic datum, and they constrain interpretation decisively. But these elementary questions about context are just those that, in the case of most poems, we cannot answer. At the opening of Galway Kinnell's poem "Wait" (127), we read:

> Wait, for now.
> Distrust everything if you have to.
> But trust the hours. Haven't they
> carried you everywhere, up to now?

Who is speaking to whom here? Are you, the reader, the one addressed? What kind of situation has occasioned the exhortation to "wait," or the talk of distrust? The poem continues, and readers may infer some answers to these questions from the rest of the text, which I give here in full:

19. Susan Stewart argues that "the notion of poetic *kinds* is tied to the specificity of their use and occasion: the epithalamion, the elegy, the aubade are at once works of art independent of their particular contexts of production and use and social acts tied to specific rules of decorum." Other kinds (ballads, pastorals, meditations) may be less clear as to what Stewart calls "social intent and consequence," but she is still right about the double aspect of poems as social acts and as "things in a world of things" (27).

20. Should we consider a text's publication as poetry to be itself a complete context of use? It is true that genre conventions are an inextricable part of any utterance's pragmatic functioning. But almost all poems refer to or presuppose contexts that are different from, or ambiguously different from, the reading context. This thin relation of a text to its own acts of deixis and presupposition is a signal part of how poetry works on us.

WAIT

Wait, for now.
Distrust everything if you have to.
But trust the hours. Haven't they
carried you everywhere, up to now?
Personal events will become interesting again.
Hair will become interesting.
Pain will become interesting.
Buds that open out of season will become interesting.
Second-hand gloves will become lovely again;
their memories are what give them
the need for other hands. And the desolation
of lovers is the same: that enormous emptiness
carved out of such tiny beings as we are
asks to be filled; the need
for the new love *is* faithfulness to the old.

Wait.
Don't go too early.
You're tired. But everyone's tired.
But no one is tired enough.
Only wait a little and listen:
music of hair,
music of pain,
music of looms weaving all our loves again.
Be there to hear it, it will be the only time,
most of all to hear
the flute of your whole existence,
rehearsed by the sorrows, play itself into total exhaustion.

The addressee of this poem is said to be distrusting, desolate, tired. We ourselves may or may not be that addressee; it depends on our own state of mind during the time of reading. Most readers' first reading of the poem will be in significant part given over to handling the uncertainty of just this question. (Is the implication that as we shift and hesitate, we alternately are, and are not, the one spoken to?)

Many readers will decide at some point—perhaps at "Don't go too early"—that they are overhearing the poem, not hearing it directly, since the line suggests an addressee not just despairing but suicidal. But even among those who react this way, there may be some who, reluctant to conclude that this gentle communication is not meant for them, will endeavor to find another way to interpret "Don't go too early," so preserving the possibility that they are being addressed. (Or they may file the poem away mentally, as a letter to be opened and read again at some harder time.) The less than fully indefinite, less than fully definite character of the poem's *you* keeps the question of address active as a question, and it will be *despite* this activity that readers settle finally into one or another stable position vis-à-vis that *you*. If a pragmatic description began by establishing the identities and circumstances of *I* and *you*, it would miss both poem and reader (see also Sell 160).[21] Yet pragmatics also supplies the best means for describing and understanding what sense we make of a poem's very deficiencies of context, deficiencies now made integral and potent by literary history and by each poet's art.

One of the tenets of this book is that for a poem to say *you* is in every case a complex act. The varieties of this complexity will emerge, I hope, as the specific interest of the close readings that follow; but a few tangles can be sketched here to give an idea of what intricacies may attend upon the question of lyric address.

Out of all the different listeners a poem can address, it might seem that the simplest and most direct *you* would be an address to the reader, the one audience that every poem we read unequivocally has by virtue of the fact that we are reading it. But there is no simplicity here. For one thing, reader address is not always explicit (say, in the manner of Jonson's "Pray thee, take care, that tak'st my book in hand"). For example, here is the famous autumnal opening of Stefan George's volume *The Year of the Soul* (1897):

Komm in den totgesagten park und schau:

Come to the park they say is dead and look:

The poem's twelve lines contain eight imperatives, urging the addressee to gaze, gather colors from the fading foliage, weave them together in a fall vision ("im herbstlichen gesicht"), and so on. Perhaps we could take this text as the poet's address to an unnamed companion who is invited into a really existing park. In that case we, the readers, would consider ourselves overhearers (ratified or not). But everything we know about George's programmatic poetics of *décadence* suggests otherwise, as does the literal implausibility of (for example) the command to carry away colors from objects ("there take the deep yellow, the soft grey / from birch

---

21. Riquelme points out that some of Eliot's poems feature a *you* (and *I*) which "indicate positions that can be variously occupied"; what can result are "perplexing effects that resist being taken as voice" (159), a rich suggestion.

and from boxwood"); or the metaphoric conclusion, "Twine [these colors and flowers] in an autumnal vision"; or not least the poem's own position as the opening piece of a collection, the book's *invitatio*, "Come and look." Everything suggests, that is, that the reader of the poem is, or is also, the one addressed (the *you*), that the park stands for the book itself, or for European high culture at the fin-de-siècle, and that the commands are therefore as much metaphors for larger attitudes and acts of mind as they are instructions for the visitor in a certain garden. The reader finds herself doing both things simultaneously: she imaginatively projects and inhabits the park, *seeing* what George describes; and she also thoughtfully interprets the park and the imperative gestures along with it. In both cases she is the poem's listening addressee, but on different levels.

The circumstances of composition and publication may introduce other complications. George's *Year of the Soul* was prepared for a private printing, deliberately restricted to a certain elite male circle. This fact directs our attention to a historical set of intended recipients among whom we cannot number ourselves: it seems to make us eavesdroppers on the poem's address. On the other hand, George knew and celebrated the enduring power of artifice, knew that the same rarefaction of style, idiom, and even typeface that removed his poetry from most readers in his time was (also) his bid for readers beyond his time. But are you the later reader to whom the poem means to speak? Similar problems are raised by "coterie publication," such as the very limited manuscript circulation for which Shakespeare wrote his sonnets.[22] Dickinson, who "published" by including some of her poems in private letters and sewing the rest into fascicles shown to no one, raises still other difficulties. Each of these poets writes poems that directly address or indirectly gesture toward their readers in posterity, notwithstanding the tiny circulation the poet faced at the moment when he or she wrote. In such cases, then—and these few examples stand for many—the poems' publication history presents an added dimension for the investigation of the address and the hearer of poetic utterances.[23]

22. On coterie publication and the "manuscript system," see Marotti 1–73. Christopher Martin's discussion of the "acute . . . sensitivity to public witness" (133) shown by the sonnets' speaker gives a different kind of complexity to their acts of address (130–91).

23. For the most part, this book leaves aside the historical investigation of poetic addressees except as these questions bear on the phenomenology of our own reading attitude. Several scholars have treated address from a historical angle; see among others Hollis, Jackson, Larson, Leverenz, Machor (109–208), and Rosenthal.

There is another still more fundamental question about how to read po-etic address. Suppose that readers generally feel, in reading *you*-poems, neither a sense of being addressed nor a sense of overhearing. This would be the case if poetry readers normally identify with the *speaker* of the verse, thereby treating this form of language like some prayers, hymns, and songs, but in a radically different way from all other kinds of utter-ance. The possibility of receiving language in this way does not figure in standard accounts of pragmatics, but it is familiar in literary criticism. He-len Vendler has argued for this kind of identification with the poetic speaker as the norm for the reading of poetry: "The lyric is a script writ-ten for performance by the reader—who, as soon as he enters the lyric, is no longer a reader but rather an utterer, saying the words of the poem *in propria persona*, internally and with proprietary feeling" (xi).[24] This claim has an intuitive truth, even if alone it does not help in understanding the varieties of poetic address. It does suggest two more facts about the effort to bring even basic linguistic categories to bear on the lyric: first, poetry frequently offers examples in which distinctions like the hearing/over-hearing contrast, or that between self-address and other-address, can be resolved in any of several, perhaps equally plausible ways; second, read-erly experience is a subtler thing than the customary distinctions of lin-guistic pragmatics are designed to catch. How is linguistics to describe the forgetfulness of one's role as reader that Vendler describes, as one "en-ters" the lyric and becomes, instead, its "utterer"? But this is the very stuff of imaginative reading. And how to relate this absorption, in turn, to the cases Vendler does not discuss—her assertion would even seem to ex-clude their possibility, though she does not mean it to—namely, poems that address their readers explicitly?

One thing is clear whether we start from Vendler's idea of the lyric as a script, from linguistic analyses of participant roles, or from the puzzle of poetry's dislocation from context: it avails nothing to discuss poetry's pronouns without involving the question of the reader's experience. These are two different domains, the formal and the phenomenological, to which two different critical vocabularies attach; but they are always, fi-nally, two sides of one coin. This book will be marked by that fact. That is, the pronoun *you* is a formal feature of the printed text, and this is one half of my concern in this study; but the other half is the poem's recipi-ent, the reader, as she finds herself in relation to the poem's acts of ad-

24. See also Schlaffer.

dress. Even where the poet addresses his dead child or his coy mistress, or indeed a Grecian urn, the position (or self-forgetfulness) of the reader with respect to that call will be essential to understanding the specific imaginative forces that are brought to expression when poems say *you*.

When the *you* designates, or could be taken as designating, the reader, then tracking pronouns becomes the formal correlate of the reader's experience: linguistic detail on the one hand, and questions of reception and response on the other, become each other's obverse. What is unexpected is how numerous are the poems that fall into the category of perhaps addressing the reader or perhaps not, since, as Bonnie Costello indicates in discussing John Ashbery's cultivation of this ambiguous *you*, "it is difficult, when reading an unspecified second person pronoun, not to take it personally first, however else we might go on to take it" (495). This is so because *you* tends to hail; it calls everyone and everything by their inmost name. The second-person pronoun is address itself. One can read unspecified *I* or *she* with comparatively small concern; encountering Byron's poem that opens, "She walks in beauty, like the night / Of cloudless climes and starry skies," we are not much bothered that we are not told who "she" is. But the summons of unspecified *you* restlessly tugs at us, begging identification.

This realization will have far-reaching consequences for a criticism that hopes to give voice to the movements of mind and emotion in reading as it is experienced, rather than as abstractly theorized or as simplified after the fact.[25] The *you* that (perhaps) calls to the reader is a wild spot in poetics, a dynamically moving gap in whatever secure knowledge about poetry we may think we have; and "live" as it is, this *you* makes palpable poetry's claim on being read, which is to say, its claim to make an accidental reader into the destined and unique recipient of everything the poem contains or is. The fascination of this topic, the need to work out a critical idiom that can engage it, and its centrality both to the powers of address and to the reasons why we read poetry at all—these grounds accord the readerly *you* the largest place in this book.[26]

---

25. Cf. Steiner, " 'Critic' / 'Reader.' "

26. Criticism focusing on "the reader" can mean several different things. The reader discussed in this book is not the abstract or faceless functionary of the cognitive operations of interpretation, as "the reader" was understood in classic reader-response theory (e.g., Iser's *Appellstruktur*). Nor do I focus on the reader in history as a culturally constructed participant in a given era's system of social codes and concerns. Each of these critical directions furnishes insights. But my interest here is something different, what I call phenomenology: namely, *what it is like to be someone reading* (here, now).

My study takes as its central thread the poetry of Rainer Maria Rilke, a writer whose work is unusually reflective about poetic "addressivity." This choice is also admittedly arbitrary, or rather personal, since Rilke is the writer I know best. But I draw supporting and contrastive examples from a wide array of American and European poetry from the classical era forward. A frequent criticism leveled at studies in poetics is that they build too exclusively on the lyric of one tradition or era; I attempt to pit the conclusions drawn from Rilke's work against a broader spectrum of lyric invention. My interest is not in asserting, much less proving, that all the diverse texts I examine are members of a single generic class, but rather in asking what reading is like if we take them that way—take all poems as, in a broadly intuited way, instances of something called "poetry."

The first chapter, "Poems Addressing Contemporaries," takes up the seemingly unproblematic case of address to a contemporary or beloved of the poet's but observes that few poems sound convincingly like natural addresses to one person. The very conventions that identify the lyric as such (the "intimate" genre) push personal address into de facto proximity with apostrophes to the dead and absent, a figure to which, in turn, lyric may be generically predisposed. Chapter 2, "Address as Greeting, Address as Spell," explores two complementary movements that could be called, in Goethean style, "Diastole" and "Systole" respectively: the first section, "Opening Out," explores conjuring poems in which the not-quite-present addressee, whether historical, mythical, or yet to be born, is not so much invoked as expanded into a greetable avatar, while the second section, "Closing In," focuses on that other sort of lyric *you* that pursues, pins, or holds in deadly fascination the one spoken to. (Often it is the reader.)

Chapter 3, "The Continuance of Poems: Monument and Mouth," recalls the mixed allegiance of poetry to speech and writing, and proposes that the archetype for this ineradicable ambivalence in poetry is the "Stay, traveler" of the gravestone inscription. The chapter aims to consider a variety of poems—even the lyric in general—under this rubric of the monument or epitaph. It is to mortality that the topic of uncertain *you* leads, as the unexpected but logical result of trying to sustain a focus on a communication between someone present and another (the poet) who is always absent. Chapter 4, "Hand-Writing and Readerly Intimacy," is a kind of coda. It develops further this thought of life-and-death as the ground on which second-person poetry stakes its claim to the seriousness of the reader's attention. The chapter pairs poetological reflections by Osip Mandelstam and Paul Celan with Keats's "This living hand" and a short fragment by Rilke as works that anticipate the writer's own death and yet in some way propose, in this circumstance, to extend the touch of the writer's hand to the reader.

A note on translations: when discussing texts not written in English, I gratefully borrow the work of other translators when I can, modifying their renditions where needed to make points about the specific original wording of this passage or that. (It will be evident that I owe a special debt to Edward Snow's versions of Rilke.) I supply the original language too for all poetry citations. Uncredited translations are my own.

I

Poems Addressing Contemporaries

A poem derives its beauty from the promise of communicative success. . . . The veracity of the speaker in poems is in part secured by the thematization (taking as subject) in lyric of absence, the search for the beloved. . . . The finding occurs at the point of loss.

—Allen Grossman

LYRIC POETRY is most often thought of in what T. S. Eliot called its "meditative" mode, "the voice of the poet talking to himself— or to nobody" ("Three Voices," 97). But it makes at least two kinds of sense to accord priority instead to what for Eliot is the "second voice" of poetry, "the poet speaking to other people" (89). First, this *I–you* lyric addressed to a contemporary of the poet's aligns itself (unlike meditative verse) with the fundamental axis of language as communication. Second, the mode of personal address has some claim also to historical precedence.[1] W. R. Johnson observes that "the most usual mode in Greek lyric (probably) and in Latin lyric (certainly) was to address the poem (in Greek, the song) to another person or to other persons. What this typical lyric form points to is the conditions and the purposes of song: the presence of the singer before his audience; his re-creation of universal emotions in a specific context, a compressed, stylized story . . . ; and, finally, the sharing, the interchange of these emotions by singer and audience" (4). The poems Johnson cites chiefly address specific persons, not generalized listeners or unknown readers. These addresses in turn are said to

---

1. When I use the phrase "personal address," I mean it to designate poems addressing contemporaries (people who are alive at the moment when the poet is writing).

figure "the conditions and purposes of song" (singer before audience) because "the person addressed (whether actual or fictional) is a metaphor
for readers of the poem and becomes a symbolic mediator, a conductor
between the poet and each of his readers and listeners" (4). In other
words, the *you* of the classical poem is one person, the reader or listener
is another; but in sharp contrast to ordinary conversation, Johnson argues
that nonaddressed listeners to lyric felt themselves not eavesdropping
but "meant," figuratively spoken to, as if by proxy, in the poem's osten-
sibly private address to another.

This idea of the personal addressee as a metaphor, an idea Johnson
introduces only in passing, is suggestive while at the same time it com-
plicates any attempt to chart out poetry's "speech situation." Eliot, who
provides the starting point for Johnson's discussion, likewise offers insight into personal address even as he moves to "dismiss as an illusion
the voice of the poet talking to one person only": "My opinion is, that a
good love poem, though it may be addressed to one person, is always
meant to be overheard by other people. Surely, the proper language of
love—that is, of communication to the beloved and to no one else—is
prose" (90). Eliot makes an observation about love poetry that he rightly
extends, by implication, to all poems that address one person. Altering
J. S. Mill's famous claim about the overhearing of poetry (Mill had had in
mind only Eliot's "first voice," the meditative lyric seemingly "of the nature of soliloquy" [12]), Eliot suggests that personal address in poetry is
in some way always felt to be public, addressed to one *you* but targeted
also at nonaddressed bystanders.[2] The more nuanced version of this insight, in a formulation that goes beyond simply dismissing personal address "as an illusion," is the last line in Eliot's *Collected Poems,* concluding
"A Dedication to My Wife" (234): "These are private words addressed to
you in public." In some way the bare fact of poetry, its stylization of the
basic gesture of address into quasi-ritual form, may be said to have placed
the "private words" into a "public" communicative framework even be-

2. I adopt the term "target" from linguistics (see, e.g., Levinson, *Pragmatics* 61–73), where
it serves to designate the intended recipient of an utterance, in contrast to the "addressee,"
who is in this terminology only and always the one designated by the pronoun *you.* (In common parlance we use "addressee" for both meanings.) It is true that the connotations of the
word "target" make it less apt for gentle or even neutral gestures than for pointed ones.
Moreover, the image also implies an unwarranted precision about who is (and is not) meant
to receive a message: in poetry, as in conversation, the intention may sometimes be approx-
imate. But the term "target" is established in pragmatics, and I have not found a better alternative.

fore, and independent of, their publication. Many occasions in life cannot be adequately described as either public or private, but that is not the bearing of Eliot's words here. His phrasing articulates the double fact: the words *are* private, even as they call attention to the way this privacy is changed by the same "listening" of nonaddressed bystanders that the words' utterance as poetry may be said to license.

We might take as a fuller example a familiar poem by William Carlos Williams, from 1934:

THIS IS JUST TO SAY

I have eaten
the plums
that were in
the icebox

and which
you were probably
saving
for breakfast

Forgive me
they were delicious
so sweet
and so cold (372)

Williams's poem is "celebrated for being nothing more than a domestic note of the kind many of his readers will have written, its language plain and direct and its purpose quotidian. It is an objet trouvé claimed by the poet in much the same way as he claimed the plums that he found in the icebox."[3] Williams's later publication, in verse form, of his wife's manifestly quotidian "Reply" (actually a foregoing note?)[4] among his own works would seem to strengthen the claim that in "This Is Just to Say" we have a limit case of personal address, a genuine one-to-one communication. But the final lines—

3. Fitzgerald 2. See A. Ferry 268 on the part that Williams's title, and the word "this," play in the double aspect of this text as poem and as note.
4. Floss's first stanza runs:
Dear Bill: I've made a
couple of sandwiches for you.
In the ice-box you'll find
blue-berries—a cup of grapefruit
a glass of cold coffee. (W. C. Williams 536)

Forgive me
they were delicious
so sweet
and so cold

—in fact exceed the genre "domestic note" (even leaving lineation aside) in ways that are palpable to any reader, presumably Florence Williams included. The triplet of adjectives, ending on "cold" (not on "sweet," which to my ear would be a plainer sequence), the repeated intensifier "so," and perhaps above all the relation conventionally entailed, and here flouted, between "Forgive me" and the kind of thing that gets said next, all distance Williams's words from ordinary discourse, and so in this case take the "message" away from Williams's wife as much as they concern the theft of her breakfast.[5] Thus William Fitzgerald is telling only half the story when he remarks on the loss of the plums:

> Because *we* weren't saving the plums that Williams ate, and which we now enjoy with enhanced orality, the addressee's loss is our gain: she must accept the loss of her anticipated pleasure for his sake and for ours. But, insofar as she is a reader, the position of Williams's addressee overlaps with our own: like us, she is asked to acknowledge that she has enjoyed the plums more in his mouth than she would have in her own. Her forgiveness depends on the delicious and unexpected enjoyment of the familiar (words like "cold" and "sweet") to which she is given renewed access through the detour of his note. (2)

The metaphor of "orality" is exact.[6] But as the words of the note themselves become delicious, granting "unexpected enjoyment of the familiar," they become in that measure unfamiliar, undomestic. Or to put it another way, as Williams's addressee becomes a reader whose "position . . . overlaps with our own," she is asked to surrender the position of sole and intimate target and so also the attending reciprocal claims that would govern the genre "domestic note."

The loss of the plum of single address also occupied Emily Dickinson,

---

5. Jonathan Culler describes the structuralist view: when this text is "set down on the page as a poem," reading conventions make us "deprive the poem of the pragmatic and circumstantial functions of the note" ("Poetics" 175).

6. For further comment on the ancient motif of what Marcel Jousse has called "la manducation de la parole," see Ong, "*Maranatha*," and Thomas 19–20 and 80. The biblical precedent is Numbers 5:23–24.

but with respect to letters rather than breakfast table notes.[7] Dickinson once chided a friend for sending a letter addressed to both her and her sister Lavinia: "A mutual plum is not a plum. I was too respectful to take the pulp and do not like the stone. Send no union letters. The soul must go by Death alone, so, it must by life, if it is a soul. If a committee—no matter" (455; letter 321). In Dickinson's terms, Florence Williams is asked by the "poeticity" of her husband's note to accept a mutual plum in place of both the singular plum of a note really meant for her and the original plums she was probably saving for breakfast.[8]

The linguist Roman Jakobson would have called the flavor of language as Williams's last stanza throws it into relief a "set (*Einstellung*) towards the MESSAGE as such," focus on the message for its own sake (356). This insight shares with Eliot's formulation—that an address like Williams's is "meant to be overheard by other people"—the idea that the poet's emphasis or intention is not, or is not just, on the addressed *you*. In Jakobson's version it is shifted centripetally into the utterance itself, while for Eliot it is shifted aside to, or shared with, a bystander (who is thereby "ratified" or targeted).

Partly for this reason, it seems wrong to say that the addressee's forgiveness in Williams's poem depends on her savoring the note's words. Linguistic structures of politeness entail that what follows the phrase "forgive me" normally should present exculpation ("there was nothing else to eat"; "I couldn't help myself") or promise recompense ("I'll bring home some more").[9] The complex tenderness of this poem lies in part in its violation of this principle by an excessive honesty ("I enjoyed, you lost") that might be called sensual innocence if it were not, rather, acknowledging how intimacy and domesticity necessarily involve us in taking: we impinge. The poignancy comes from the fact that there is—pace Fitzgerald—no *reason* why the addressee should forgive; her forgiveness depends on nothing, and for that reason it can be relied upon and bluntly confronted with the speaker's theft of her pleasure.

7. Daria Donnelly points out the extraordinary importance Dickinson attached to letters, even trivial ones, and argues that in Dickinson's own writing practice, the distinction between letters and poems is a porous one.

8. Contrast the lines from the fifth section of Stevens's poem "The Comedian as the Letter C," earlier than Williams's poem (I do not quote the full context): "The words of things entangle and confuse, / The plum survives its poems" (33).

9. See Brown and Levinson. "They were delicious" is not a way of saying "I couldn't help myself" because it already presupposes the eating (contrast "they looked so delicious," which could be an excuse).

Fitzgerald also neatly suggests some of the ways in which Williams's poem seems to bear on the theft-and-gift of language that is poetry: "But the poet also returns what he has stolen to a kind of second-order icebox that is the poem itself, through which we can experience vicariously the moment when he opened the door to find the plums in a state of sweet, cold, and delicious preservation." The crucial difference between what was "taken" and what is "returned," Fitzgerald goes on, is that the contents of that "second-order icebox" cannot be consumed, since "our aesthetic positioning means that we cannot *have* the poem" (239). No more could Florence Williams, who, if she might have expected an apologetic note in token recompense for her stolen breakfast, finds instead yet another thing that she cannot have. The poem is not hers—nor any reader's—to dispose of, and in this way too it is unlike a household message (which is truly "consumable," with its single target and narrow purpose).[10]

The paradoxical position of the addressee of a personal lyric can be summarized in various ways; here we might observe that the note becomes a "something," and hence potentially a gift for the addressee, by withdrawing from her as recipient in preoccupation with itself as language or with other potential readers "beyond" her. Its power to speak keenly of intimacy is won by momentarily defaulting on the ongoing discourse in which that intimacy is played out. Theft and gift are of one root.

Most of the poems discussed in this chapter are love poems of one kind or another, but that need not have been so. As an illustration, we can place a dedicatory poem from a thoroughly different world next to Williams's "This Is Just to Say." The introductory poem to the Roman poet Catullus's collected works (1) shows remarkable similarities to Williams's "note." The stakes are higher in Catullus's dedicatory piece, and at the same time the tone is more jocular; but the conundrum of who can "have" the poem—of what having means—is the same:

> Cui dono lepidum novum libellum
> arida modo pumice expolitum?
> Corneli, tibi: namque tu solebas
> meas esse aliquid putare nugas

10. Henry Widdowson puts this neatly when he points out that as a poem, "This Is Just to Say" is *not* just to say that which, as a note, it would say: namely, that its author has eaten the plums (*Practical Stylistics* 26–31).

iam tum, cum ausus es unus Italorum
omne aevum tribus explicare cartis
doctis, Iuppiter, et laboriosis.
quare habe tibi quidquid hoc libelli
qualecumque; quod, <o> patrona virgo,
plus uno maneat perenne saeclo.

To whom do I give this chic new little book
freshly smoothed by the dry pumice?
Cornelius, to you; for it was you
who used to think my trifles *were* something
when you yourself had dared, alone
of the Italians, to expound all history
in three most learned and laborious volumes.
So have this little book for what
it's worth; and, O my virgin patroness,
may it remain fresh for more than one generation.[11]

The opening question evokes the process of arriving at a dedicatee for
Catullus's work. The choice is, for a moment, held open; the book was apparently not composed or assembled with a particular recipient in mind.
To this extent the poem already looks past its principal addressee, Cornelius Nepos, here at its beginning: the question "To whom do I give?"
implies a range of other friends and patrons Catullus might have chosen
but, in the end, did not. Yet the words "chic new little book" ("lepidum
novum libellum") seem to speak of the volume any reader at all may be
holding, a sense that recalls W. R. Johnson's assertion that a lyric's personal addressee is a stand-in for the general reader.

As Fitzgerald suggests, Cornelius Nepos specifically occupies a crucial
relation to Catullus's text: "The dedicatee . . . stands at a nodal point between the production of Catullus's *nugae* [trifles] and their reception by
posterity: because he approved them, or saw something in them, they
have now been published and committed to the care of time" (39). Simultaneously, though, the act of publication, which is what prompts the
writing of a dedicatory poem, removes these works from Cornelius's
"possession," and indeed from any reader's. Thus the poem's abrupt turn
at its end to a "virgin patroness"—Catullus must mean his Muse, whom
he aptly invokes as unpossessed herself ("virgo")—brings to expression

11. Trans. Fitzgerald 39, modified. On the question of which "libellus" might have been
meant, see Quinn 10–20.

what was implicit from the beginning, namely, the poem's simultaneous advance toward its personal addressee and past him toward posterity:

> Quare habe tibi quidquid hoc libelli
> qualecumque; quod, <o> patrona virgo,
> plus uno maneat perenne saeclo.

> So have this little book for what
> it's worth; and, O my virgin patroness,
> may it remain fresh for more than one generation.

The legal-formulaic bequeathing of property ("habe tibi")[12] joins with a colloquial display of modesty ("this little book for what / it's worth"), only to turn swiftly into an earnest prayer. That prayer abandons the address to Cornelius and instead reenacts or revises the gesture of entrusting the book—this time not to a friend, but to the Muse and so to those other future generations of readers that only she can ensure. The turn from Cornelius to the protector-virgin corresponds to the movement of thought from the word "new" and the book as object (l. 1) to "perenne" 'lasting' and the book as oeuvre (l. 10).[13]

This movement dramatizes the ambivalence—Fitzgerald calls it "teasing" (41)—that must inform *every* poem addressed to a contemporary, as I tried to show in my reading of Williams's text. "This Is Just to Say" seeks preservation (the "second-order icebox"), which must mean preservation from its readers as much as preservation for them; Catullus too entrusts his poems to a *patrona* (protectress, defender) whose virgin power makes her the fit preserver of his poems' provocative enticements. Though not all poems addressing an acquaintance of the poet's reflect so explicitly on their own contradictory status as transactions, the lyric's inability to "belong" fully to its personal addressee is universal.

The continuity or lastingness that Catullus seeks ("may it remain fresh") is not a version or extension of the duration of life, the sequence of events in time. Rather this poem, altogether an occasional one—in a later tradition we might expect it to be handwritten on the flyleaf of someone's copy, not published together with the collection—"revolves around that occasion" with a persisting concern.[14] This concern can also be felt

---

12. Fordyce 86.

13. See Latta on the debate about the suddenness of the address to the Muse.

14. Frye uses this phrase in discussing the occasional character of much lyric ("Approaching" 32).

as informing the otherwise puzzling present indicative of the poem's first line, "Cui dono?" 'To whom am I giving / do I give?' Read in light of the poem's ending, the question may not be merely a rhetorical set-up for the answer in line 3, "Cornelius, to you," but may rather reflect a genuine, perhaps amused bewilderment. To whom, indeed? The presentational copy, "polished" literally with pumice to smooth the scroll ends and emend errors, is placed in the hands of Cornelius Nepos, the volume's "begetter" insofar as he certified Catullus's poems to be "aliquid" 'something' (and has established his creditability as a judge with his own labors as an author [ll. 5–7]). But for all that, the poems themselves cannot really be *given* to Nepos.[15] In light of the last two lines, the answer to "Cui dono?" is the Muse, whom Catullus styles *à la romaine* as protectress rather than source of inspiration (Catullus 90). Under her aegis the poems—*expoliti* now in the sense of "polished, refined"—may be "given" to further generations ("saecla"), as well as distributed outward to unknown readers in the poet's time. And yet if the poems as poems cannot finally be bequeathed to Nepos, neither is there any obvious way that the book-in-hand, the *libellus,* can be presented as an object either to the Muse or to unborn generations of readers. The bind holds both ways.

Northrop Frye distinguishes such poems of occasion from another tradition, an "epitaphic" one, in which the "block" that diverts the continuum of experience into the sustained preoccupation that makes up the poem pertains not (as in occasional verse) to the poet, but rather to the reader. In the epitaphic tradition, writes Frye, "the reader is assumed to be a traveler, pursuing his normal course through time and space, who is suddenly confronted with something he should stop and read. What he reads is the verbal essence of a life which has once had its own context in space and time but is now enclosed in a framework of words" ("Approaching" 32). I will devote a later chapter to such epitaphic poetry; but curiously, there is more than one way in which Catullus's "Cui dono" fits this description too, despite its undeniable status as a poem of occasion. (So, in a different way, does Williams's poem.) Cornelius Nepos, the personal addressee, represents stopping and reading, first in having seen *aliquid* (something to stumble over) in *nugae* ("trifles," something to pass on by), and now in ceremonially receiving the volume; and at the same

---

15. Compare Genette's comments (139–40) on Rilke's dedication of the *Duino Elegies,* which reads, "Aus dem Besitz der Fürstin Marie von Thurn und Taxis-Hohenlohe" 'Property of Princess Marie von Thurn und Taxis-Hohenlohe').

time he also represents the ambition to publish something with claims on all time. The "omne aevum" 'all history' which his own work of scholarship will unfold ("explicare") serves to anticipate the phrases Catullus hopefully predicates of his own work, "plus uno . . . saeclo" 'more than one generation' and "perenne" 'lasting.' The unexpected appeal to the Muse in Catullus's concluding prayer is a sudden plea for this divine patroness, too, to stop in her tracks and listen. Finally, any poem explicitly concerned with its possible readers in a later age acquires, when it is read by such a later age, a touching currency of reference at once to itself and (at whatever oblique angle) to its audience.

I have been arguing in part that looking past the one you are addressing is a way of withdrawing your words from him or her (though it may set opposite forces in motion as well). Let us now turn to the field of love poetry, which throws these questions of exclusiveness and intimacy into occasionally nervous prominence. Anne Ferry has remarked on how dramatically even a subtle gesture toward readers—and so away from the beloved addressee—will shift a poem's presentational stance. Marvell's "To His Coy Mistress" (published 1681) has long been cited to illustrate the notion that reading poetry puts us in the position of "overhearers." But as Ferry argues, the title of the poem should complicate this notion in two ways. The word "his," first, "conveys a greater sense that the speaker can look at 'his' mistress with some detachment than would *my mistress,* and it pointedly holds 'his' persuasion up before the reader as a performance of 'I' addressing 'you.' We are distanced as an audience, but we are invited to be present" (123). The "dramatic tone" to which critics such as J. B. Leishman attribute their impression that in this poem "we are overhearing one of the speakers in a dialogue," then, is affirmed by the grammar of the title to be performance, flagged as such and so targeted above all at readers as nonaddressed bystanders.[16] The mistress, if she exists, could as little be the poet's genuine interlocutor as is one's fellow actor on the stage. The point is driven home by Ferry's gloss on the unusual word "coy" in the title, which in this period "could mean displaying shyness, modesty . . . , or making a display of it, so that the most striking word in the title has a double edge like many expressions in the verses." Thus,

---

16. Cited by A. Ferry 123. For a scrutiny of the term "dramatic monologue" and its over-application, see Rader; and see Culler, "The Modern Lyric," and Tucker.

by that adjective in the title, we are let in on the speaker's rhetorical strategy. We are told in advance that he will appeal to the listener as if she were truly shy and modest, while allowing that she may be only putting on a show of reluctance. As a result, there is a kind of complicity between the titler and the reader . . . which excludes the *you* of the poem who hears only the verses. . . . The title . . . draws us into [the poem] as an audience ready to listen to the lover's dazzling argument with an informed appreciation for its fusion of passionate intensity and witty detachment. This would not be the lady's likeliest response to it, either if she were genuinely or affectedly coy. (123–24)

In this respect the title focuses and confirms elements also present in the verses as they play on courtly love conventions; but Ferry's observation is that in this case, the title operates over and above these conventions to underline the exclusion of the poem's *you* from the full obligations and rights of being, besides the addressee, the authentic target of what is said. As a speaker shifts the role of target away from even (let us say) a real, hearing addressee, the effect is to abstract or "fictionalize" that speaker's use of *you* until it only weakly means the interlocutor who is genuinely present and the reversibility of *I* and *you* is frozen.[17]

This is the communicative situation of the vast body of European poetry in the courtly love and Petrarchan traditions (of which Marvell's poem is a late representative). Even in convention-bending poems like Shakespeare's sonnets to his young man, the stylized evocation of an addressee is first an element of the traditional form, and only secondarily— if at all—an appeal to a genuine hearer. The seventeenth-century poet Richard Crashaw titles a poem "Wishes: To his (supposed) Mistresse," and in the same era Robert Herrick wrote "The Parting Verse, or charge to his supposed Wife when he travelled." As Ferry notes, such titles show the late Petrarchan poets' "playful skepticism . . . toward their own self-conscious conventionality" (71). Many of the innumerable mistresses appearing in poetry of the courtly and Petrarchan types were "supposed" persons only.[18]

17. This observation narrows the validity of Alastair Fowler's suggestive remark (21) that "the literary artist can be thought of as using a nonreversible communication link, like a speaker with a megaphone, say, or Roland at Roncesvalles."

18. This point bears on our general framework for understanding lyric, since it shifts the locus for an account of poetic address, in such poems, partly to intertextuality and so away from the notion of poems as contained "fictive utterances" like dramatic monologues. Compare Culler's comments on intertextuality ("Changes in the Study of the Lyric"). See Dubrow's essays on the addressees of Shakespeare's sonnets.

There is a kind of poem, though, in which the stylization of the addressee works chiefly within the individual text, as in Else Lasker-Schüler's 1910 poem "Ein alter Tibetteppich" (*Sämtliche Gedichte* 103):

EIN ALTER TIBETTEPPICH

Deine Seele, die die meine liebet,
Ist verwirkt mit ihr im Teppichtibet.

Strahl in Strahl, verliebte Farben,
Sterne, die sich himmellang umwarben.

Unsere Füße ruhen auf der Kostbarkeit,
Maschentausendabertausendweit.

Süßer Lamasohn auf Moschuspflanzenthron,
Wie lange küsst dein Mund den meinen wohl
Und Wang die Wange buntgeknüpfte Zeiten schon?

AN OLD TIBET-CARPET

Your soul, which loveth mine,
Is entwined with it in Carpet-Tibet.

Ray in ray, enamored colors,
Stars that courted circling heaven-long.

Side by side on precious stuff our feet rest there,
Thousanduponthousandstitchesfar.

Sweet lama-son upon a muskplant throne
How long this kiss your mouth to mine
And cheek to cheek for brightly knotted ages gone?[19]

The opening address takes up and modifies a recurrent phrase from the biblical Song of Solomon, "du, den meine Seele liebet" ("O thou whom my soul loveth," 1:7), and its syntactic interlocking of *I* and *you* inaugurates a string of interlocking and chiastic figures that mimic in grammar the two souls' interwovenness with each other as with the exotic carpet that is both a governing metaphor and, it seems, a thing physically present to the lovers (l. 5). That is, in "Deine Seele, die die meine liebet," the relative clause can mean either "which loveth mine" or "which mine loveth." The indifferently nominative or accusative form "die" stands doubled at the line's center as if to present the "forfeitness" and interwo-

19. My translation borrows in places from Newton's (Lasker-Schüler, *Your Diamond Dreams* 137).

venness ("verwirkt" means both) of the two souls' separate identities. The archaism "liebet" 'loveth' betokens the line's biblical origin, but is also here for the sake of rhyme—which is to say that, bringing the word for the emotion into phonetic concord with the (coined) word for the thing ("Teppichtibet"), it simultaneously discovers in the soul-word "liebet" a conformance to the antiquity of the thing itself ("an old Tibet-Carpet").[20] The phonic resonance that makes love rhyme with Tibet (the country's name is accented on the long first syllable in German) suggests a correlate semantic resonance: this love is like that country (exotic and mysterious, elevated, vast, inaccessible to outsiders) and also like the carpet (old and of stylized design, beautiful in color and form), which seems to have "imported" the country into the poem to begin with.

Though "dein" 'your' belongs in one sense to the forms of address, it is used, like "mein" 'my,' only in third-person (i.e., in nominal) constructions. The line "Deine Seele, die die meine liebet" 'Your soul, which loveth mine' holds a third-person distance from both the addressee and the self, both of which are observed objects like the carpet itself; the speaker steps outside I/you to see I and you (lost) in relationship.

The second stanza presents a still stronger version of disorientation:

> Strahl in Strahl, verliebte Farben,
> Sterne, die sich himmellang umwarben.
>
> Ray in ray, enamored colors,
> Stars that courted circling heaven-long.

The light-imagery of "ray," which can be read after the fact as anticipating "stars," on first reading lends only an unexplained luminescence to—perhaps—the threads of the carpet ("enamored colors") and to the lovers' entwined souls which those threads represent. In the phrase "ray in ray," we cannot say, nor can the lovers, which "ray" is you, which I. The enmeshment of love raises those pronouns' potential reversibility to a meta-

---

20. The echoes of the Song of Solomon in this poem are many. Compare "Er küsse mich mit dem Kusse seines Mundes" 'Let him kiss me with the kisses of his mouth' (1:2); "Ich bin braun, aber gar lieblich, wie die Teppiche Salomos" 'I am black, but comely . . . as the curtains [*Teppiche* 'carpets, tapestries'] of Solomon' (1:5); "Mein Freund ist mein, und ich bin sein" 'My beloved is mine, and I am his' (2:16, 6:3); "Sein Mund ist süß, und alles an ihm ist lieblich" 'His mouth is most sweet: yea, he is altogether lovely' (5:16). The "brightly knotted ages" of the lovers' vast and beginningless communion invoke a Solomonic biblical age, and its ritual-sacramental feeling, together with the atmosphere of a playfully orientalized "old Tibet."

physical oscillation which checks any endeavor to name distinct roles. "Stars" joins this stanza's verbless concatenation of substantives (which uncertainly function as appositives for souls or for attributes of the carpet) by uniting the dyads "ray in ray" and "your soul [and] mine" into a single plural. Together with the coinage "heaven-long," "stars" invokes a spatial vastness; but equally and also, "heaven-long"—with the past tense "courted"—may be taken to indicate the unimaginable reaches of cosmic time (and in this sense the line represents an amplification of the expanse of time signaled by "old" in the poem's title).

In the third stanza, the addressee (who had "disappeared" along with other grammatical deletions in the second) is recaptured under the adjective "our," which continues to refuse any distinction of person: Whose feet are whose? From the metaphors of souls and stars and from the carpet itself as metaphor, this stanza emerges into a physically concrete scene involving bodies and a real carpet: "our feet rest there." The next line, however—the witty "Thousanduponthousandstitchesfar"—stands in uncertain grammatical relation to what precedes it: Is the carpet, or are the feet, seen as at a great distance (*weit*)? Or is it the carpet itself which seems to be an endless expanse, as the printed shape of the word— "stitching together" lexemes into a single bolt of verbal fabric—might suggest?

The last stanza constitutes the focal point of the poem as a poem of personal address. Even here, no pronoun *you* appears as such, but its first line as a whole constitutes a vocative, a nominal string used not in any third-person grammar but rather as a means of directly addressing, while simultaneously describing, the beloved: "Sweet lama-son upon a muskplant throne." The provenance of the carpet has again become salient— just as the title's "Tibetteppich" 'Tibet(an) Carpet' became, in a chiastic crossing of verbal threads, the second line's "Teppichtibet" 'Carpet-Tibet'—to style the beloved, by a remarkable chain of metonymies, as a reincarnate Tibetan monk. Human figures are not represented in Tibetan carpets, but traditional painting and sculpture do show bodhisattvas and lamas on lotus thrones.[21] Lasker's vision of a "muskplant throne" turns this received iconography back to the realm of the heavily sensuous and intoxicating, and works a still greater imaginative change on the ad-

---

21. Heselhaus is therefore mistaken to say that the last stanza "refers to an image-motif of the carpet" (215). Lasker, as a cosmopolitan Berliner in the heyday of German *Orientalistik*, would certainly have known what Tibetan carpets look like.

dressed beloved. As a "Lamasohn" he is young, tingeing their relationship with the maternal; also, as Gerhard Kaiser suggests, "Sohn" 'son' here may evoke the lama as reincarnate bodhisattva, returning after death to be discovered in a child, repeating this process for all eternity in an endless striving to save all beings from suffering.[22] This image then fuses the bridegroom of the Song of Songs, who in Judaic tradition points to the Messiah, with Tibetan depictions of the *yab-yum*, the enlightened being figured in sexual embrace. Eros and divine love merge in the eternal kiss of the god, implicitly answering "How long?" with the endless past and endless future.

That line, "How long this kiss your mouth to mine," hangs suspended between future (*wie lange noch*: "how long will . . . ?") and past (*wie lange schon*, as line 9 will eventually resolve the construction: "how long has . . . ?"). "Your mouth to mine"—the German "dein Mund den meinen" lacks even the preposition—recalls the syntax of line 1, as it also echoes the Bible again ("Let him kiss me with the kisses of his mouth" [1:2]). In these last lines,

> Wie lange küsst dein Mund den meinen wohl
> Und Wang die Wange buntgeknüpfte Zeiten schon?

(here an English rendering cannot be literal enough to make my point), most readers probably infer the verb "kisses" again as the implied connection between "cheek" and "cheek" ("Wang die Wange"). But the phrase retains something of the bewilderment of entwined selves felt earlier in the poem (do cheeks "kiss"?) where the *Verwirktheit* ("interwovenness" and "forfeiture") of embrace masks distinction in an uncertain knotting—*buntgeknüpft*—of *I* and *you* (and carpet); mine and yours; present, past, and future; "here" and the Tibetan utopia of Shambhala.[23]

For our understanding of personal address in poetry, the vital question has to do with the identity of this poem's *you*. Something seems to make us quite confident that the poem is *not* spoken to a genuine Tibetan lama's son; a good deal of its imaginative force would be lost if it were. Interestingly, a linguistic scrutiny of the workings of address in the poem will not reveal how we know this fact. Lasker's poem depends upon the sustained articulation of a fantasy addressee who is a fictive version of the poem's

22. My discussion of this poem is indebted in places to Kaiser 1: 379–82.
23. One more strand to this poem cannot have escaped Lasker's attention: German *dichten* 'to write poetry,' cognate to English *text*, etymologically means "to weave."

true listener and "allocutee." So the stylization, in this text, works by an oscillation between the spoken *you*, who is not there, and the unspoken *you*, who is.

In a sense, the address in "An Old Tibet-Carpet" involves an apostrophe in the narrow sense: an address to a nonhearing, fictional entity, which however here stands in the closest metaphorical relationship to the implicit hearer, the real beloved. There is in this variant of apostrophe a germ of invocation, only superficially at odds with the fact that the person meant is, in a commonsense way, already present. Behind or beneath the poem's playfulness is a gesture of urging the beloved to be present, or to see himself and allow himself to be seen, in the manner of ray, star, colored thread, lama-son on muskplant throne. The poem asserts this view of the addressee *sub specie* to be already so; it exists as and for the departure from a prosaic way of perceiving the erotic relationship. In this detour, simultaneously performed by and urged upon the imagination, we can see something like that "block" or discontinuity that Northrop Frye argued is fundamental to the personal lyric. A poem, he writes, "often takes off from something that blocks normal activity, something a poet has to write poetry about instead of carrying on with ordinary experience. . . . Here the blocking point makes the lyrical poem part of what biologists call a displaced activity, as when a chimpanzee crossed in love starts digging holes in the ground instead" ("Approaching" 32). "An Old Tibet-Carpet" belongs, more specifically, to that sort of poem in which the block has, in Frye's terms, become "transparent," poetry that "turns away from sequential experience and superimposes a different kind of experience on it. The superimposing provides an intense concentration of emotion and imagery, usually on some concrete image" (33). Lasker's poem interrupts the continuum of relationship in order to present the relationship, deepened and condensed, through the sustained diversion of the image of the carpet; and that act of presentation is at the same time an invocation, aiming to bring forth and linger over something of eroticism's sweet strangeness. The poem's performance is meant for an overhearing audience, but since the beloved is both addressee *and* overhearer, it's far from clear that the address is a public one.

Another way in which love poems can interrupt the sequence of experience in the relationship is to turn their attention not to what Frye calls a "concrete image," but to the act of address itself as an emblem of the lovers' connectedness. Unexpectedly, the most vivid way to do this is to imagine the address fallen silent. (A variant I will consider in a moment involves address that gives us to understand that the beloved cannot hear.) The real virtuoso at the affecting art of setting something present against the background of its own imagined absence is Rilke, nowhere more so than in his poem "Lullaby," from the second volume of the *New Poems* (1908):

SCHLAFLIED

Einmal wenn ich dich verlier,
wirst du schlafen können, ohne
dass ich wie eine Lindenkrone
mich verflüstre über dir?

Ohne dass ich hier wache und
Worte, beinah wie Augenlider,
auf deine Brüste, auf deine Glieder
niederlege, auf deinen Mund.

Ohne dass ich dich verschließ
und dich allein mit Deinem lasse
wie einen Garten mit einer Masse
von Melissen und Stern-Anis.

LULLABY

Some day when I lose you,
will you be able to sleep
without me to whisper over you
like a crown of linden branches?

Without me to stay awake here
and put words, almost like eyelids,
on your breasts, on your limbs,
down upon your mouth.

Without me to lock you up
and leave you alone with what is yours
like a garden thickly sown
with mint-balm and star-anise.[24]

The curious double play of absence in this poem is best seen if we first examine it without the opening line. Starting in line 2, "Lullaby" is given

---

24. Rilke, *Kommentierte Ausgabe* 1: 576; *Other* 191, slightly modified. The *Kommentierte Ausgabe* of Rilke's works will henceforth be abbreviated *KA*.

over to evoking the loving attentions of the speaker within a framing conception that he is not there speaking. Invoking a future "some day" wherein no lullaby will be sung, the poem stages a withdrawal of its own verbal act; but the repeated gesture by which the *I* is subtracted—"without me to . . . " (ll. 3, 5, 9)—encloses, each time, a description of what, in the present words, the speaker *is* enacting nonetheless.

Line 2 ("will you be able to sleep?") is in tension with the poem's title, since it makes this a lullaby explicitly evoking, of all things, insomnia. The poem plays with rich inversions: it evokes insomnia, itself a reversal of sleep, by hollowing out this the speaker's present sleep-inducing lullaby, which, however—despite these repeated, negating "without" gestures— is soporifically enacted upon the addressee even by the very words that tell her to imagine it gone and herself wakeful.[25] The peculiar thing about the poem's first line is that it is itself a negative of what the rest of the poem would make us expect. "Some day when I lose you," that is, imagines the scene of departure—the separation of I-and-you that the poem, though it *now* links I and you very intimately, forebodes—as a withdrawal of the addressee, not (as in the rest of the poem) a withdrawal of the speaker. The expected line would be, instead, "some day when you lose me." Reversing the pronouns here, Rilke seems to introduce illogic, because his wording "I lose you" designates the event as an experience of the *I*, and as one, furthermore, that involves losing track of the *you* (not, as the poem does instead, turning to focus on the effects on the *you* of this being-lost). But this illogic—the fact that "I lose you" goes on to tell nothing about the condition of "[me] without you," but rather dwells on the idea of "you . . . without me"—is offset by the "contents" of the *you*'s experience; as the poem spells them out, those contents are exclusively about the *I*. The poem is structured after the manner of Chinese boxes, *I* (l. 1) containing *you* (l. 2) containing *I*, in fact three successive images of the *I* (ll. 3–4; 5–8; 9–10). The actions of the *I* which constitute the whole poem from line 3 onward are—we come by a detour to understand—occurring at present. At the same time they are to be imagined, from the perspective of "some day" in the future when the lovers' togetherness will have given way to their separate alonenesses, as *not* happening. The abandoning addressee is to imagine herself forsaken in turn by the speaker, having to do without him—except that everything, abandon-

25. Another poem discussed later in the chapter develops, as it happens, the idea of insomnia as an upside-down condition. Paul Claes also notes the incongruity of the first line of "Lullaby."

ment, sleeplessness or grief, and (logically) the comforting gestures of the lullaby itself, are all just a "what if," just a dream, just something heard, as we say, in a lullaby.

This poem goes far toward rescinding its own existence in the same gesture with which it comes into being. Both movements are fundamentally connected to the fact that "Lullaby" is a poem of address. It is an easy experiment to rewrite the poem, changing each form of *you* to a form of *she*: "Some day when I lose her, / will she be able to sleep / without me to whisper over her . . . " and so on. Although this experiment leaves the first-person grammar as it was, the new, rewritten version becomes chilly and egotistical in a way that the addressed poem was not. The grammatical alteration makes visible, in other words, the way that *I–you* statements are profoundly different from—since they are not—*I*-statements: the voice that speaks in address speaks from a foundation of mutuality rather than of self. The addressed sentences actually participate in and extend the activity of the relationship between *I* and *you*.

This fact produces the poignancy of *I–you* poems that speak, like Rilke's, of the dissolving of the *I–you* relationship. The content pulls in the opposite direction from the act. Like parting itself in Rilke's poem of that name ("Abschied," *KA* 1: 479; *New* 109, modified), a poem like "Lullaby" is one "by which a tender coalescence / is once more shown and held out and torn apart."

Some commentators have taken the first line's "When I lose you" to mean "when you die." Judith Ryan writes, in a passing reference to this poem, that "the speaker imagines himself whispering or rustling like a linden-tree over the grave of a lost loved one and laying words 'wie Augenlider' (like eyelids) over the dead woman's breast and limbs while she 'sleeps'" (*Modernism* 225). Ryan, in general one of our best readers of Rilke, reads a little too hastily here.[26] The speaker's whispering attentions are explicitly the things the beloved must do *without* when she is dead; the rustling and kiss-like caresses with words cannot belong to a scene at her deathbed or grave. They are occurring here and now (as "hier" [l. 5] declares). The addressee is a lover dropping off to sleep. As she does so,

---

26. Also, neither Ryan nor Berendt (326), who likewise proposes that the poem envisions the addressee's death, discusses the disturbing implication that the addressee, once she is in the grave, is imagined as restlessly needing to be sung back to death. I think the poem risks including this possibility less out of an interest in the macabre than because it is utterly refusing to admit that the symmetry of *I* and *you* could be broken. If one person loses the other, they nevertheless remain two interconnected solitudes, preoccupied with one another.

the poet's lullaby sings to her, spinning a fantasy about separation, wake-fulness, silence—the total inversion of their present situation. (This is so regardless of how we take the phrase "I lose you.")

The image of sleep as an enclosure into which one is shut (as by clos-ing eyelids, "Augenlider" [l. 6]) is a familiar one: "Turn the key deftly in the oiled wards," writes Keats in his "Sonnet to Sleep," "and seal the hushed casket of my soul" (275).[27] The door-locking gesture makes an ap-propriate conclusion to Rilke's lullaby, because the speaker's "leaving alone" the addressee does suggest that she may, at the end of the poem, have fallen asleep.[28] As it happens, this observation brings out a basic pe-culiarity of the lullaby as a genre with respect to address: by its nature a lullaby targets someone who is meant to hear but not entirely to heed what is said. It's not that anyone else is meant, nor that one is singing to oneself; and yet a real lullaby is sung in the hopes that its listener will turn her back on the utterance and leave the speaker and his words, at the last, unheard and alone. Brigitte Bradley remarks that already in the second stanza, if the dropping of "Words, almost like eyelids" on the out-stretched body of the addressee conveys the closing of eyes, it also thereby suggests that the speaker gradually becomes invisible to her as the words of the lullaby continue to fall (201).

The implications of the lullaby genre, together with the specific images of eyelids closing and of leaving someone alone, are that the withdrawal is completed on her side—the speaker does not refer to himself in the poem after the words "leave you alone"—as she accedes to the song by ceasing to listen to it and leaving the *speaker* alone, singing. The threat in line 1 (if threat it is) of his losing her turns out to be fulfilled by the end of the poem itself, but in the gentlest way; and everything in the poem's middle—her insomnia, his repeated subtractions of himself by the phrase "without me"—looks in retrospect like so many displaced invitations to

27. Rilke's image "I lock you up" (in his last stanza) seems like a response to the idea of "I lose you" back in line 1. But the later phrase comes nested in a grammar that subordinates it to the event it "answers": *When* I lose you, will you be able to sleep without me to lock you up as I now do, prior to losing you? In other words, closing the door behind me as I leave you belongs to the set of things that *are* happening now but will no longer happen once I lose you. This is a characteristic freedom of poetry: the second gesture (*ich verschließ*) pre-cedes the first one (*ich verlier*) temporally, but it follows it—reacts to it, even—both psycho-logically and in the unfolding of the poem itself.

28. Claes explores the herbological lore of all three species of plant named in this poem and finds them aptly chosen beyond the suggestiveness of their names: all are reputed so-porifics (150–151).

enter, in sleep, a mirror world, where the echoing question "Will I be able to sleep?" becomes itself the portal to sleep, to a place where the poem's speaker is not heard nor seen singing the lullaby that he is, nevertheless, still singing to the end. One sign of how far the end of the poem loses the concerns of its beginning is that although the second and third stanzas depend syntactically on the question in line 2—"will you be able to sleep?"—the question mark falls away, in both cases, as if the images of each stanza had come to stand on their own, as complete thoughts in some sense other than the syntactic one.

Eudo C. Mason, in a pithy excursus appended to one of his studies of Rilke, identifies the "gesture of withdrawal" as deeply characteristic of Rilke in his life and work alike.[29] Mason indicates that Rilke knew this fact about himself: "On one occasion [Rilke] describes himself as 'a place where giving and taking back have often been almost one and the same thing, so swiftly would the most genuine impulse swing round to its opposite.' "[30] Mason comments, "The moment of withdrawal is for him the creative moment"; as "Lullaby" withdraws, simultaneously on the speaker's side and on the addressee's, it opens up negative spaces in which an intimate tenderness comes to be because it has gone missing, so to speak, while it is still there.

In contrast to Rilke's discovery of hypothetical negation as a means of affirming, other sorts of poems can withdraw so decisively from their addressees that they exclude them from hearing the poem at all. A small subgenre of modern poetry centers on this paradoxical thwarting of the communicative gesture.[31] Often the marked refusal or retraction of effective address only sharpens, in such works, the palpability of the "other" with whom the poem shows itself preoccupied, as if negation and absence generated a peculiarly potent virtual presence. Jürgen Theobaldy's 1976 poem "Something" works along these lines, while also neatly ex-

29. See his essay "Rilke and the Gesture of Withdrawal" (176–78). Mason observes, for example, that Rilke "always withdraws himself from his own professions of faith—which is something different from simply repudiating them" (176).

30. Mason (177–78) attributes the quotation to Rilke's letter to Ilse Erdmann of October 9, 1915, but this reference is evidently erroneous.

31. I am thinking of such works as Dylan Thomas's "To Others Than You"; Adrienne Rich's "To a Poet," with its line "I write this   not for you"; or Donald Justice's "Poem," which begins, "This poem is not addressed to you." The Expressionist poet Ludwig Rubiner begins his poem "Die Ankunft" (Arrival) with an address to "Ihr, die Ihr diese Zeilen nie hören werdet" 'You (plural) who will never hear these lines.'

emplifying Frye's notion of poetry as a "displaced activity," "something a poet has to write poetry about instead of carrying on with ordinary experience" ("Approaching" 32):

IRGEND ETWAS

Irgend etwas hält mich davon ab
dich zu lieben. Du bist schön. Ich
mag dich. Gern sitze ich neben dir
im Kino und versuch, die Menschen
auf der Leinwand zu verstehen.
Und gern bin ich mit dir am Tisch
schaue dich an und lausche auf
den Wein, wie er langsam in den Abgrund
hinter unsren Augen rieselt. Ich kann
dir auch sehr viel erzählen, zum Beispiel
wie ich die Leiche deines Vaters
vergraben habe, im Traum natürlich
oder wie das Licht anging, als ich
auf dir lag, auch im Traum, denn ich
kann dich nicht lieben. Es geht nicht.
Eine Mauer oder sowas, eine unsichtbare
Wand aus Glas, oder sogar
ein kurzer scharfer Schnitt zwischen
meinem Kopf und meinem Körper. Und
jetzt, anstatt dich zu lieben
schreibe ich dieses Gedicht. Umgekehrt
wäre besser, würdest du sagen, wenn du
dieses Gedicht gelesen hättest. Aber
du hast es nicht gelesen, das heißt
ich habe es dir nicht gezeigt.

SOMETHING

Something keeps me
from loving you. You're beautiful. I
like you. I like sitting next to you
at the movies, trying to understand
the people on the screen.
And I like sitting at the table with you
looking at you and listening to
the wine trickling slowly into the abyss
behind our eyes. I can also
tell you lots of things, like
how I buried your father's

> corpse, in a dream of course,
> or how the light came on as I
> lay on top of you, also in a dream, because I
> can't love you. It won't work.
> A Wall or something, an invisible
> wall of glass, or even
> a short sharp cut between
> my head and my body. And
> now, instead of loving you
> I'm writing this poem. The other way around
> would be better, you'd say, if you
> had read this poem. But
> you haven't read it, which is to say
> I haven't shown it to you.

The poem, as it announces in lines 20–21, comes into being because of the inability to love that it takes as its theme. With the closing lines in mind, we could also say that this is a message that originates in its own undeliverability; the poem addresses a *you* because of and concerning its inability to address that *you* in the ways it does here, the ways that might matter.

The tone struck is a remarkably flat parlando, a not-quite-complete anesthesia. There is an odd passivity, too, verging on simple-mindedness, in the first two "interactions" the speaker describes: "sitting . . . trying to understand"; "sitting at the table . . . looking at you and listening." This bewildered passivity seems to drop away in lines 9–10: "I can also / tell you lots of things." But the apparently aggressive or shocking ("I buried your father's / corpse") together with the erotic content of these anecdotes is muted by the doubled retraction "in a dream" (ll. 12, 14), and is still further "cut off" from the addressee by the indication that even these dreams are something the speaker "can" tell (l. 9) but, as that same word implies, has not told. These lines anticipate in miniature the poem's concluding retraction or emptying of its own communicative shape: "I haven't shown it to you."

The disconnections and displacement are rife. The attempt to understand is focused not on the addressee but on the literally "projected" images of the movies (ll. 4–5). Grammatically, too, the poem keeps *I* and *you* entirely distinct, never speaking of "us" except once, and then to posit a shared "abyss" ("Abgrund" [l. 8]), which is to say a gap where something shared should be. The scene of (attempted) sexual congress—dreamed merely—appears in strikingly passive, static form: "I / lay on top of you" (ll. 13–14). The "event" which could (but will not) be narrated is not a shared sexual encounter but "how the light came on as I / lay on top of you." This image itself involves a curious ambiguity: does this "light" have a figurative meaning? If we suppose instead that the light overhead really does come on unexpectedly, the effect might well be one of interruption, not insight. Even if we took "the light came on" as metaphor, it would still leave us in doubt as to the realization attained (was it perhaps the inability to love? or was it an answer to that dilemma?). This long sentence ("I can also / tell you lots of things . . . "), in its ending, casually turns a corner to find itself back at the poem's beginning (which was "Something keeps me / from loving you"). But at that moment it also rings an unanticipated change on the motif "can't love":

> Ich kann
> dir auch sehr viel erzählen, zum Beispiel
> wie ich die Leiche deines Vaters
> vergraben habe, im Traum natürlich
> oder wie das Licht anging, als ich
> auf dir lag, auch im Traum, denn ich
> kann dich nicht lieben. Es geht nicht. (ll. 9–15)

> I can also
> tell you lots of things, like
> how I buried your father's
> corpse, in a dream of course,
> or how the light came on as I
> lay on top of you, also in a dream, because I
> can't love you. It won't work.

The logic of "because" (l. 14), implying an equivalence between loving and lying on top of, introduces a physical meaning to "lieben": I cannot make love to you. The lines that follow reinforce the perception that impotence is among the poem's expressions of disconnection. The verbless sentence begins with that most charged noun, in German, of unwilled division, "a Wall" ("Mauer" [l. 16]) and downgrades it first with the hedge "or some such," then with the image of a finer, or rather an invisible partition: "an invisible / wall of glass" (*eine Wand*, in contrast to *eine Mauer*, means a wall found indoors, or the wall of a house). The sentence ends by internalizing the division into the speaker's own body:

> oder sogar
> ein kurzer scharfer Schnitt zwischen
> meinem Kopf und meinem Körper. (ll. 17–19)

> or even
> a short sharp cut between
> my head and my body.

Impotence and the missing emotional connection here serve as metaphors for each other, as we cannot say which side of the "cut"—head or body—loves and which does not.

This version of disconnection gives way in the next lines to the either-or of writing and loving: "now, instead of loving you / I'm writing this poem." But in these terms, as we know from having read this far, the wall (or cut) really has only one side:

> Umgekehrt
> wäre besser, würdest du sagen, wenn du
> dieses Gedicht gelesen hättest. Aber
> du hast es nicht gelesen, das heißt
> ich habe es dir nicht gezeigt. (ll. 21–25)

> The other way around
> would be better, you'd say, if you
> had read this poem. But
> you haven't read it, which is to say
> I haven't shown it to you.

The poem's logic supposes that a reversal of the writing/loving opposition ("The other way around / would be better") is inherently contrary to fact, not least because such a reversal would recommend the poem out of existence. But this reversal is doubly negated by being made dependent on another, independent contrary-to-fact condition: "if you / had read this poem." If writing the poem is a compensatory act of creation, allowing it to be read would expose it to destruction ("The other way around / would be better")—a notion that does violence to the fundamental idea that writing is communication. In this way we arrive at the curious doubleness of the poem's *you*, wherein the speaker addresses a genuine other—someone specific is meant—but at the same time shields the poem from contact, from "addressing" its addressee: "I haven't shown it to you."

Theobaldy's poem, then, comes like Williams's "This Is Just to Say" as

a substitute or compensation for a lack where the addressee will have expected to find something. Like Catullus's poem, also, it belongs to a presentational type, taking as theme its own significance as an object in
expressive transaction between *I* and *you*. Catullus's "Cui dono?" 'To
whom do I give?' wittily alludes to the oxymoronic sweet "inedibility" of
poetry: the willing gift of the book cannot but simultaneously reserve it
for other, later readers. Theobaldy's "Something" brings a suggestion of
impotence where Catullus's poem had invoked the preserving energies
of virginity, and this difference may stand for others. The failure of desire
("because I / can't love you") is a drama of the self, the inability to discover oneself in the terms of relation, or even in the "conversation" that
Theobaldy's colloquial tone might seem to summon up. The enacted presentation of Catullus's "to whom do I give?" to his friend Cornelius
draws after it the thought of the Muse, guarantor of readers beyond this
one; addressed as "virgo," an emblem of desire's frustration, she stands
for the poems' continued freshness, not just their enduring ability to generate new relation and desire but their inability not to do so.

But in "Something" a thought of posterity is absent, as if the failure of
personal address, far from shunting the communication toward some
gallery of "overhearers," were instead dampening that possibility too. A
great many poems give no explicit attention to their later audiences. If in
this case the omission is significant, the significance lies in the impression
it gives us that just as the energy of Catullus's bequeathing his book to his
friend occasions, instead of obstructing, a prayer that the book may be
kept ("may it remain") for other readers, so the inhibition of a poem's personal address ("I haven't shown it to you") limits also its concern with listeners beyond its (non)addressed *you*.

Something like this principle may hold the clue to explaining, in turn,
why it should be that certain poems of loss—poems addressed to the
dead, or to a deserting (unhearing) lover—come still closer to contro-
verting Eliot's maxim that poems "addressed to one person" are nevertheless "always meant to be overheard by other people." It is in these
cases, where the addressee—grievously—cannot hear, that the act of address becomes most convincingly singular.

Elizabeth Bishop's "Insomnia" is such a poem:

INSOMNIA

The moon in the bureau mirror
looks out a million miles

(and perhaps with pride, at herself,
but she never, never smiles)
far and away beyond sleep, or
perhaps she's a daytime sleeper.

By the Universe deserted,
she'd tell it to go to hell,
and she'd find a body of water,
or a mirror, on which to dwell.
So wrap up care in a cobweb
and drop it down the well

into that world inverted
where left is always right,
where the shadows are really the body,
where we stay awake all night,
where the heavens are shallow as the sea
is now deep, and you love me. (70)

This poem, aptly enough given its central motif of the "world inverted" (l. 13) by reflection, asks to be reread "upward" from its last three words. Here at the bottom of the "well" (l. 12) that is the poem, the words "you love me"—half a deliberate pronouncing of the longed-for condition as if to wish it into being, half the anguished reverse image of the true state of affairs—culminate and shed light backward on the last stanza's accumulating inversions, and on the poem as a whole.

The title and first stanza already project reflections within reflections. If it is partly the moon—not the real one but the moon in the bureau mirror—that suffers from insomnia, "far and away beyond sleep" (l. 5), it is just as evidently also the speaker, looking all too wakefully into that mirror, she whose own circumstances the mirror-moon is made to reflect. The poem proceeds by avoidance of the *I* in favor of its displacement into the image of the moon in the bureau mirror. The speaker's reflection is unmistakably visible in the opening of the second stanza, since the contrastive, italicized pronoun *she* tells us—by indirection—everything about the speaker's own desolate situation.

By the Universe deserted,
she'd tell it to go to hell

But no signal before the last line reveals that the poem is not uttered within the self alone. Heartbreak is in a sense *about* the I-you relationship, but talk of heartbreak need not therefore take the form of address. Rather, address to the unloving partner takes on, formally speaking, a special pathos, since in the courageously sustained appeal to the beloved are already present the vulnerability of the speaker, the yearning for reciprocal intimacy which is, or may feel like, the radical of all address, and the anguished suppression of that same yearning.

But "Insomnia" does not, after all, really "speak to" the beloved; or better—since here again we are encountering the problematic conflation of two separate senses of "address"—the beloved does not "hear." Earlier the poem invoked another addressee altogether, namely the speaker herself, arguing from the case of the reflected moon in the mirror to her own case and urging an attempt at indifference:

> By the Universe deserted
>
> . . . .
> ... she'd find a body of water,
> or a mirror, on which to dwell.
> So wrap up care in a cobweb
> and drop it down the well (ll. 7, 9–12)

Dwelling on at least one mirror herself, the speaker issues half-hearted advice; but the self-imperatives, and the will to them, last no more than these two lines (ll. 11–12). Insomnia, and gazing at the moon in the bureau mirror, remain solitary activities, and with the words "you love me," the conflict between the form of the utterance (address to the beloved) and its context (lying in bed alone) expresses poignancy as much as does the "inverted" indirection. The reality that this mirrored "you love me" reverses is "I love you" but also, alas, "you don't love me."

The image of the mirror combines two elements: the reversal of the way things naturally are (insomnia is not mere wakefulness but rather the reverse of sleep where sleep should be); and the idea of loneliness (since the being in the mirror is just an illusion of twoness manufactured in isolation). If the mirror-world offers the illusion of an alternative to the speaker's present misery, the illusion is thin, and the speaker's language itself repeatedly betrays her by simultaneously reflecting her present lonely state: the putatively self-sufficient moon is, annihilatingly, "deserted" by the entire "Universe" (l. 7) (hence the loss of the beloved looks like the loss of everything); the word "body" recurs tellingly (ll. 9, 15); through the escape through the looking glass it is hoped that being "left" will turn out to have been all "right" (l. 14). Even where the insomniac self seems really to have entered the inverted world—"where we stay awake all night" (l. 16)—both the treacherous pronoun "we" and the erotic cliché "all night" send this line into an unreliable oscillation between what is and what is wished for.[32] Before the poem's last three words, the imagery of inversion is already beginning to collapse: in the mirror or the well, it is said, "the heavens are shallow as the sea / is now deep." In each of the two ways we are invited to take this enjambment, whether pausing at the line break or not, the sense is elusive, since first the sea must be shallow, and then "shallow" and "deep" must find an (unavailable) common measure. The intrusion of the real "now" into the elaboration of the unreal world ("the sea / is now deep") marks yet another threadbare spot in the scenery of escape.

Bishop's poem requires, in a way, its turn to the second person. Equally important, though, is the awareness that the addressee does not hear, is not in that other sense "addressed" at all. (We might say that the addressee—the *you*—is not, in "Insomnia," a genuine interlocutor or "allocutee.") In this sense the poem's *you*, like the *you* of Theobaldy's "Something," would seem to meet a usefully narrow definition of apostrophe, namely, address to nonhearing entities. Yet much would be sacrificed if Bishop's *you*, which aches with the memory of genuine allocution and with the desire for its return, got assimilated to invocations of the state, a sunflower, or (as in a sonnet of Sidney's which "Insomnia" self-consciously recalls)[33] the moon.

Even between Bishop's poem and Theobaldy's, the difference in the feeling of the address is great. The emotional dead end of "Something" works twelve forms of *I* and fifteen of *you* into its twenty-five lines, as if the speaker were vainly assailing his numbness with volleys of "personal" pronouns. "Insomnia," by contrast, cannot bring itself to say either *I* or *you* but once, when it has reached the very bottom; and with that reticence the poem seems to open up "a million miles" of yearning, as if the beloved really were a boundless "Universe" receding in all directions. Such address recalls Rilke's theory that the purest love is that which goes unanswered or, even more, a devotion in which the beloved is "a direction of love, not an object of it."[34]

A poem Rilke wrote in 1913 but never published depicts this deliber-

32. Wheeler, taking a different cue from the word "inverted," reads the poem as one of Bishop's "lightly coded explorations of the experience of homosexuality" (126).

33. *Astrophel & Stella*, sonnet 31 (1582).

34. *Die Aufzeichnungen des Malte Laurids Brigge* (The notebooks of Malte Laurids Brigge [1910]), §70, *KA* 3: 628.

ately intensified sense of loss in personal address. It invokes, as it happens, a simile of the moon:

> Wie das Gestirn, der Mond, erhaben, voll Anlass,
> plötzlich die Höhn übertritt, die entworfene Nacht
> gelassen vollendend: siehe: so steigt mir
> rein die Stimme hervor aus Gebirgen des Nichtmehr.
> Und die Stellen, erstaunt, an denen du dawarst und fortkamst,
> schmerzen klarer dir nach.

> The way that bright planet, the moon, exalted, full of purpose,
> all at once surmounts the peaks, filling in serenely
> the outlined night: look: just so my voice
> rises purely out of the mountains of no longer.
> And the places—astonished—that you occupied and left
> ache more clearly for you.[35]

The moon's appearance above mountain peaks is said to complete "die entworfene Nacht," the night as something sketched out, provisionally drawn up. In the terms of the simile, the poet's "voice / rises" like the moon, over an enjambed line, above "the mountains of no longer"—rises, then, out of and over a massif that is not there. Or rather, the image is not one of absence, merely, but one of loss: the mountains, nothing themselves, are memories, looming in and as the place where what once was is no longer. The voice that comes up from this lack, lunar, unbidden, not claimed by the poet except through the dative "mir" (l. 3), must in its turn "serenely complete" a night that was but provisional without it.[36] It is a voice appearing out of disappearance.

The last two lines bring attention to the specific loss of the addressee:

35. *KA* 2: 65; *Uncollected* 77, modified slightly. Compare these lines from a trio of poems Rilke had written in 1911 (but not shown!) to Lou Andreas-Salomé: "Selbst, dass du nicht da bist, / ist warm von dir und wirklicher und mehr / als ein Entbehren" 'Even your not being there / is warm with you and more real and more / than a privation' (*KA* 2: 18; *Uncollected* 15).

36. The force of the dative in "steigt mir ... hervor" is hard to capture in English (and a little uncertain in German; it is Rilke's invented construction). An analogy might be "Da entfuhr mir ein Seufzer" 'a sigh escaped me': the effect is notably passive, as if the pure rising of the voice were something the speaker had to undergo, rather than his being "serenely" (l. 2) in charge of it. "Steigt hervor" (translated as "rises") is a coined expression mixing "steigt herauf" 'climbs up' and "tritt hervor" 'steps forth': it might be more literally rendered as "rises forth." I thank Johannes Wich-Schwarz for help with these observations.

Und die Stellen, erstaunt, an denen du dawarst und fortkamst,
schmerzen klarer dir nach.

And the places—astonished—that you occupied and left
ache more clearly for you.

Astonishment is like the afterimage of presence, the apprehension of the existent in the light of its own "gratuitousness," by which I mean the grateful fact that a thing was, at all, when it did not have to be. To be "erstaunt" (in a context like this) is to know being and non-being together, as twin and inseparable aspects of phenomena. Far from being mere nothingness, the places at which the beloved "was present," but is no longer, show forth now *what* was lost, entire, etched in the finest line, "serenely perfected" by the falling away of the obscurations and entanglements that attend our usual perception of things and people around us.

But the clarity of Rilke's own words here has above all to do with the fact that his lines do not "portray," as I have been doing, from a third-person perspective: they address. The rising voice speaks to, not of, the one lost, *to* the one whose inability to be a *you* any more is the epicenter of the speaker's pain. Addressing the empty place directly, seeking the knife as it were, the poet speaks "purely" ("rein"), taking not-being into himself and discovering "aching after" (*nachschmerzen*, Rilke's coinage) as a kind of knowing, a way of limning the one who is gone and a sort of lucidity.

The gesture "look," in line 3, holds up to the addressee the image of the moon, but also—since colons both precede and follow it—it holds up in the visual field the poet's voice, which must suggest the "rising" of voice into print. The poem draws attention to its own moment-to-moment appearance: this means both, as if they were the same thing, its coming to be under the composing pen and its word-by-word entry into the reader's, or rather the addressee's, consciousness. The hesitation in that last phrase (reader? addressee?) itself shows Rilke's enigma, since the lost addressee does not hear, and one would like to say even more emphatically does not read, the poem. A lyric addressing the absent and unhearing is in this way just the converse of a letter: reading, which in epistolary practice makes communication with the absent possible, here seems beside the point. If contact is made, then this occurs not at some later time of receipt (there is none) but exactly in the moment of composition.

And what of *our* position as readers? Here there are two things to be said. First, we may, in reading, "blur" ourselves into the addressee position even where the logic of the discourse deters such identification—a topic I also raise elsewhere in this book. Second, and more fundamentally: to the extent that in reading we become aware of ourselves and try to find our own position vis-à-vis speaker and addressee, we might speak of "overhearing" Bishop's poem, or Rilke's. But at least in these poems, I think this notion presumes too much self-consciousness on the reader's part. When I read "Insomnia" or the Rilke poem, the question of my own position strikes me as intrusive, a confusion of levels. The poem does not know of us, and reading it, we may not know of ourselves either.

The poems I have discussed are not meant to represent prototypes of a category of personal address to a contemporary of the poet's, but neither are they eccentric. They illustrate some of the intricacies of what could have seemed to be the most straightforward form of address in lyric.

Williams's "This Is Just to Say" approaches ordinary communication, the "prose" with which (as Eliot says) we routinely and genuinely address one another. But it wins its power to say more than domestic notes say—it makes visible or palpable, makes into a gift, the matter-of-factness of taking that is the tenderest part of intimacy—by withdrawing, as poetry, from the person it addresses. Catullus's dedicatory verses raise these same matters to the noisier level of the poet looking for a patron, praise for his work, and fame. His is no love poem; it gives exemplary voice to the ambivalent social energies generated by poets' acts of address in pursuit of their survival. The comparison with Williams shows how porous the distinction is between private and public transactions of this kind. Framing words that mean to have value (to be kept for their own sake), Catullus at the same time means to do communicative work, managing his relations to other people, by talking to his friend—and in a different way, perhaps by talking past him in the final verses, too. The autonomous and communicative aspects of the work (the terms are Jan Mukařovský's) are always opposed, and always interlaced.

Else Lasker-Schüler's "An Old Tibet-Carpet" illustrates the frequent case that a poetic addressee is addressed "as" something, and this example turns out unexpectedly to complicate the intuition—introduced earlier in the terms of Mill and Eliot, and seconded by W. R. Johnson—that poetry is something prototypically "overheard." Lasker's poem addresses a real, "listening" beloved, who is also a bystander to this same address. The stylization of the addressee through the vocative shows how personal address can be colored with something akin to apostrophe-in-the-sense-of-summoning, that sort of second-person hailing that describes (as if it were, rather, third person) as much as it calls. The listener is genuinely addressed, but as someone he may not have been before—even as someone he may not "be" at all outside this instance of address.

Rilke's "Lullaby" anticipates Bishop's "Insomnia" by finding in sleeplessness and sleep a mirroring inversion that suggests, in turn, the play of other reversals—some of them treacherous—between *I* and *you*, together and apart, the poem itself and silence. The poem does not withhold itself so much as it depends on and stages scenes of withdrawal, in which the addressee drifts away from the speaker into sleep while he, still close by, sings to her about their being far apart, reflecting presence in a pool of its own loss.

Theobaldy's poem "Something" also negates or inverts its own act of intimate address, but with anguished success; in this way it renders literal the idea of poetry's communicative "withholding." It comes in the place of the things it itself says to the beloved, because the beloved is unbeloved, is not a true *you* despite being a real person in the speaker's daily life. The failure of relation and desire could more easily have been recounted in a third-person account, but the dampened emotion of Theobaldy's poem is felt in its rehearsal of address to the *you* who is meant not to hear.

Bishop's poem and Rilke's "Wie das Gestirn" (The way that bright planet), addressing a beloved who is lost to the speaker, seem at first to be out of place as examples of address to contemporaries. Elegiac address to the absent or dead has traditionally been thought of as a classic instance of apostrophe, which as a category appears to be the contrary of address to a living friend or lover. But the intensity of focus on the lost addressee in "Insomnia" and in Rilke's poem suggests that, on the contrary, being heard is distracting to the purity of address. The isolation of the speaker from his or her addressed target unexpectedly goes hand in hand with the ability really to intend the addressed other, really to speak—if we apply T. S. Eliot's words against his own argument—"to the beloved and to no one else."

When a poet speaks to other people, then, the address may often betray the complicatedness of this endeavor—very often just where the poet's address to a friend or beloved becomes itself the poem's chief concern. Poems that seem most obviously like communication undercut that connection, while deeply communicative lyric may be born out of the difficulty or impossibility of communication. Public and private spheres crisscross in a perplexing manner that the helpful distinctions of linguistic pragmatics can bring to light but not, finally, resolve. In an account of reading lyric, there will be places where the participant roles of speaker, intended hearer, and bystander melt together or away; these are moments of wonder.

The next chapter also begins with poems addressing people who are not there to hear, but who, in these cases, never were known to the poet. The projective character of converse with past, future, or mythic figures—people inaccessible, in a commonsense way, to the poem's message—gives the poems examined here an impetus to open or expand the addressee in the gesture of invocation. Complementary to that outward motion, and still more richly attested, is the second topic of the chapter: that other lyric *you* which targets, and constricts, its object with pinpointing authority. Such tenacious poems are also, characteristically, works in which the one who has difficulty staying clear of the poem's insistent call to *you* is the poem's reader.

2

Address as Greeting, Address as Spell

> Calling brings closer what it calls.
> —Martin Heidegger

1. Opening Out

I CONCLUDED the previous chapter by proposing that when the person addressed in the poem is lost to the speaker, the elegiac spaces opened up can be pure, vast distances, and the withholding reflex that characterizes poems addressed to living contemporaries falls away or ceases to be palpable. But there are other kinds of sentient addressee, too, not just lost ones, who are structurally unable to have the poem; they are beyond the reach of communication in other ways. In poems addressing historical figures, for example, history contained and "done with" may turn, by the poet's address, into something still open or not yet done. Or it reveals a new, open dimension without losing its character of containment or fixity, making the poem into a temporal crossroads.[1] The first section of this chapter takes up examples of lyric address to various sorts of figures (historical and otherwise) that follow this pattern of expanding what is closed and inaccessible into a flexible present tense by means of the gesture of address.

Many poems calling upon celebrated figures from the annals of history (to take this example first), as opposed to elegies for our own dead, adopt

---

1. Readers interested in apostrophe to historical and (especially) religious figures should see Diehl 137–40 on "as-if-there apostrophe" and "do-as-you-did apostrophe" (which I think should be seen as overlapping categories). Sharon Olds's poem "I Go Back to May 1937" provides a secular modern version of the "do-as-you-did" idea.

an oratorical air befitting the public status of the famous addressee, as in the many English addresses to Shakespeare. But Constantine Cavafy, who was fond of both poetic address and the figures of classical antiquity, brings these together in a tone that is intimate and psychological.[2] In his poem "Ides of March" (1911), the text undertakes an explicitly counter-historical urging, conjuring Julius Caesar not to do as he famously did. The poem becomes a meditation on tragedy and history:

> Τα μεγαλεία να φοβάσai, ω ψυχή.
> Και τες φιλοδοξίες σου να υπερνικήσεις
> αν δεν μπορείς, με δισταγμό και προφυλάξεις
> να τες ακολουθείς. Κι όσο εμπροστά προβαίνεις,
> τόσο εξεταστική, προσεκτική να είσai. (48, ll. 1–5)

> Fear honors and wealth, O soul.
> And if you cannot overcome your ambitions,
> With hesitation and precautions
> Follow them. And the farther you advance,
> The more searching, attentive you must be.

The poem begins as if it were Caesar's self-address—"O soul"—though the thoughts are uncharacteristic of the Caesar of historical and literary tradition. "When you reach your peak, Caesar at last" (όταν θα φθάσεις στην ακμή σου, Καίσαρ πια [l. 6]), the poem goes on (and these later verses become increasingly hard to square with the notion of self-address),

> αν τύχει και πλησιάσει από τον όχλο
> κανένας Αρτεμίδωρος, που φέρνει γράμμα,
> και λέγει βιαστικά «Διάβασε αμέσως τούτα,
> είναι μεγάλα πράγματα που σ' ενδιαφέρουν»,
> μη λείψεις να σταθείς· μη λείψεις ν' αναβάλεις
> κάθε ομιλίαν ή δουλειά· μη λείψεις τους διαφόρους
> που χαιρετούν και προσκυνούν να τους παραμερίσεις
> (τους βλέπεις πιο αργά)· ας περιμένει ακόμη
> κ' η Σύγκλητος αυτή, κ' ευθύς να τα γνωρίσεις
> τα σοβαρά γραφόμενα του Αρτεμιδώρου. (ll. 10–19)

> if it happens that from the populace
> some Artemidoros comes near, carrying a letter,

---

2. Cavafy's frequent addresses to figures out of his reading inflect, among other precedents, the medieval rhetorical exercise of *suasoria*, or deliberative eloquence. See Curtius 69, 155; Diehl 140–41. On "Ithaka," the most famous of these advice poems, see my "Poetic Address and Intimate Reading" 213–16.

and hurriedly says, "Read this at once,
it is a grave matter that concerns you,"
do not fail to stop; do not fail to postpone
all talk, every task; do not fail to turn away
the various people who greet you and pay homage
(you are seeing them later); let even
the Senate itself wait, and know at once
the grave writings of Artemidoros.

Artemidoros was the Sophist who, on March 15, "vainly tried to hand Caesar a message disclosing the murderous plot of Brutus and Cassius" (Keeley and Sherrard 225). This poem's fine-grained account of the future ("if it happens that . . . ") must draw its information, and its urgency, from the pastness of this future (what we know befell Caesar on the Ides of March). More specifically, the language of advice-giving and choice springs, both in motivation and in content, from the fixity and fatedness of tragedy, whose nature it is not to be able to be otherwise. The poem works through the two aspects of history: on the one hand, history is something completed, a closed whole, which cannot be altered but only gone over again; on the other hand, history means experience in time, not static but serial, open to change at each moment. Like tragedy, Cavafy's poem plays on the pathos that emerges when these two sides are taken together, when we reexperience the open choices that seal a fate shut.

These conflicting viewpoints with respect to time are responsible for the difficulty of identifying the speaker of this poem.[3] The words "O soul" in the first line set up a scene of self-communion, which is to say that they seem at first to make the poem into a role-poem (a dramatic monologue) whose speaker is Julius Caesar.[4] But when we read about "some Artemidoros" who, "if it [so] happens" (αν τύχει), may approach the *you* saying these specific words, we feel the poem pull away from the framework of self-address that "O soul" seemed to signal. The one who knows this much cannot himself be Caesar, and cannot caution Caesar either, since what the poem says is knowledge bought only with Caesar's incaution

3. The ironies of time are present even in a casual aside like "(you are seeing them later)": since Caesar—as we cannot help knowing—does *not* put off his petitioners now to read Artemidoros's letter, he cannot ever see them later. Futurity is undone for Caesar (he dies) because of his unwillingness to "postpone" (l. 14) into it, to put his arrival in the Senate into that future, taking the time to heed a message that, like this poem itself, would give him time.

4. In the Greek, the adjectives in line 5 ("searching, careful") are feminine in form, continuing the appeal to the soul.

and death. The resulting utterance is neither in accord with history nor at odds with it: this Caesar seems to narrate himself from a timeless vantage concerned with the disposition of the soul, with selfhood abstracted from all sequence and hence detached from the conundrums of time and knowledge which, taken narrowly, the poem would make proliferate.[5] Because of this abstracted perspective, there is no dramatic irony in Cavafy's poem, no knowing look exchanged with readers over the head of Julius Caesar, just a fateful gap between these words and Caesar's actions in the temporal continuum. Although the counsel is framed as his own self-admonition, on the Ides of March Caesar will not (cannot) heed this warning any more than he heeded the prophet who told him to beware that day to begin with, or any more than he heeds Artemidoros himself. The second-person form, the inward address to his own soul, is conspicuously at odds with his fixed or fated inability to hear.

It is unexpected that there can be such proximity or even overlap between self-address—where the lyric *you* never leaves an individual consciousness—and a mode of poetic retrospection calling upon a celebrated historical figure. But it is not hard for the reader imaginatively to share in Caesar's plight and to hear the words of this poem (to feel addressed by them) all the more acutely because knowing that this is the message that passed Caesar by. Inhabiting Caesar becomes, in Cavafy's poem, a way of expanding the figure's possibilities, at least for the one long, temporally dislocated moment of the poem's counsel.

If the fate of Caesar is always something we finally know too much about to open the closed book of history on his page, the case is different where the chronicles have left a blank. A largely unknown historical figure can be explicitly conjured through the poet's imagination, and the life that is long past can be rendered immediate and open. This is the mode of another Cavafy poem, "Caesarion" (1918), whose title refers to the seventeen-year-old son of Caesar and Cleopatra, executed as Octavian took power. In the text's first fourteen lines, we have a first-person account of the poet reading in his study; the last sixteen lines switch to second-person address. This turn stands also for other, simultaneous turns between the poem's two parts. Here are the opening lines:

---

5. Alternatively, Cavafy's "Ides of March" may be the counsel that a modern reader sometimes wants, vainly, to impart to the tragic figures of the past—a message not just unheard but radically unhearable because it can be formulated only by virtue of the subsequency it dreams of undoing.

Εν μέρει για να εξακριβώσω μια εποχή,
εν μέρει και την ώρα να περάσω,
την νύχτα χθες πήρα μια συλλογή
εμιγραφών των Πτολεμαίων να διαβάσω.
Οι άφθονοι έπαινοι κ' η κολακείες
εις όλους μοιάζουν. Όλοι είναι λαμπροί,
ένδοξοι, κραταιοί, αγαθοεργοί·
κάθ' επιχείρησίς των σοφοτάτη.
Αν πεις για τες γυναίκες της γενιάς, κι αυτές,
όλες η Βερενίκες κ' η Κλεοπάτρες θαυμαστές. (100–101, ll. 1–10)

In part to verify what one epoch was like,
in part to pass the time as well,
last night I took down a collection
of Ptolemaic inscriptions to read.
The abundant praises and the flatteries
fit all of them. All are brilliant,
glorious, powerful, beneficent;
each undertaking of theirs most wise.
If you speak of the women of the line, they too,
all the Berenices and Cleopatras, are marvelous.

The way the flattering inscriptions "fit all of them" (l. 6) depicts history as closed and unalive. Given what the speaker learns from his evening's study—that the Ptolemies were uniformly glorious, wise, and admirable—the phrasing of line 1 becomes ironic when he repeats it in line 11, wrapping up his reading: "When I'd succeeded in verifying what the epoch was like . . . " The verb here, εξακριβώνω, conveys exactitude and precision. But in this case history (as represented by the first half of the poem) brings no exact or even reliable knowledge. This failure prompts a second, compensatory attempt to get the details right, through the methods not of study but of "art" (τέχνη, l. 20).

Όταν κατόρθωσα την εποχή να εξακριβώσω
θάφινα το βιβλίο αν μια μνεία μικρή,
κι ασήμαντη, του βασιλέως Καισαρίωνος
δεν είλκυε την προσοχή μου αμέσως . . .

Α, να, ήρθες συ με την αόριστη
γοητεία σου. Στην ιστορία λίγες
γραμμές μονάχα βρίσκονται για σένα,
κ' έτσι πιο ελεύθερα σ' έπλασα μες στον νου μου.
Σ' έπλασα ωραίο κ' αισθηματικό.
Η τέχνη μου στο πρόσωπό σου δίνει

μιαν ονειρώδη συμπαθητική εμορφιά.
Και τόσο πλήρως σε φαντάσθηκα,
που χθες την νύχτα αργά, σαν έσβυνεν
η λάμπα μου—άφισα επίτηδες να σβύνει—
εθάρρεψα που μπήκες μες στην κάμαρά μου,
με φάνηκε που εμπρός μου στάθηκες· ως θα ήσουν
μες στην κατακτημένην Αλεξάνδρεια,
χλωμός και κουρασμένος, ιδεώδης εν τη λύπη σου,
ελπίζοντας ακόμη να σε σπλαχνισθούν
οι φαύλοι—που ψιθύριζαν το «Πολυκαισαρίη».
(11–30; ellipsis in original)

When I'd succeeded in verifying what the epoch was like
I would have left the book, if one mention, small
and insignificant, of the King Caesarion
hadn't suddenly caught my attention . . .

Ah, so you came, with that indefinite
fascination of yours. In history only a few
lines about you can be found,
and so I shaped you more freely in my mind.
I shaped you as handsome and emotional.
My art gives your face
a dreaming, likeable beauty.
And so completely did I imagine you
that last night, late, as my lamp
went out—I let it go out on purpose—
I believed that you came into my room,
it seemed to me you stood before me; as you would be
in conquered Alexandria,
pale and tired, ideal in your sorrow,
hoping still that they would have pity for you,
the vile ones—who whispered, "Too many Caesars."

In these lines the creative or projective powers of the poet's address become explicit. On the one hand, Caesarion "came" before the poet unbidden (l. 15); on the other hand, the poet "shaped" him (l. 18) to suit his own taste and imagination, which is to say his "art" (l. 20). The poem finds its own lines in the paucity of "lines" (l. 17) furnished by history, and Caesarion steps out of both the book of inscriptions and the poet's reflection as the poet "on purpose" lets the "lamp" of his "verifying" (l. 11) faculties go out (ll. 23–24).

The changed project does not entail "leaving" or "abandoning" (αφίνω [l. 12]) the book of inscriptions—which is to say it is still about desire for contact with people who really once lived—but everything else is now different: the "insignificant" (l. 13) comes to the fore, while the "brilliant, / glorious, powerful" (ll. 6–7) fall away. The "epoch" (l. 1) arrives to inhabit the poet's "hour" (ὥρα [l. 2], translated as "the time") not through its own inscriptions commemorating itself, but through an erotics of shaping memory, whose character it is to be "immediate" (αμέσως [l. 14]), while the inscriptions dating from the Ptolemaic era itself are, in contradiction to our usual way of talking about what we call "primary sources," mediated. Whereas the book was "taken down" deliberately and for a purpose (ll. 1–3), the vision of Caesarion "came" (l. 15) of its own accord. And most powerful and crucial in this list of the ways in which the poem turns halfway through from history (study) to art is the unexpected switch to direct address:

> Ah, so you came, with that indefinite
> fascination of yours.

It's not that desire is a second-person matter where history is third person; there are plenty of poems of desire that do not say *you*. But given the systematic contrasts between mediation in the poem's first half and immediacy in the second half, the move from *they* to *you* takes on and performs this contrast as the most convincing and affecting of the poet's means.

Cavafy's personalizing of history is not distorting or arbitrary;[6] his addresses to historical figures, like all his passionate study of Hellenic history, are a means of drawing close the elusive actuality of the factual past. On the one hand, the Caesarion of his poem *is* the historical son of Cleopatra and Caesar, named and known through (among other documents) Ptolemaic inscriptions (l. 4), dead two thousand years and decisively inaccessible to speech. On the other hand, this Caesarion is expressly a manufactured fiction of the speaker, molded "freely" (l. 18) to the dictates of the speaker's own desire and finally located (if anywhere) only within the speaker's consciousness.[7] The poem, as in "Ides of March," becomes a mediator between closedness and openness, between the static figure of history and the fresh possibilities of a living interlocutor.

Cavafy's "Caesarion" shows, in other words, that knowing the ad-

6. See Keeley 99.

7. Here is another caution against demanding of poetry certain kinds of commonsense communicative distinctions. It seems wrongheaded to ask if Caesarion, in this poem, is or is not in a position to hear what is said; or as I am suggesting, it is unhelpful to categorize him as either a phantom in the speaker's mind or a historically attested figure.

dressee to be sealed in another time can prompt the effort to conjure him or her into the speaker's present. This effort means making the poem into an attempt at greeting, or making the *you* into someone greetable. Such is also the mode—with an important twist—of a riddle poem by Sylvia Plath, from *Ariel* (60):

YOU'RE

Clownlike, happiest on your hands,
Feet to the stars, and moon-skulled,
Gilled like a fish. A common-sense
Thumbs-down on the dodo's mode.
Wrapped up in yourself like a spool,
Trawling your dark as owls do.
Mute as a turnip from the Fourth
Of July to All Fools' Day,
O high-riser, my little loaf.

Vague as fog and looked for like mail.
Farther off than Australia.
Bent-backed Atlas, our traveled prawn.
Snug as a bud and at home
Like a sprat in a pickle jug.
A creel of eels, all ripples.
Jumpy as a Mexican bean.
Right, like a well-done sum.
A clean slate, with your own face on.

All the vital syntax operates between the title and the body of the poem, since everything in the poem (except the vocative in line 9) is a predicate of the title, "You're." That is to say, the poem has no other topic than the identity of the *you*. It is a poem about guessing, in two senses: it is a riddle poem for the reader; but also, its addressee, who when the riddle is solved must be the speaker's unborn child, is an object of wonder and speculation (a different kind of riddle) to the speaker herself. Shelley's words to the skylark are even more appropriate for Plath's poem: "What thou art we know not; / What is most like thee?" Her metaphors swing from the cosmic ("Feet to the stars, and moon-skulled") to the oozy ("a creel of eels"). But they belong chiefly to two categories: the body, appropriately for both pregnant speaker and developing fetus ("hands," "feet," "skulled," "gilled," "thumbs," "backed," "face"), and—wittily for the proverbially hungry expectant mother—food ("fish," "turnip," "loaf," "prawn," "sprat," "pickle," "eels," "bean"). The sheer proliferation of images leaves the addressee unidentified with any one of them in the end, and this and other differences from the mode of, say, Cavafy's "Caesarion" may be attributable to the salient fact that this addressee, though in a sense she too belongs to a time other than the present, *will* come forward to meet the speaker as she intrinsically is. She resides in the future, not in the past. At the same time, of course, in another sense with which the poem is also much concerned, she lives also now inside her mother's body. The child in the womb, though in one sense begun in independence (and fireworks) on the Fourth of July, remains, for all that, wholly and genuinely interior to the speaker.

The last two lines stand out from the rest of the poem. "[You're] Right, like a well-done sum" sees the child as a cumulative result, something already complete. It also affirms her as being—whatever the confusion of her identities in the poem so far—finally as she should be and necessarily must be. The final line then continues the mathematical thought, by itself summing up and at the same time retorting to the twenty or so preceding predicates that the text has proposed before this: "[You're] A clean slate, with your own face on." It is because the unborn child is "a clean slate," without face or voice, that the pregnant mother can project so many faces onto her; the poem as a whole is an extended gloss on the notion of prosopopoeia, which etymologically means "face-making." The phrase "clean slate" also plays with Locke's notion of the child at birth as a tabula rasa—another kind of book, as yet "unimprinted" by the world. But in sharp contrast to "Caesarion," in which the poem avowedly gives its addressee a face *not* his own, this child can be counted on to appear in time with her "own face on." She is an individual, an other, perhaps "a clean slate" in one sense but certainly not a blank face: she is someone, in short, who can be known as herself.

Past figures and unborn ones, then, are sometimes addressed in poetry as a way of understanding them, bringing them closer, opening up their self-enclosure, and making them, with invocatory power, a greetable avatar of themselves. Mythological and religious figures, too, lend themselves to this expansive address, either directly or through painted or sculpted depictions of them. As with Cavafy's Caesar, a poem addressing a mythological person—as Rilke addresses Orpheus, say—looks back to a set of familiar narratives and seeks to speak life into them once again. The mythic dimension is inherently a flexible one in ways that history is not; and the address to such figures takes up their significance, not their historicity. Charles Segal summarizes Rilke's particular conception of the Orpheus myth in the *Sonnets to Orpheus* like this:

> Orpheus's power of song embodies the power of language to impose form on the formless through naming and classification. In him song—poetry— can also view and hold the fleeting moment in stable cohesion and fixity. In speaking that which cannot be contained in the abstractive structure of words, Rilke's Orphic voice seeks to open our excessively conceptualized world to hidden or excluded aspects, especially the knowledge of death, the "subjective" side of the phenomenal world, the validity of nonrational understanding and experience. . . . "Orpheus" is that potential surfacing of being in the world of change, that coming together, ever unreconciled, of the transient and the eternal in art. (126–27)

The only sonnet of the fifty-five that is explicitly addressed to Orpheus throughout—1.26, the last of the first part—is an instance of how poetic address can unfold a mythic figure by retelling his story; but still more, it is a poem *about* amplification, because Rilke's Orpheus is a principle of expansion in himself: "It is by overstepping that he obeys" (sonnet 1.5). Even his death by dismemberment at the hands of the envious Maenads (Ovid tells us he would pay no attention to their enticements, so steady was his grief for his lost Eurydice [*Met.* 10.78–81]) is a transcendence, not an annihilation. Rilke addresses Orpheus—greets him in farewell—as a god:

> Du aber, Göttlicher, du, bis zuletzt noch Ertöner,
> da ihn der Schwarm der verschmähten Mänaden befiel,
> hast ihr Geschrei übertönt mit Ordnung, du Schöner,
> aus den Zerstörenden stieg dein erbauendes Spiel.
>
> Keine war da, dass sie Haupt dir und Leier zerstör',
> wie sie auch rangen und rasten; und alle die scharfen
> Steine, die sie nach deinem Herzen warfen,
> wurden zu Sanftem an dir und begabt mit Gehör.
>
> Schließlich zerschlugen sie dich, von der Rache gehetzt,
> während dein Klang noch in Löwen und Felsen verweilte
> und in den Bäumen und Vögeln. Dort singst du noch jetzt.
>
> O du verlorener Gott! Du unendliche Spur!
> Nur weil dich reißend zuletzt die Feindschaft verteilte,
> sind wir die Hörenden jetzt und ein Mund der Natur.[8]

8. For this poem I have followed the punctuation of the first printing (1923) in preference to that of the manuscript (which was adopted by Ernst Zinn for the *Sämtliche Werke*,

But you, O divine one, you to the last still resounding,
When the mad swarm of rejected maenads assailed you,
you outsounded their shrieks with Order, you beautiful one;
from among the destroyers arose your upbuilding play.

None of them there could destroy your head or your lyre,
however they wrestled and raged; and all of the sharp
stones they threw at your heart
became something gentle before you and gifted with hearing.

In the end they battered and broke you, harried by vengeance,
while your resonance lingered in lions and rocks,
in trees and in birds. Still now you sing there.

O you lost god! You infinite trace!
Only because, at the last, enmity tore and scattered you
are we the hearing ones now and a mouth of the world.[9]

Orpheus's song and his absorption in it—which, according to Ovid,
brought about his death—already stand under the sign of loss and lament
(for Eurydice); Rilke's sonnet in turn elegizes Orpheus himself as lost. But
song itself—like this poem, for example—was made possible only by the
sacrificial death of the god here mourned, who "distributed" himself into
the world in that event.[10]

---

and reprinted in *KA* 2: 253). See the 1997 critical edition with variants by Groddeck, from
whom I take the German text (78).

9. The motif of the head and lyre drifting safely downstream after the dismemberment,
still singing, is Ovid's. My translation of the sonnet borrows phrases from Segal (147–48).

10. The generative redistribution of the sacred figure in death is prefigured in Rilke's
work by the image of Saint Francis, that other holy tamer of wild animals, at the closing of
the *Book of Hours*:

> Und als er starb, so leicht wie ohne Namen,
> da war er ausgeteilt: sein Samen rann
> in Bächen, in den Bäumen sang sein Samen
> und sah ihn ruhig aus den Blumen an.
> Er lag und sang. (*KA* 1: 252)

> And when he died, as lightly as without a name,
> he was distributed: his seed ran
> in brooks, in the trees there sang his seed
> and from the flowers it quietly gazed at him.
> He lay and sang.

In "Orpheus. Eurydice. Hermes" (*KA* 1: 500–503) it is dead Eurydice who is already "aus-
geteilt wie hundertfacher Vorrat" 'distributed like a hundredfold supply' (l. 81). Compare,
in Auden's elegy for Yeats (247–49), "the words of a dead man / are modified in the guts of
the living" (ll. 22–23) and the observation that at the moment of Yeats's death, as "the current of his feeling failed," "he became his admirers" (l. 17).

Even in the first stanza, Orpheus's song comes up free of him in the poem's description of how he "outsounded" the Maenads' howling "with Order": "from among the destroyers arose your upbuilding play." Although he is drowning them out—the German *übertönen* shows his song "on top of" their cries—his playing seems rather to arise, building something up, out of the destroyers themselves. This "Apollinian singer," as Ovid calls Orpheus, transforms—for a moment—the character of his assailants by being not himself but them, by developing or disclosing the order latent even in their rage (*Met.* 11.8).

This capacity of Orpheus's to affect the world by losing (or loosing) himself into it comes to expression again in lines 7–8, a small tour de force of sound painting. Throughout, the sonnet adheres to a perfect dactylic pentameter; the exception is line 7, which tells how "alle die scharfen" (l. 6)

> Steine, die sie nach deinem Herzen warfen,
> wurden zu Sanftem an dir und begabt mit Gehör. (ll. 7–8)

As the jolting rhythm of the seventh line's sharp stones ($-\cup/-\cup/$ $-\cup\cup/-\cup/-\cup$) enters the music of Orpheus's playing, line 8 ($-\cup\cup/$ $-\cup\cup/-\cup\cup/-\cup\cup/-$) embodies the way the assault becomes, instead, part of the harmony.[11] But at the same time, what the line says is not that the projectiles sing—though they seem to—but that they become "gifted with hearing." Deaf, they become able to hear by having heard the sheer demand for reception in Orpheus's art, as if the music contained its own uptake within itself.[12] (As the final lines will make clear, it is actually with the poet's own ears that the world hears him.) His "sound" lingers even through his death, in "lions and rocks / in trees and in birds" and not as an echo, but as a continuing song.

For this reason the great final tercet can celebrate the "lost god" as an "infinite trace," always already gone, but also always still here, and to be unendingly sought for in the world. He is a trace of both song and hear-

11. In fact, the disruptiveness of line 7 is the greater on first reading because the word "die" could very naturally be taken as unstressed, permitting the impression that the dactyls are continuing. The rhythm of the word "deinem," however, brings this impression to a jerky halt, and forces one to re-scan the line from the beginning.

12. The reference in Rilke's lines 6–8 is to Ovid: "Another [Maenad's] missile was a stone, which, even as it was thrown, in the very air was conquered by the harmonious song of voice and lyre and like a suppliant asking pardon for such deeds of furious violence fell before his feet" (*Met.* 11.10–13; trans. Segal 147). Orpheus's power to create hearing is also the theme of the first sonnet in Rilke's cycle (1.1).

ing, both mouth and ear. His sacramental dismemberment at the hands of "enmity" (l. 13) creates a new bond, which is like Orpheus's own song, connecting human beings and "the world" (l. 14) most intimately.

It is unexpected that the last line does not say that we are "an ear of the world" but rather its mouth.[13] One would expect that we (later humans whose lives have, in some secret way, to do with the story of this lost figure) would be his hearers, listening to the inexplicably still-singing voice of the god in the ordinary goings-on of nature, as we listen also to the sonnet (the word means "ringing" or "little sound") which brings us this news of what concerns us.[14] The metaphor of hearkening, one of the great themes of Rilke's late poetry, comes together in this poem with his abiding absorption in the way we are moved by, and move among, absences, the hollows where something just now was (or seemed to be). And the Orpheus sonnets as a whole celebrate Orpheus as less a self than the oscillation between presence and absence, between his helpless death and his song's triumphant continuance—as the vibration that is song (poetry) itself and simultaneously an insight into our basic condition of being. ("Be," another of the sonnets exhorts, "a ringing glass that shattered even as it rang.") All this points to hearing, to the invocation of Orpheus as that profoundest "breath about nothing" to which our lives are a way of attending.[15]

Sonnet 1.26 frames questions about what kind of "hearing" poetry is susceptible to, or requires, or makes possible. These questions haunt all lyric, though Rilke gives them a particular mythic habitation. Generally they are taken up by criticism as questions about the status and position of the speaking *I*, but the complementary emphasis—listening or reading, or the addressed *you*—offers better entry to these old enigmas.

The invocation itself reminds us that in these existential depths, reception and expression are not necessarily distinguishable things.[16] In a late, posthumously published piece called "Gong," Rilke speaks of a sound

---

13. Compare Hölderlin's note to his hymn "Friedensfeier": "On a fine day almost every kind of song makes itself heard, and Nature, from which it originates, also receives it back again" (163); or Novalis, in *Heinrich von Ofterdingen*: "The mouth is only a moveable and answering ear" (257).

14. Notice the causal relation between the past *second*-person and present *first*-person, between myth and life: "nur weil *dich* . . . sind *wir*."

15. *Sonnets to Orpheus* 2.13, 1.3.

16. "Rilke often emphasized in the sonnets that under Orpheus's rule, when Being returns to its originator, cause and effect coincide—as in the poem of the 'fountain-mouth' (2.15), where the earth at once *speaks* and *hears*" (Leisi 174).

"no longer for ears," one "that, like a deeper ear, / hears us, apparent listeners" ("Klang / der, wie ein tieferes Ohr, / uns, scheinbar Hörende,
hört" [1–3]).[17] Sounding us, poetry resonates within the particular quality of hearing we offer to it; moreover, it "listens" to our response. The unfamiliar idea here is that our response *matters,* that we are heard when we
had thought to be alone, connected when we imagined ourselves separate. Orpheus's music makes the unhearing things of the world "gifted
with hearing" (l. 8), as if his song brought its hearing (its being-heard)
with it; again, it is with the poet's own hearing that the world hears him.
Conversely, the resonance of your reception is sound in its own right; as
you speak over the poem, as it makes of you a mouth, the listener who is
not there where you are addressing him arises, instead, on your side, in
your verbal act ("Only because, at the last, enmity tore and scattered
you / are *we* the hearing ones now and a mouth"). We do not think, as we
may think when poets address urns, skylarks, and the like, that the *you*
only highlights the poet's aloneness. To this extent the address to Orpheus feels "heard"; but it is a hearing that does not involve two distinct
presences in colloquy with each other.

2. Closing In

> The whole theory of the universe is directed unerringly to one
> single individual—namely to You.
>
> —Walt Whitman, "By Blue Ontario's Shore"

In this section I take up a series of works that depict the world turning in
on the addressee with disquieting force, texts that are small allegories of
the way in which the word *you* itself may seem to bear down upon, ambush, or hover unshakably around the self or reader who is the poem's
target. This is a *you* that tightens.

Readers familiar with the ideas of the French neo-Marxist philosopher
Louis Althusser may wonder whether his notion of authoritarian *inter-*

---

17. *KA* 2: 396; *Uncollected* 231. Compare, to the conflation of hearing and emitting sound
in these texts, the way that Rilke's poem "Archaic Torso of Apollo" conflates seeing and emitting light. On that poem, see my "Answerable Aesthetics."

pellation, or "hailing," is relevant to these pinning powers of the lyric second person. Althusser's concept of the way ideology "hails or interpellates individuals as subjects" (49) is summarized like this:

> Ideology "acts" or "functions" in such a way that it "recruits" subjects . . . by that very precise operation which I have called *interpellation* or hailing, and which can be imagined along the lines of the most commonplace everyday police (or other) hailing: "Hey, you there!"
>
> Assuming that the theoretical scene I have imagined takes place in the street, the hailed individual will turn round. By this mere one-hundred-and-eighty-degree physical conversion, he becomes a *subject.* Why? Because he has recognized that the hail was "really" addressed to him. (48)

Althusser puts his finger on the power of the second person to nominate its target, as well as on a certain complex psychological truth about the vulnerability of persons. The particular quality of the scene Althusser evokes depends especially on staging: his imagined individual is hailed from behind. This staging (like a nightmare reversal of Frye's sense that "the poet . . . turns his back on his listeners": here the *listener* has unwittingly turned his back on the speaker and must turn again to acknowledge the call) helps to suggest an air of paranoia or guilt. Also contributing to this impression are the specific connotations of Althusser's verb *interpeller,* which in French means to call or shout out to someone, but also "to heckle" and, in police or judicial contexts, "to question."[18]

But if we try to set the uncanny *you* of poems into Althusser's terms— terms that are describing the workings of ideology, after all, not poetry— matters of doubt arise that are related to his choreography. Far from always bringing us up short, the voice of the poem, often more enticement than arrest, may draw us forward or inward. The opposition between authority and intimacy itself admits of wavering and middle ground.[19] Most centrally, Althusser asserts of his primal scene of subjectification that "nine times out of ten" it will be the correct suspect who turns around in response to the call "Hey you!"; but the character of poetry—even of those relatively few poems that do abruptly hail their *you*—makes of the reader instead that tenth person, startled but uncertain, who sometimes

18. English "interpellation" is known to the *OED* only in specialized or obsolete usages that do not match the modern French sense, but Althusser's anglophone translators and followers have reimported the word as a technical term.

19. On this opposition, see Altieri.

looks around but then is and is not the one meant, who now locates and now loses the source of the voice calling "you." The readings in the remainder of this chapter set out to illustrate this situation with works that may or may not intend their address for that uneasy reader.

The beginning of John Ashbery's "At North Farm," the opening poem to his 1984 collection *A Wave*, gives acute form to the discovery, if one can put it like this, that the world intends you. It is best to discuss with the whole poem before us:

AT NORTH FARM

Somewhere someone is traveling furiously toward you,
At incredible speed, traveling day and night,
Through blizzards and desert heat, across torrents, through narrow passes.
But will he know where to find you,
Recognize you when he sees you,
Give you the thing he has for you?

Hardly anything grows here,
Yet the granaries are bursting with meal,
The sacks of meal piled to the rafters.
The streams run with sweetness, fattening fish;
Birds darken the sky. Is it enough
That the dish of milk is set out at night,
That we think of him sometimes,
Sometimes and always, with mixed feelings?

"At North Farm" consists of five sentences, which represent phases of the poem's movement; but the broader divisions are first the very striking difference between the two stanzas, and second a turn within each stanza from statement (ll. 1–3; 7–11) to question (ll. 4–6; 11–14). In the first stanza this turn may at first seem puzzling, as if the tremendous focus and exertion depicted in the opening three lines ought to have preemptively answered all these questions (with a retort like "of course he will find you"). But the interrogative form enters the poem, tellingly, together with the switch from present to future tense. In that way it marks—more, it names and establishes, even in the face of this drive bearing inexorably down on you like destiny—the ineradicable uncertainty that characterizes every "not yet." Perhaps the awe-inspiring surety of the messenger is made possible, contrary to what we might expect, by the indefiniteness of the word "somewhere." Whereas in ordinary experience one's zeal to deliver a pressing message might become more urgent with proximity, fueled by anticipation of the imminent goal, in Ashbery's poem the hurtling force and unwavering certainty of the messenger are purchased by his distance from you. It is as if things became more viscous with the approach to meeting, or rather as if that approach necessarily erased certitude, diminishing it in direct proportion to the distance left intervening. In a way this situation reflects the root facts of encounter: face-to-face with another being, in the *you* situation, certainty (which Martin Buber calls the knowledge proper to the "I-It" relation) must evaporate.[20]

Ashbery's questions in lines 4–6 form a syntactically parallel sequence that bears a closer look. The gap opened up between "traveling . . . toward you" and "know[ing] where to find you" highlights the slightly inhuman quality of that first phrase; objects in nature "travel toward" one another, but people "travel to meet" each other (if I describe myself as "traveling toward" someone, it might be to emphasize chance: I do not know that this person is there where I am going). Knowing "where to find" someone, in this connection, adds a purposive seeking and—in the future-tense question form—a corollary doubt.

As this question moves to the next, "Will he . . . / Recognize you when he sees you," the possibility of slippage is repeated even as contact ("he sees you") seems to be established. Here it is taken for granted that the messenger will find you, but to see is not, dismayingly, to recognize. Recognition, that most potent moment of human consciousness (one thinks of the centrality of *anagnōrisis* to Greek tragedy),[21] in a sense replicates the drama of "know[ing] where to find you," this time on the psychological plane. But "will he . . . / Recognize you" could imply more specifically that you have changed, which introduces the thought that it could be from your side, rather than from the messenger's, that the meeting is put into doubt. Perhaps you might fail to be recognized because you don't look like you used to (when?); or, an alternative more rife with implications, maybe you don't look like yourself. With appearance opposed to reality, perhaps one is not so much missed by the Messenger as one evades him? The terrible pace of his approach, resembling, after all, nothing so much as the implacable certainty (or the "fur[y]") of death, might well prompt fear.

The question concluding the first stanza brings to a head both the se-

20. Buber, *Ich und Du* 37–40.

21. Aristotle, *Poetics*, esp. 1452a–b (chap. 11, nos. 4–8) and 1454b–1455a (chap. 16). See Steiner, *Real Presences* 180–82, on the quality of recognition in aesthetic encounters generally.

ries of interrogatives and the furious drive of the messenger: Will he "give you the thing he has for you?" In this act of giving, it seems, the mission of the ambassador is (would be) fulfilled. The noun "the thing" recalls the indefiniteness of line 1 ("Somewhere someone"); as there, what is referred to is particular ("definite" in that sense) but unknown or as yet unrevealed. Insofar as Ashbery's question allows the possibility that this "someone" might, upon finding and recognizing you, nevertheless fail to present, or might even withhold, the thing he has for you, it continues and culminates the abrupt slowing that lines 4–6 have enacted in place of the expected contact—almost a collision—that had seemed inevitable after lines 1–3.[22]

The stanza division is an extraordinary caesura in this poem; one can easily get the feeling of entering a different poem altogether in moving from the first to the second strophe. Part of the reason is the apparent sudden change of subject, signaled in various ways. Most striking may be the disappearance of both "you" and, especially, "he"—which had been the subject of every clause in the first stanza:

> Hardly anything grows here,
> Yet the granaries are bursting with meal,
> The sacks of meal piled to the rafters.

The effect is lurching: everything comes to a halt, or shifts with supreme abruptness down to the slowest possible gear. "Incredible speed" (l. 2) gives way to the paradigmatically slow pace of plant growth, here made slower or compromised by the deterrents to growth implied in the first three words. (Imagine the difference had the line read "Things grow riotously here"; it would seem to continue the furious energy of the first stanza, as if channeling it through Dylan Thomas's "green fuse.") The first stanza showed us a figure "traveling furiously"; the second is fixed in space ("here"). That spatial deictic "here" is abrupt, too. Whereas the first stanza played out wholly in the realm of "he" and "you," the proximal "here" suddenly re-centers the poem on a speaking subject (an implied *I*) of whose role we have till now had no hint.

The second stanza connects, in a number of ways, with the poem's ti-

22. This drag with which the velocity of lines 1–3 is countered may not be so apparent on a first reading as I have described it here; the strongest impression is left by the relentless pace of the messenger as the poem's opening evokes it. Rather, the reader's first sense of shock at the poem's change in direction comes at the start of the second stanza.

tle: "At North Farm." What this observation points up is how the first stanza (a stanza entirely of "toward," with no "at") interrupted that connection.[23] Insofar as "North" is a relational term, it signifies "off-center," a topography at odds with the first stanza's situating *you* at the center of the world's intent, you as "a hub," in Whitman's phrase, "for the wheeled Universe."[24] At North Farm, it is both that you are outside this center, positioned north of it, and that—insofar as the onomastic function wears away at (tends to absolutize) the relational one, and insofar also as you are "at" the place—your presence there bids to re-center the world upon you there. The word "North," in that sense, anticipates the distance between lines 1–3 (absolute, unerring, present) and the questions of lines 4–6 (uncertain, interrogative, future).

Discontinuity or dislocation of another kind becomes the focus of the second stanza with the baffling turn in its second line:

> Hardly anything grows here,
> Yet the granaries are bursting with meal,
> The sacks of meal piled to the rafters.
> The streams run with sweetness, fattening fish;
> Birds darken the sky.

The abundance of yield is inexplicable, out of joint with the farm's northerly barrenness, and the word "yet" seems to recognize the contradiction and implicitly sanction a search for an explanation. But the poem moves not an inch toward this explanation. Cause and effect are set free of each other, and the multiplying imagery of abundance instead evokes a miraculous Land of Cockaigne, generating plenty where by rights there should be want and famine. The poem seems to have eating on its mind, as "meal" (twice), "sweetness," and—especially—"fattening" attest. Smaller dislocations are also at play, since while the phrase "hardly anything grows" finds its magical counterpart in "the sacks of meal . . . piled to the rafters," the quantities of fish and birds need have no direct correlation to agricultural yield, but come as associative expansions of the mysterious "fattening" plenty of the unearned, unharvested, self-milling and self-bagging grain. The series concludes in an echo of the cliché of lost natural abundance in the American landscape: like the herds

23. Though the title may offer the answer to line 4, "will he know where to find you," as if it were your postal address. Later I discuss another element of this "postal" allusion.
24. *Selected* 63, "Song of Myself" (1855), l. 1269.

of bison darkening the plains, or rather like the passenger pigeon, Ashbery's birds "darken the sky."

This second stanza, for all its feeling of being a non sequitur to the first,
loosely forms an upside-down correlate to it, with lines 1–3 corresponding to lines 8–11, and lines 4–6 to line 7 ("but" [l. 4] and "yet" [l. 8] are
the pivot words dividing each stanza).[25] The "incredible speed" and focus of the messenger find their counterparts in the granaries' inexplicable accumulation of meal, excess corresponding to overwhelming excess.
The other half of each stanza's picture opposes to this high index of certainty and abundance a difficulty that hinders and reduces: in the first
stanza, "But will he know where to find you" (etc.), and in the second,
"Hardly anything grows here." But in the second stanza—the second half
of this *abba* grouping of images—the disproportion is in sharper relief; it
is both of greater degree and, in its explicit flouting of cause and effect,
more troubling to reason.

Overlaid on this stanzaic inversion is a contradictory movement by
which the poem shifts in linear progression from dynamism to stasis,
most strikingly in these same images of lines 8–9:

> . . . the granaries are bursting with meal,
> The sacks of meal piled to the rafters.

While the phrase "hardly anything grows" remains, however barely, pro-
cessual, the sacks of meal piled to the rafters (with even their verb elided)
convey a sheerly static quality. All of this excess abundance is waiting.[26]
Wholly inactive, the stores point to a future use—the surfeit seems des-
perate for consumption—and the sweet streams, fish, and birds vainly
await their reaper.

The poem concludes with a question:

> Is it enough
> That the dish of milk is set out at night,
> That we think of him sometimes,
> Sometimes and always, with mixed feelings?

25. This observation might prompt another: the entire poem could be seen as a kind of
upside-down sonnet (albeit in free verse), with the two tercets preceding the octave.

26. The lines also recall Keats's thought of a poetic oeuvre as a long lifetime's harvest, at
the end of which "high piled books, in charactry, / Hold like rich garners the full ripen'd
grain" (166). The remembrance of Keats traces a suggestion, in Ashbery's second stanza, of
great unread libraries.

The question of sufficiency ("Is it enough") is related to the matters of abundance and scarcity that have occupied the stanza so far. The line break after "Is it enough" briefly seems to make the question ask directly about the emblems of surfeit in the lines preceding it, absurdly wondering whether this unnatural glut, so emphatically too much, is "enough" after all.

The movement of setting out milk at night seems to bring action into this changeless scenery; and yet the passive form "is set out" underscores the absence of agency in the whole farm scene: we have seen no people at this farm, and unnoticed in the disproportion between "hardly anything grows" and "granaries . . . bursting with meal" was the simultaneous elision of harvesting, threshing, and so on—all signs of work, of human doing.

With the word "him" (l. 13), the poem is finally making an explicit connection between its two stanzas by referring back to the speeding figure of the opening lines. Another reading is hardly possible, but readers may be surprised by this recollection, at the poem's leisurely end, of the figure moving at such a torrential pace when it opened. Moreover, the dish of milk brings to mind a different sort of character altogether from the furious and distant messenger: "Milk is left out in a saucer or other vessel for the house spirits in many parts of western Europe" (Joffe). Brownies, goblins, kobolds, and the like are helpful, sometimes mischievous domestic agents; by definition they do not travel, they know where you live (living there too), and they bring no gifts or messages, much less death. But they do, when properly fed and respected, accomplish work. Are theirs the invisible hands that provide such supernatural plenty?

The consequence of this humble image of the milk is dramatic, since it must also mean that the angelic messenger "becomes," in the asymptotically increasing slowness of his approach, nothing more than a household sprite who has been with you from the beginning. If Ashbery is thinking of the figure in this poem as Death, then in these last lines it is a conception of death reminiscent of Auden's vision, in "As I Walked Out One Evening" (1937), of how "vaguely life leaks away" among the things of the everyday:

> The glacier knocks in the cupboard,
> The desert sighs in the bed,
> And the crack in the tea-cup opens
> A lane to the land of the dead. (134)

Is it enough, the poem goes on, "that we think of him sometimes, / sometimes and always, with mixed feelings?" The change from *you* to *we* is typical of the shifting pronominal sands of Ashbery's writing; here it has the effect of suggesting a generalizability that the poem has until now withheld, a relaxation of the fierceness of the first stanza's *you*. Such a slackening accords, in turn, with the demotion of the angel of death into a homely boggart.

It is a puzzling conclusion to the poem. In several ways, the question "Is it enough" makes a parallel to the first stanza's concluding questions ("will he know where to find you," and so on). The relationship of interrogative to foregoing statement is more than a trivial part of this correspondence: in each case the stanza moves from describing a scene (declarative, taken as factual) to a question about upshot, about the success or failure, sufficiency or inadequacy, of relation. They are questions about "meeting" in ontological terms, and as such they are—in their yes / no form—finally unanswerable.

Although one can imagine various ways of taking the question "Is it enough," one reading would take it as a question about the sufficiency of "our" response to the knowledge that "somewhere someone is traveling furiously toward" us. How, indeed, would one respond to the awe and fury of such a messenger, whose arrival is nevertheless still distant in time and perhaps finally uncertain? With routine, Ashbery answers, and with the sporadic and "mixed" constancy that inevitably characterizes daily life: "the dish of milk is set out at night." The routinization of the gesture may account for the fact that the dish of milk is not explicitly said to be put out "for him": it has lost (if ever it had) the sense that it is set out in expectation of the messenger. Now it is just set out.

Similarly, if we say we "think of" someone sometimes (or always), we place the person concerned in the category of absent people, people we do not see and whose arrival we do not expect. The sentence "we think of him sometimes" suggests that we don't really think he will show up.

"At North Farm" must be partly a gloss on Milton's sonnet on his blindness (ca. 1655):

> When I consider how my light is spent,
>   E're half my days, in this dark world and wide,
>   And that one Talent which is death to hide,
>   Lodg'd with me useless, though my Soul more bent
> To serve therewith my Maker, and present

> My true account, least he returning chide,
> Doth God exact day-labour, light deny'd,
> I fondly ask; But patience to prevent
> That murmur, soon replies, God doth not need
> Either man's work or his own gifts, who best
> Bear his milde yoak, they serve him best, his State
> Is Kingly. Thousands at his bidding speed
> And post o're Land and Ocean without rest:
> They also serve who only stand and waite. (66–67)

Ashbery's opening lines specifically recall the words with which Milton's figure of Patience reminds the doubting speaker of the work of God's servants:

> Thousands at his bidding speed
> And post o're Land and Ocean without rest

Merritt Hughes compares these lines to a passage from Hooker's *Ecclesiastical Polity* (1593), which describes as "unweariable and even insatiable" the "huge, mighty and royal armies" of angels intent upon the errands of God.[27] Ashbery's "someone" is an archetypal messenger, whose strivings may—typically for this poet—fuse the way Milton's sublime thousands "post" with the motto of the U.S. Postal Service, raising that cliché in turn to its highest power. As the Messenger—Greek *angelos*—Ashbery's figure compresses Milton's angelic thousands into one agent, and so simultaneously concentrates God's bidding, the purposive action of the universe, into the stupendous intensity of this single messenger's striving to reach, precisely, you.

The incomplete gift in Ashbery's poem—will he "give you the thing he has for you?"—again echoes Milton's sonnet, wherein it is said (against Matthew 25:14–30) of the Talents God lodges with men, "God doth not need / Either man's work or his own gifts" (9–10). Not needing corresponds to Ashbery's theme of supersufficiency, and it is "man's work" that is shown to be superfluous by the magically self-piling sacks of meal in Ashbery's poem. Finally, Milton's famous last line gets rewritten into the inactivity, standing and waiting, of the abundance in Ashbery's second stanza. And the substance of Milton's words—the sufficiency of faithful expectation—engages on an existential scale the same question on which Ashbery concludes: "Is it enough?"

27. Richard Hooker, *Of the Laws of Ecclesiastical Politie* 1.4.1; cited in Hughes 168.

There is also a twentieth-century text that informed Ashbery's poem, or makes a breathtaking parallel to it. The progress of Ashbery's messenger toward a *you* who only stands and waits recalls a story of Franz Kafka's titled "An Imperial Message" ("Eine kaiserliche Botschaft"), published in 1919.[28] (Kafka's story itself involves other Miltonic themes, most prominently that of an authority whose "State / Is Kingly" and who is served, in different ways, by his rushing messengers and his waiting subjects.)

"An Imperial Message" is a one-page story telling of a message reportedly sent by the emperor on his deathbed to—specifically—you: "The emperor—so it is told—has sent to you, the solitary, his wretch of a subject, the minute shadow that has fled from the imperial sun into the furthermost distance, expressly to you has the emperor sent a message from his deathbed."[29] The fleeing of the emperor's subject traces before the fact—and introduces—the same distance that the messenger will labor to traverse in the narrative proper. That traverse is a bodily or spatial enactment of the emperor's singling out of you—"gerade Dir"—as the recipient of his deathbed message (and the narrative switches from past tense to present, to "now," as the messenger begins his task): "At once the messenger set out on his way; a strong, an indefatigable man; striking out now with one arm, now the other, he cleaves a path through the throng; if he meets with resistance he points to his breast, which bears the sign of the sun; and he forges ahead with an ease that none could match." But in transmission, in mediation, the sure directness of the emperor's choice (*gerade* also means "straight" or "direct") is replaced with a never-ending and futile effort to bridge a suddenly infinite intervening distance. Kafka, after stressing the messenger's mighty progress ("he forges ahead with an ease that none could match"), evokes this distance in a long sentence pinned up in his characteristic hesitating semicolons:

> But . . . how vain are his efforts; he is still only forcing his way through the chambers of the innermost palace; never will he get to the end of them; and if he succeeded in that, nothing would be gained; down the stairs he would have to fight his way; and if he succeeded in that, nothing would be gained; the courtyards would have to be traversed; and after the courtyards the sec-

28. Posthumously published manuscripts show that Kafka extracted this text from the unfinished story "Beim Bau der chinesischen Mauer" (Building the Great Wall of China) (75–76).

29. Translation slightly modified from Pasley 175.

ond, outer palace; and again stairs and courtyards; and again a palace; and so on for thousands of years; and if at last he should burst through the outermost gate—but never, never can that happen—the royal capital would still lie before him, the center of the world, piled high with all its dregs. No one can force his way through here, least of all with the message of a dead man. —But you sit at your window and dream up that message when evening comes.

As Ashbery's poem began with the messenger in furious progress, then suspends it with questions about his arrival, and gives over the second stanza to the static non-expectation of the not-really-waiting target, so Kafka's prose seems only to separate the messenger from you more with each mighty step of his, as if his efforts to reach you themselves generated the intervening obstacles. In both Ashbery's text and Kafka's, the passage culminates in a cinematic jump cut to the static dreaminess of the no-longer-expectant addressee.

Part of what makes these short works so compelling is the way in which the angel or messenger comes like a figuration of address itself, the word of the other meant for and profoundly concerning oneself, the universe's meaning appearing in and as the word *you* (Buber calls it "das Grundwort" 'the fundamental word' [*Ich und Du* 9]), spoken to you in utmost confidence. But Kafka's last sentence shows even more clearly than Ashbery's second stanza what both texts know as the other side of this confidence: if the angel is himself the word *you*, for all that there must also be a preexisting person sitting by the window somewhere who is meant by this address. To preexist is to belong already to a complete world that must be "traversed," but that, since it is world, has no outside from which such a messenger could come. Two faces—the word and intention *you*, and the reality of yourself—are in this sense incompatible. Kafka marks the unbridgeable gap with a dash: "—But you sit at your window and dream up that message [und erträumst sie Dir] when evening comes." The window, as always in Kafka, concretizes the dilemma of consciousness expectant (etymologically "looking out"), caught by the distinctions inside / outside, self / other, captive / free. What comes is not the messenger but evening, another kind of threshold; and in the text's only indicative verb forms predicated of *you*, the Kafkan addressee does not "stand and wait" but sits and dreams up the imperial message meant only for herself.

This verb *erträumen* seems to me crucial: you dream up this "message of a dead man," invent it as a wished-for fiction opposed to fact. Yet the message is really out there and on its way to you. Your version corresponds to the truth—though it can never be that truth—and since the messenger can never arrive, since his message is (like a Kantian *Ding an sich*) forever unknowable, your dreamed-up substitute for it is itself the only message worthy of the name.

The content of the message remains, on the one hand, carefully unspecified; on the other, it has the shape of its circumstances, as Kafka's text describes them: finality, the bewildering importance of oneself as recipient and (perhaps) topic of the communiqué, fierce urgency, and so on. The "blankness" of the content works toward several ends. You, as waiting dreamer and as reader of Kafka's text, can and must fill the message with intuitions of what pertains to you in all your particularity. At the same time, the content is left blank so that you can wonder what it is.[30] Finally, as we will see in other contexts too, the message that promises to bear most intimately on oneself, on the very fact of one's uniqueness, is a message from the dead. When the emperor spoke it, of course, he was alive; but Kafka's penultimate sentence shows that the intervening death has altered the character of the message (as wholly, perhaps, as if that death had preceded the message and it were a communication from beyond the grave): "No one can force his way through here, least of all with the message of a dead man." This "least of all" ("und gar") could be taken to suggest that such messages are literally not so pressing as others. But since we have been told that the messenger is "a strong, an indefatigable man" who "forges ahead with an ease that none could match," it seems less likely that the message of the dead is irrelevant or the envoy weakened by a sense of futility than that the message has somehow become the one that the dead would give to the living. By the nature of things such messages may be dreamed of but cannot ever cross their boundary and arrive.

There is one more dimension to Kafka's thought about mediation and transcendence in this work. The larger, unfinished story from which Kafka excerpted this passage for publication introduced it with a con-

---

30. This is the point of the little staging of the messenger's re-uttering of the message: the dying emperor, writes Kafka, "made the messenger kneel by his bedside and whispered the message to him; so much store did he set by it that he made him repeat it in his ear. With a nod of his head he confirmed the accuracy of the words." That re-saying also provides a model of the mode of existence of a "legend"—said and re-said through the centuries—which is what Kafka's manuscript context (in the draft story "Building the Great Wall of China") announces this parable to be.

nective sentence: "There is a legend that expresses this relationship well" ("Beim Bau" 75). The word *Sage* ("legend," also with a relevant figurative sense of "rumor") is utterly paradoxical applied to this story, and Kafka took pains to see that the paradox was preserved by another means when he removed this introductory sentence for the published version. Three inconspicuous interpolated words (four in the translation) are radically at odds with the messenger's single-minded commitment to exactly you: "The emperor—so it is told—has sent to you, the solitary, his wretch of a subject, the minute shadow that has fled from the imperial sun into the furthermost distance, expressly to you has the emperor sent a message from his deathbed." With the words "so it is told" ("so heißt es"), attention shifts to the narrative for the narrative's sake. One listens in order to find out what has been told, in order to hear the traditional story—the legend—that others have heard before oneself. That is the paradox: others have heard before you this tale of the emperor's vital communication for you and only you ("gerade Dir"). If, I may reason, they heard the tale in the very same words as I now read, that word-perfect sameness is a guarantee that they heard a different tale from mine, since each listener would necessarily have taken the pronoun *you* as a reference to himself and not to me.[31] But the text is charged with opposition to just the kind of bland cognitive democracy that would allow each reader or hearer to be addressed equally. Although the legend has been told and retold anonymously through the generations, the tale of the emperor's envoy must on my receiving it concern a message for me and only me, pertinent to myself alone of all times and persons.

The grounds for this necessity may be suggested by a remark of Malcolm Pasley's regarding the period when Kafka was assembling the stories—of which this parable was one—to be published in the collection he eventually titled "A Country Doctor": "It was a time when the theme of a great task or calling had come to the fore in his writing; he considered the title: 'Responsibility' " (vii). To know oneself the only intended recipient of the emperor's dying message could well be to feel oneself "called," or responsible, even if the message never reaches one. Especially then: as you find yourself wondering if an envoy from "the center of the world" has been laboring or will labor "through millennia" to reach you, obliged

31. On the other hand, it is unlikely that the traditional legend always pointed messianically to me, even through the ages before my birth, and that others would have read the tale with my name or some other designate (like "a certain person in the future") appearing in place of the pronoun *you*.

in your solitude to "dream up" what he might say, your attitude remains receptive in a way that would be abolished by actually knowing the message. The sense of being called, because it will forever lack the specific content to define it more narrowly than that, is pure. The result—that the continuous sensation of existence is reexperienced as a state of responsive expectancy—comes very close to Milton:

> They also serve who only stand and waite.

Ashbery's version, in which the willed steadiness of Milton's "serve" has become an intermittent anticipation (and incidentally pagan ritual) enacted with "mixed feelings," accords—like Kafka's "dream up"—with the modern temper:

> Is it enough
> That the dish of milk is set out at night,
> That we think of him sometimes,
> Sometimes and always, with mixed feelings?

Finally this uncertainty about uptake or the sufficiency of our response to the postulated angelic messenger is ineradicable, a duratively open question which criticism cannot seek to resolve. Is Kafka's "Imperial Message" a parable of the oblique and even dubiously self-generating ways that are the only ways in which a nevertheless real calling may be experienced? Or is it rather a parable of responsibility shirked, of a deluded life spent dreaming of consolation instead of actually living? I incline to the former reading because it takes better account of the full text, but the inability to rule out the second reading is as essential as are the disorienting implications of the distancing phrase "so it is told."

Since the era of archaic Greek epitaphs, the most persistent shape taken by the "message of a dead man" has been (to cite the message in its shortest, best-known wording) *memento mori*.[32] A poem by the nineteenth-century German poet Eduard Mörike works this tradition into a portent that shares with Ashbery's and Kafka's imagery the idea of something bearing down upon a *you*. In this case, though, the approaching figure is the grave itself.

32. I say more about the earliest Greek inscriptions in chapter 3.

DENK' ES, O SEELE!

Ein Tännlein grünet wo,
Wer weiß, im Walde,
Ein Rosenstrauch, wer sagt,
In welchem Garten?
Sie sind erlesen schon,
Denk' es, o Seele,
Auf deinem Grab zu wurzeln
Und zu wachsen.

Zwei schwarze Rösslein weiden
Auf der Wiese,
Sie kehren heim zur Stadt
In muntern Sprüngen.
Sie werden schrittweis gehn
Mit deiner Leiche;
Vielleicht, vielleicht noch eh'
An ihren Hufen
Das Eisen los wird,
Das ich blitzen sehe.

THINK ON IT, O SOUL!

A small fir is greening somewhere,
Who knows, in the forest,
A rosebush, who can say,
In what garden?
They are already selected,
Think on it, O soul,
To take root upon your grave
And grow there.

Two black ponies graze
On the meadow;
They return home to the town
In lively leaps.
They will step slowly
With your corpse;
Perhaps, perhaps before
From their hoofs
The iron comes loose
That I see flashing.

Mörike's poem illustrates how an instance of address becomes the axis around which a lyric poem organizes itself as a whole. "Think on It, O Soul!" contains no second-person forms beyond this title, which repeats in line 6, and the two phrases "your grave" (l. 7) and "your corpse" (l. 14). But these are more than sufficient to make us read every word and line as address, to read them, that is, intensely and exclusively in light of their relation to the addressee. In Mörike's poem this grammatical focus is also the verses' own theme, the gathering of the world to bear on the self or the place where the self once was.

The title leaves it up in the air whether the soul addressed is the speaker's own, or rather the reader's. The first lines begin in a welter of additional, explicit uncertainties. "A fir" and "a rosebush," with their indefinite articles, nevertheless here serve to single out specific items while cloaking them from any knowledge (including that of the speaker) that could locate them. The first line's "wo," for example, serves as a poetic version of "irgendwo" 'somewhere'; but it also seems to make the first line's statement ("A small fir is greening") swerve into the interrogative ("where?"), as if anticipating its alliterative follow-up question, "Who knows?"[33] This puzzled questioning is explicitly the mode of the next lines, where the verb itself falls away:

> A rosebush, who can say,
> In what garden?

A certainty within a context of unknowns ("certainty" because the so-called indefinite article here names a specific, definite entity) is like the subject matter of the poem, which is one's own death.

The progression from "is greening," at the stanza's beginning, to "take root . . . / And grow," at its end, represents no significant change for the fir tree and the rosebush; but against this smooth continuum no discontinuity could be greater than that between the implied presence of a *you* and the evocation of "your grave." In light of the startling appearance of the noun "grave" in line 7, the proliferation of alliterating interrogatives (*wo / wer weiß / wer sagt / in welchem*) can seem sinister, as if announcing a hidden menace that might emerge from any direction. The word "selected" (l. 5), too, suggesting an agency at work on one's funeral arrangements while one is still alive and well, may share something of this effect. In fact the planning is "already" (l. 5) finished; and the statal passive "are already selected" sets off not the past action of selecting but its ominously continuing relevance.[34] (There may also be a pun in line 5 on the word "read" [*lesen*] in *erlesen* 'selected': the rosebush and fir are "already read"

---

33. Compare, in Ashbery's poem, the indefinites ("Somewhere someone").
34. German grammatically distinguishes statal, or stative, passives (*sind erlesen* 'are [already] selected') from dynamic passives (*werden erlesen* 'are being selected').

before you reach this line, and your chance reading turns out to have been your selection as addressee; you have been snared into the process of composing the scene of your own burial.)

Although "is greening" (l. 1), "take root" (l. 7), and "grow" (l. 8) are all of a botanical kind, the interpolation of the word "selected" divides the sequence into images present ("is greening") and future ("to take root / and to grow"), while insisting that the innocent, natural "before" picture (fir in the woods, rosebush in the garden) already invisibly carries the knowledge of the "after" picture (your planted grave). What grows wild in the woods, or by cultivation but without special meaning in the garden, will be shifted from the category *it* to the category *you*: on your grave they will signify you, come in your place and betoken your existence when you are not there to affirm or dispute the adequacy of this signification. This jump from *it* to *you* is like an inverse image of the progression of your death itself, that impossible and inevitable transformation of every *you* into an *it* which also, however, represents the funneling of life toward death, its sole unifying point, where its meaning is secured, and also dissolved. The approach to death is an approach of the world to oneself, the encroaching of the world on the riddle of what it has meant, after all, to be someone—a question made urgent, perhaps made visible, only by the felt certainty of having to become no one.

The second stanza begins in an echo of the first, but the persistent uncertainty is—chillingly—gone:

> Two black ponies graze
> On the meadow;
> They return home to the town
> In lively leaps.

As before, the stanza starts by describing something with no obvious relation to the addressee. Unlike the rose and fir, though, these ponies are not "somewhere" but rather described as if immediately present; their grazing and frisky gait are both witnessed. The next two lines draw the connection between "this" sight and *you*, seizing the attention as suddenly as did the first stanza ("They are already selected, / Think on it, O soul") and more terribly:

> They will step slowly
> With your corpse

The shock comes partly from the subtle acceleration Mörike performs by inserting the name of death earlier than the parallelism of the two stanzas would have led us to expect ("your grave" appears in the seventh line of its stanza, but "your corpse" already in the sixth of its stanza). But more, the corpse (l. 14) is more awful than the grave (l. 7). The grammar of the phrase "your corpse" contains the mystery in miniature: despite the possessive adjective, a corpse is "unpossessible," since it can appear only when its owner cannot, and it appears as the sign that the one who "owns," or better "is," the body neither owns nor is, that there is in short nothing to which the personal form ("your") may refer.

The parallelism between the two stanzas also underlines a contrast between the ponies' earlier friskiness ("in lively leaps"), which is associated with the wild growth of fir and rose from the first stanza, and their measured pace ("step slowly") in funerary service, which is associated with the transplantation of fir and rose to grow on the grave. Both are cases of taming. Time is drastically foreshortened in the last four lines, whose slightly out-of-control feeling comes partly from their break with all relations of symmetry between the two stanzas. Together with the preceding pair of lines they read:

> They will step slowly
> With your corpse;
> Perhaps, perhaps before
> From their hoofs
> The iron comes loose
> That I see flashing.

In line 15 "perhaps"—with *vielleicht* phonologically echoing *Leiche* 'corpse'—seems at first to bring back into the poem what has been absent from the second stanza, namely, the uncertainty so prominent earlier ("where," "who knows," "who can say," "in which . . . ?"). But this impression is mistaken. In replacing interrogatives about spatiality (ll. 1–4) with an adverbial "perhaps" about time, the second stanza has clenched around the fatal dimension—temporality—itself. The echoing "perhaps, perhaps before" threatens with imminence (it is the repetition of "you can't argue with this") rather than softening it. The loosening of the horseshoes seems to take on some of the same metonymic function as, earlier, the forest tree and garden rosebush: like them it has no relation to the addressee. The poem may seem to be saying that like them, it will nevertheless in time converge upon the *you* even as death itself does so. In fact, though, the loss of the horseshoe will occur at some unspecified and meaningless interval after the ponies draw the coffin cart, and unlike the grave plantings, it continues to lack any evident relation to that death. Instead, the insinuation that the addressee may die before the shoes are off the horses serves mostly to accelerate drastically the approach of death, which had seemed, in the first stanza, to have a vegetative pace.

The most alarming line in the poem is the last, that relative clause specifying the horseshoes as "the iron . . . / that I see flashing." The poem's increasing momentum culminates (as the lines' trotting 3-beat-2-beat rhythm abruptly reverses) in the utterly unexpected appearance of an *I*, an embodied speaker of the poem who stands over against the addressed *you* but inhabits the same world. It is the last turn in the poem's endeavor to name metonyms for death. Here at the end metonymy builds on itself as we move from corpse to ponies to horseshoes to an observing *I* speaking in the punctual or immediate present tense.

The I-statement can be read in two rather different ways, depending on whether we take *I* and *you* to be two entities or one and the same. On the one hand, the advent of a speaking *I* different from the *you* all at once certifies that in saying *you*, the poem has been turned outward, in search of its target. Disturbingly, the *I* who comes to prophesy your early death and vouches for it by invoking the concreteness and immediacy of his own physical sense-perception ("I see") establishes himself as the guarantor of this world, and so as the guarantor of your death, who, like the young horses, will outlive you. This speaker sees the horseshoes "flashing" or "glinting" ("blitzen"): the sensory impression that connects to *I* and so makes fast the chain of metonymies is ephemeral, the flash of a split second. The flash not only provides a contrast to the garden-slow uncertainties of the poem's opening lines but also betokens the kind of phenomenal perception—instantaneous, reflecting by nature—that seems to stand for consciousness and to certify one's aliveness. The world as seen *now*, in a flash, is the world whose metonymic convergence upon one's death (the moment when the place you occupy will become just more world) has already begun, a convergence the poem claims to be readable even in the innocuousness of roses, fir, and ponies. But this is not human knowledge, as the beginning of the poem acknowledged, and the speaker who locates himself at the eternal instant of phenomenal perception and links himself, by knowledge and by voice, to the circumstances of your funeral—this speaker becomes by these facts a demonic one.

If, on the other hand, we take "Think on It, O Soul!" to be self-address, then this sudden switch to *I* in the flash of phenomenal perception places the speaking self adjacent to (making it stand for) the token of its own death (the horseshoes' flashing).[35] The distinction between *I* and *you* (my soul), in this case, turns on the "flash" of perception: where I, now and here embodied, see this instantaneous materiality of the world, my addressed soul is instead detached, immaterial, perhaps timeless. But this explanation leads to new complications: first, the immaterial soul cannot have a "grave" (l. 7), much less a "corpse" (l. 14), except by those conventions—severed here—that temporarily ally souls with bodies. Second, since neither grave nor corpse can, strictly speaking, belong to an *I*—and least of all to that *I* which in the poem's last line vouches for its own aliveness in the world—"self" is here split into not two entities but three: speaker, soul, and (lifeless) body.

In other words, taking this poem as self-address does not, as we might have expected, unify the poem; instead it multiplies entities and contradictions that would not be present if this poem were read, like Ashbery's "At North Farm," as a message from someone else bearing down on the youness of you. The explanation is not that self-address always doubles the self, however, as we shall see in our next example. In "Think on It, O Soul!" the splintering of self has rather to do with the inclusion of both a *you* and an *I*. It is also characteristic of poems that revolve around the encounter of the addressed self with some object in the world. This structure tends—as the next examples will show—to divide the self against itself, or to ensnare consciousness, even where the *you*-form is maintained throughout. The demonic theme continues to make itself felt there, too, since the uneasy power of many of these poems of self-address comes in part from the lingering ambiguity of whether—again, like Mörike's poem—they might not, instead, be addresses to you the reader.

A substantial tradition of criticism identifies Rilke as a "monologic" poet who, it is assumed, addresses himself except where the contrary can be demonstrated. This notion is itself a response to the fact that Rilke's poems so often turn to the second person (no one thinks to call those po-

35. Hötzer 164 reproduces the earliest manuscript version of the poem (1852), which lacks any *you*-address and speaks instead of "my grave" and "my corpse" (the version is titled "Thoughts of Death"). Mörike's revisions, for publication as part of the 1855 novella "Mozart on the Way to Prague," introduced new possibilities of reference into the poem without removing the possibility of self-address.

ets "monologic" who never invoke a *you*). Rilke is a poet, in other words, whose addresses are frequently unidentified; criticism seeks to settle the question, and (correctly) sees self-address as a plausible answer. But that answer also, just as often, prematurely closes off other possibilities for construing address. The ways in which these unidentified *you*'s pull at the reader are especially worth our attention—perhaps all the more so when a body of scholarship works as hard as some Rilke critics have worked to deny the validity of this way of reading.

I turn to three of Rilke's *New Poems* (1907–1908) which are frequently, and to varying degrees of plausibility, read as self-address.[36] All three are poems that "capture" their addressees and hold them bewitched by their objects (thus showing the sinister side of Rilke's famous celebration of "Things").

The first poem is called "Snake-Charming":

SCHLANGEN-BESCHWÖRUNG

Wenn auf dem Markt, sich wiegend, der Beschwörer
die Kürbisflöte pfeift, die reizt und lullt,
so kann es sein, dass er sich einen Hörer
herüberlockt, der ganz aus dem Tumult

der Buden eintritt in den Kreis der Pfeife,
die will und will und will und die erreicht,
dass das Reptil in seinem Korb sich steife
und die das steife schmeichlerisch erweicht,

abwechselnd immer schwindelnder und blinder
mit dem, was schreckt und streckt, und dem, was löst—;
und dann genügt ein Blick: so hat der Inder
dir eine Fremde eingeflößt,

in der du stirbst. Es ist als überstürze
glühender Himmel dich. Es geht ein Sprung
durch dein Gesicht. Es legen sich Gewürze
auf deine nordische Erinnerung,

die dir nichts hilft. Dich feien keine Kräfte,
die Sonne gärt, das Fieber fällt und trifft;

36. Müller best takes account of the pervasive addressedness of the *Neue Gedichte* (including the many poems in which the sole token of address is one vestigial imperative, often "look!"). His pages on the topic are scrupulous and useful, though he retains traditional notions (such as the *verstecktes Ich* 'veiled I') that I find untenable.

von böser Freude steilen sich die Schäfte,
und in den Schlangen glänzt das Gift. (*KA* 1: 544)

SNAKE-CHARMING

When in the marketplace, swaying, the charmer
pipes on the gourd-flute that lulls and rouses,
it sometimes happens that he lures himself
a hearer, who steps straight from the tumult

of the stalls into the circle of the pipe,
which wills and wills and wills until at last
it makes the reptile stiffen in its basket,
and fawns upon the stiffness till it softens,

alternating ever more dizzyingly and blindly
what startles and stretches with what unloosens—;
and then just a glance: and the Indian's
infused in you a foreignness,

in which you die. It's as though a blazing
sky crashed in on you. A crack
runs through your face. Spices pile themselves
upon your Nordic memory,

which is of no avail. No power's a charm,
the sun ferments, the fever falls and strikes;
the shafts rise up with malicious joy,
and poison glistens in the snakes. (*Other* 97)

This poem vividly exemplifies Rilke's virtuoso use of syntax, in the *New Poems*, to mimic the object described and simultaneously to index the responses of the experiencing mind. The first thirteen of the poem's twenty lines contain a single, serpentine sentence repeatedly delayed and propelled by eight relative clauses. Then in the fourth stanza, three short and jarringly enjambed sentences follow, each one repeating the impersonal "es" form; and in the last stanza the poem swells to its malicious end in five packed independent clauses.

This syntactic structure, reflecting and enacting the stages of deadly fascination and crisis, works in counterpoint to a formal organizing principle that divides the twenty-line poem into two ten-line halves, the first governed by the sound of the flute, the second by the sharp switch to the visual at the word "Blick" 'glance' (l. 11). The flute mediates between the listener and the source of peril, the glance is immediate and brings the danger to a head. Whereas the first half's images are acoustic, rhythmic, kinetic, the second half turns to vision, scent, and body feeling.

Given this scheme of a mediation dropped in the course of the poem, it is most apt that the poem begins with no sign of a directly addressed *you*, but with a "hearer" who is not only third person and generic but also just incidental, casually possible: "it sometimes happens that he lures himself / a hearer" ("so kann es sein, dass er sich einen Hörer / herüber-lockt" [ll. 3–4]). Several elements of this line bespeak mediation or the absence of compelling relation: the obliquity of the third-person reference; the take-it-or-leave-it quality of the phrase "it can happen" ("so kann es sein"), which is already in tension with the purposefulness of "lures himself" ("sich . . . / herüberlockt"); even the appellation "hearer," which sets up a relation of the passerby with the flute rather than with the charmer or with the snakes (and this relation also usurps—despite the poem's title—a relation *between* the charmer and the snakes). The way this possibility—"it sometimes happens"—then becomes an actual event is like the insensible turning of mild interest into deadly enthrallment. The objectless universality of "lulls and rouses" (l. 2), inaugurating the poem's strongly sexualized portrayal of seduction as the alternation of stimulus and sedation, makes the pipe's effect both ambient and inescapable.

In the second stanza the "reptile" is the one roused and lulled, but as we move to the pivotal third stanza, it again becomes ambiguous whether the flute "which wills and wills and wills" is affecting the snake or the human bystander:

> alternating ever more dizzyingly and blindly
> what startles and stretches with what unloosens—

The dash marks the even midpoint of the poem and brings to a climax the first, seductive phase. But the stanza continues, as does the disorientation in the first half of line 11, "and then just a glance": we may at first be unsure—"blind" (l. 9) to—who is looking, and at what, or whom. Then, having driven the poem's tension, characteristically, to its peak with a colon, Rilke reveals at last the snare. The sudden revelations come too fast to keep track of in these extraordinary, foreshortened lines that all at once close down the protracted thirteen-line sentence:

> und dann genügt ein Blick: so hat der Inder
> dir eine Fremde eingeflößt,

in der du stirbst.

and then just a glance: and the Indian's
infused in you a foreignness,

in which you die.

Roles precipitate swiftly out of the cloudy ambiguities that have gone before: the "Indian," appearing as it were in the place of his cobra, occupies
the position of controlling subject vis-à-vis—and here is the poem's most
daring moment—not the indefinite "a hearer" of lines 3–5 but, abruptly,
you; in the coils of the flute's seduction, the third-person narrative frame
has metamorphosed into direct address.[37] Or, in psychological terms, we
could say it is as if you realized too late that it has been you addressed
all along; the casual chance of the phrases "it sometimes happens" and
"a hearer" introduced—so hindsight shows—a figure of the self not
fully known or recognized as self, veiled into a third-person guise by ignorance. (Thus grammar may both express and conceal psychological
truth.)

   Like every strophe break in the poem, this one is enjambed, but in this
case line 12 is also a foot short (tetrameter in place of pentameter), an effect that hurtles the reader onward to the shocking conclusion in line 13:
"in which you die." In the subsequent lines, this death is as it were repeated, striking over and over. Five instances of the second person in the
final quatrain mercilessly confirm five times that the addressee is caught
and pinned, and that the complete absence of address in the poem's first
eleven lines—one would have said it was an "impersonal" poem, not an
address at all—was a disastrous misreading, a trap. Now it is sprung:

> It's as though a blazing
> sky crashed in on you. A crack
> runs through your face. Spices pile themselves
> upon your Nordic memory,
>
> which is of no avail. No power's a charm,
> the sun ferments, the fever falls and strikes;
> the shafts rise up with malicious joy,
> and poison glistens in the snakes.

37. In the German, the poem's first use of the pronoun *you* is stressed by its appearance
at the beginning of the line (12), where it forces a trochee.

The unleashing of a fascinating and fatal Orient upon a hapless European—a Nietzschean Orient complete with blazing sky, spices, fermenting sun, fever, and fell erotic imagery—occurs here in images like those Thomas Mann will invoke four years later in *Death in Venice* to bring down his character Aschenbach with a symbolically freighted "Gangetic" cholera.

In the context of the problem of the poem's address, the crucial lines are 15–16: "Spices pile themselves / upon your Nordic memory." The northern memory of the addressee here stands for something like phlegmatic rationalism, and as a pendant to the foreignness of line 12 ("Fremde"), it is meant to represent the addressee's sense of self. As such, it goes further than any other element of the text in narrowing the range of potential addressees. It is also salient that the poem itself accords no special emphasis to this phrase: it forms part of a rapid sequence of images that convey the addressee's helplessness in the face of an alien malice. The poet, in other words, is not highlighting this new information (that the addressee belongs to a "northern" culture) *as* new information. Poems regularly deploy presupposition for economy—as when I say just "C" and "D" and know that my listeners cannot help reconstructing an "A" and "B" from them—but in Rilke's poem the words "Nordic memory" do no pointed work of this kind and are genuinely incidental, presupposing but without apparent intention to do so.

The upshot is either—so readers will reason—that the German poet has been addressing only himself throughout the poem, or that he was presuming a generalized addressee who identifies ("as we all do") with a Germanic heritage.[38] Possibly for some Germans, especially of an earlier era, this line 16 was so to speak invisible and dovetailed the poet's self-address with address to the reader so nearly that a distinction between these choices seemed irrelevant: the poem addressed one of these (self, reader) and the other was *mitangesprochen* (simultaneously ad-

---

38. The complex hermeneutical position of those readers for whom this presupposed identification on the part of the poem becomes, instead, an object of awareness is only roughly characterized by such writers on intercultural reading as Rainer Kußler: "Foreign-language texts do not invite identification in the same measure as native-language texts do. They are read in a much more distanced way, because the foreign-language reader does not see himself as their immediate addressee" (12). This idea, though current in the field of intercultural language studies, is sometimes mistaken. American students reading canonical literature in German can get caught up in the world of the text with no trace of consciousness of the sociocultural distance, or *Fremde*, of which so much has been made by theorists. The word "addressee" in formulations like Kußler's cannot do the work required of it.

dressed). In this reading, prompted by the fact—of which the text itself is unconscious, however—that the poem is written in German, a reader can remain undecided between or half-committed to either of these conceptions of the poem's addressee.

Otherwise, and for the rest of us, the effect of line 16 will be in part to discomfit. I would not believe the testimony of readers (if there were any such) who claimed that on a first reading they immediately took the unexpected "dir" of line 12 to be only the speaker's self-address, not to touch themselves as readers. In oral conversation, address is more often mistaken than it is meaningfully ambiguous, so that in the course of a given exchange, we use later cues to correct earlier miscues on this count. In literary writing, ambiguity is likely to be meaningful and as such should not be unthinkingly corrected out of our initial readings on the strength of subsequent disambiguations. The embarrassment of a reader well aware that she herself has no "northern memory" comes from being torn between, on the one hand, acceding to the text's mighty efforts, at just this moment, to seize upon its addressee and sweep resistance aside—for this is the experience being described—and, on the other hand, obscurely feeling the gap between her real-world identity and the one addressed. Bonnie Costello's remarks concerning John Ashbery's poetic meditation on Parmigianino's painting *Self-Portrait in a Convex Mirror* apply well (mutatis mutandis):

> Art is an experience of absorption, but when the image is one of self-absorption, the beholder feels excluded, denied. This problem is raised on several levels in the [poem]. Ashbery shifts in and out of certainty about whether he is invading the privacy of Parmigianino, or whether he as beholder is the true object of the artist's absorption. Similarly we move in and out of certainty as we respond to the *you* in Ashbery's poems, uncertain whether we are addressees or bystanders. The effect is a repeated experience of embarrassment, as when we answer to a call directed to another. (502)

But "self-absorption" in Rilke's poetry is never just that. In the *New Poems* in particular, the self is always and everywhere found in active relation to an other, as "what draws the self takes on the power to question, displace, evade, estrange, undo, or otherwise disrupt it" (*Other* xiv). Certainly in "Snake-Charming" the metamorphosis of third person ("a hearer") into *you* enacts the drawing tight of relation beyond fascination and into helpless vulnerability. The reader, then, is not confronted with an image of self-absorption (Rilke's poems are not self-portraits), even where she may take a poem as Rilke's self-address. The nature of poetry is such that seeing the picture of a *you* held captive may provoke the feeling that one is held captive oneself. To describe this tendency as "identification"—we identify with the poem's pronoun *you*—is possible in a loose psychological vocabulary but misleading if pressed literally, since the pleasurable thrill of poems like "Snake-Charming" arises from the reader's certainty that she and the poem's addressee can never be wholly one and the same. The poem is fictive, and therefore what the reader experiences is simultaneously expressive of reality and at odds with it.

"Snake-Charming" also illustrates another consequential fact about self-address in poetry generally: to understand a *you*-poem as self-address entails no particular relation to the "lyric I," as critics' allusions to notions of a *verstecktes Ich* (a veiled *I*) would have it.[39] Self is here *you* all the way down. An experiment of rewriting some lines in the first person should make this point clearer:

> Es ist als überstürze
> glühender Himmel mich. Es geht ein Sprung
> durch mein Gesicht. Es legen sich Gewürze
> auf meine nordische Erinnerung,
>
> die mir nichts hilft.

> It's as though a blazing
> sky crashed in on me. A crack
> runs through my face. Spices pile themselves
> upon my Nordic memory,
>
> which is of no avail.

This rewritten version, far from revealing the naked truth behind Rilke's *you*, rather adds something of which Rilke's poem is free: it introduces an obtrusively reporting *I* whose presence is at odds with the event the poem seeks to describe. The first-person forms put an overlay of self-possessed reportage onto the depicted loss of self (and of self-control). The use of *I*, in other words, distractingly doubles experiencing self with speaking self, and so illustrates the special ability of the *you*-form, by contrast, to stage the experiencer alone.

"Snake-Charming," in summary, may be seen as a poem of self-address which becomes difficult to distinguish from reader address for reasons

39. E.g., Müller 76 n. 55.

having to do with the poem's theme: writing about the alien overthrow of the self, Rilke characteristically works to describe by exemplifying. His poem, seeking to enact the enthrallment that it recounts, naturally discovers, in syntax, the electricity produced by a turn from third to second person; and this turn itself suggests, in pragmatics, the power of a poem over its reader.

The poem immediately following "Snake-Charming" in Rilke's *New Poems: The Other Part* was placed so as to continue the theme of the vulnerability of the self to what it watches, and here too the observer appears in the second person. But in "Black Cat," self-address is shadowed by impersonal *you* as much as by reader address:

SCHWARZE KATZE

Ein Gespenst ist noch wie eine Stelle,
dran dein Blick mit einem Klange stößt;
aber da, an diesem schwarzen Felle
wird dein stärkstes Schauen aufgelöst:

wie ein Tobender, wenn er in vollster
Raserei ins Schwarze stampft,
jählings am benehmenden Gepolster
einer Zelle aufhört und verdampft.

Alle Blicke, die sie jemals trafen,
scheint sie also an sich zu verhehlen,
um darüber drohend und verdrossen
zuzuschauern und damit zu schlafen.
Doch auf einmal kehrt sie, wie geweckt,
ihr Gesicht und mitten in das deine:
und da triffst du deinen Blick im geelen
Amber ihrer runden Augensteine
unerwartet wieder: eingeschlossen
wie ein ausgestorbenes Insekt. (*KA* 1: 545)

BLACK CAT

Even a ghost is like a place
your glance bumps into with a sound;
but here, when it encounters this black fur,
your strongest gaze will be dissolved:

the way a madman, when he in fullest
rage pounds into the blackness,
stops short at the sponge-like padding
of a cell and drains away.

All the glances that have ever struck her
she seems to conceal upon herself
so that she can look them over,
morose and menacing, and sleep with them.
But all at once, as if awakened,
she turns her face straight into your own:
and you unexpectedly meet your gaze
in the yellow amber of her round eye-stones:
closed in like some long-extinct insect. (*Other* 99)

German does not have a distinctive possessive form of the impersonal pronoun like the English form *one's,* but the impersonal valence of "dein" in lines 2 and 4 can be gauged by noting how smoothly "one's" could substitute for "your" in the English translation there. Later in the poem, when the form *you* returns suddenly, we may mentally narrow the range of *you* to a single addressee, as the Rilkean "volta" isolates a punctual, single event ("But all at once" [l. 13])—and also (in the German) straitens space with "mitten in" ("into the middle of" [l. 14]). That is, this poem, like so many of the *New Poems,* turns from an imperfective aspect—the first twelve lines describe not an event but generally valid conditions—to a perfective one; and a singular event—"she turns her face straight into your own"—implies a specific *you* unlike that of the opening stanza. But since the so-called impersonal *you* can in principle stand for each person's private and individual experience as easily as for the public and general, this turn in the poem could represent its tightening of the scope and bearing of the still impersonal *you.*[40]

In addition, nothing in the text prevents reading it as self-address. In my view, the poem also offers little incentive to reading it in this way, despite the assertions of, for instance, Wolfgang Müller to the contrary ("This 'You' is . . . an 'I' transposed into the second person" [79]; Lockemann 91–92 had made the same claim). The same experiment hazarded in the discussion of "Snake-Charming," testing Müller's theorem by rewriting the poem into the first person, generates in the case of "Black Cat" a dreadful and self-conscious poem. Müller's notion could be admitted only if it could be modified to take account of the great differences between addressing yourself and talking about yourself. More broadly, what second-person lyrics in general help to show is this: self is not al-

40. That is, it would be possible (if a bit forced) to preserve the reading "one's" in line 14 and "one" in line 15, but this "one" will of necessity represent a specific person's momentary perception in a way that the poem's opening lines need not have done.

ways a matter of "I." Saying *I*—talking about oneself—is one enunciatory pose of the person, not personhood itself.

"Black Cat" is like "Snake-Charming" in the way its content—the evocation of an animal as an emblem of fascination disruptive to the observing consciousness—governs the poem's pragmatics: the pronoun *you* hinges together the cat's effect on its observer and the poem's effect on its reader. It can do this so well because, once again, discourse in the second person tends to perform what it describes, most of all when, as here, what it describes is a drama of self confronting other. Narrative in the *you*-form easily produces in the reader a slightly claustrophobic sense of being controlled.[41]

Both "Snake-Charming" and "Black Cat" are about the captivity of the *you*-observer to the animal it watches (they reverse the zoo cage of that more famous cat-and-gaze poem "The Panther"); this captivity is figured in both works as your involuntary ceding of "subject rights" to the other (the snake, or the "Indian"; the cat). You are not in charge of the situation to the extent you thought you were. This in turn we cannot help applying to our relation as readers to the poem's pronoun *you*, as the poem's ambiguous address bids to occupy, or co-opt, our uncertainties about who we are and are not. The imagery in "Black Cat" is breathtakingly apt: what the poem describes is not just (as in a poem like "Archaic Torso of Apollo") the observed object looking unexpectedly back at you, but its doing so with your own gaze.

My gaze is by definition mine in that I am its subject and it "brings me" objects and knowledge of them. But when the cat turns her face into the observer's (and the ambiguity of that phrase has its analogue in Rilke's German with the play on the two meanings of "Gesicht" in lines 13–14: "face" and "vision"),

> . . . da triffst du deinen Blick im geelen
> Amber ihrer runden Augensteine
> unerwartet wieder: eingeschlossen
> wie ein ausgestorbenes Insekt. (ll. 15–18)

> . . . you unexpectedly meet your gaze
> in the yellow amber of her round eye-stones:
> closed in like some long-extinct insect. (ll. 15–17)[42]

---

41. See the history of unsettled critical reactions to Michel Butor's novel in the *vous*-form, *La modification*, a history summarized in Kacandes's article "Narrative Apostrophe" (332–35) and traced more fully in her dissertation (9–35).

42. Snow's translation condenses these four lines into three.

The alien eyes of the cat present your own subjecthood back at you as an object, coming (impossibly) from another, fixing you even as it itself is entombed ("eingeschlossen") and frozen thinglike within the eye of the animal. Rilke's image of the extinct insect preserved in amber is rich in implication: *ausgestorben* (died-out) first plays off *eingeschlossen* (closed in) by answering confinement *in* with a prefix *out* that, however, brings anything but release.[43] But the word *extinct* conveys much more than impotence, more even than deadness. The prehistoric insects preserved in amber would be lost wholly to knowledge and memory if not for this same vessel that announces their extinction. They are not mourned for as a loss but marveled at as a startling remnant, a recovered and estranged presence where we did not even know there had been anything missing. Your gaze, which at the beginning of the poem had disappeared without "sound" (l. 2), "dissolved" (l. 4) into the blackness of the cat's pelt, comes back at you with this distance, as across millennia in which it has long since ceased to be remembered. "Eye-stones" (l. 16) reflects the depth of this alienation by showing minerality in the place we look to for aliveness and subjectivity.

The word "eye-stones" also suggests the several ways in which "Black Cat" is a negative pendant to "Archaic Torso of Apollo" (*KA* 1: 513). In that sonnet, where "Augensteine" 'eye-stones' might have been expected in the description of a statue, Rilke speaks instead of "Augenäpfel," or "eye-apples," an image not just organic but weirdly horticultural. The statue's missing head occupies the first two lines of the sonnet, just as the first two lines of "Black Cat" concern something that is likewise not there, "a ghost"; and in each text this opening proves to have been a calculated feint from which the poem promptly turns, with the word "but," to its real subject. ("Calculated" because the opening image, which in each case introduces the key theme of vision, remains as an afterimage through what follows it.) The "Torso" poem further describes the putatively static surface of the stone as bestially alive, "glistening like wild beasts' fur." Most telling of all for the inverse relationship between these two texts is their respective uses of the word "Stelle" 'place' (appearing in both as the rhyme of "Felle" 'fur'). In "Black Cat" the place in question is the thing (or "not-thing") seen:

---

43. "Rilke uses *Amber* here as a synonym for *Bernstein*, which is also called 'yellow Ambra'" (*KA* 1: 977).

Ein Gespenst ist noch wie eine Stelle,
dran dein Blick mit einem Klange stößt

Even a ghost is like a place
your glance bumps into with a sound

In "Archaic Torso of Apollo," the word "place" marks the moment at the poem's end where—just as at the end of "Black Cat"—the object observed becomes the gazing subject, reducing the poem's *you* to the status of object:

denn da ist keine Stelle
die dich nicht sieht.

for here there is no place
that does not see you.

The difference between the return gazes of statue and cat is in accord with the ways in which Rilke seems to have interchanged the properties of sentience and stone between the two poetic figures. In front of the stone torso, we are in no doubt that we are confronting a genuine other. Before the living cat there is no such certainty: the two predicates the text attaches to the cat herself are thrown into doubt even as they appear, as "she *seems* to conceal upon herself" all glances that have struck her and as she turns her face "*as if* awakened" (my emphases). The "eye-stones" that meet our gaze estrange the cat not just from sentience but from animacy, even from the organic. Finally, the torso of Apollo "beholds" us with breathtaking intimacy: the unseeing piece of statuary works upon us by being irrevocably over against the viewer, expressive (with our own lost expressiveness?) in the highest power. The contrast with "Black Cat" may be found in the two poems' use of "da" (translated as "here" or "there") in their closing lines. To the torso sonnet's "here there is no place / that does not see you," "Black Cat" opposes "there you unexpectedly meet your gaze [again]." The cat, which should by ordinary lights be a true other in contrast to the inanimate statue, instead only reflects back the viewer's own gaze, or rather shows it back as conquered and utterly trivial. To the end, Rilke withholds certainty that the encounter with the cat *is* an encounter, that any living entity inhabits those eyes.

To sum up, "Black Cat" shares with "Snake-Charming," as with "Archaic Torso of Apollo" and several other of the *New Poems,* both the grammatical form of a second-person address devoid of first-person references and a focus on the addressee's fascination with and eventual submission to a visually perceived object. These are different things: a poem like "The Reliquary" ("Der Reliquienschrein," *KA* 1: 530) can present a similar scene in the third person. Where the *you*-form is present, it becomes a grammatical modeling or restatement of the meeting (which is always itself nonlinguistic). What these poems finally depict is not "someone's" encounter but encounter itself: Rilke's fascination is not with autobiographical events but with the possibilities of mind and world. The *you*-form, able to address each comer, permits this level of inclusiveness while yet retaining the insistence on the solitary, particular, one-time nature of meeting. The architecture of Rilke's verse draws the reader in, eliciting the absorbed encounter that the poem describes and that its second-person grammar replicatingly calls forth.

Such absorption of the addressee is not always as dramatic or as total as in the *New Poems* discussed so far. For example, some texts portray the *you* lost not by capitulation to an overpowering other but rather lost, as we say, in perplexity, or in thought. The most effective example of this mode is Rilke's "In a Foreign Park":

IN EINEM FREMDEN PARK
Borgeby-Gård

Zwei Wege sinds. Sie führen keinen hin.
Doch manchmal, in Gedanken, lässt der eine
dich weitergehn. Es ist, als gingst du fehl;
aber auf einmal bist du im Rondel
alleingelassen wieder mit dem Steine
und wieder auf ihm lesend: Freiherrin
Brite Sophie—und wieder mit dem Finger
abfühlend die zerfallne Jahreszahl—.
Warum wird dieses Finden nicht geringer?

Was zögerst du ganz wie zum ersten Mal
erwartungsvoll auf diesem Ulmenplatz,
der feucht und dunkel ist und niebetreten?

Und was verlockt dich für ein Gegensatz,
etwas zu suchen in den sonnigen Beeten,
als wärs der Name eines Rosenstocks?

Was stehst du oft? Was hören deine Ohren?
Und warum siehst du schließlich, wie verloren,
die Falter flimmern um den hohen Phlox. (*KA* 1: 479)

IN A FOREIGN PARK
Borgeby-Gård

There are two paths. Neither takes you.
Sometimes, though, in thought, the one
lets you go on. It's as if you'd erred;
yet suddenly you're in the ring of flowers
left alone again with the stone
and again reading on it: Baroness
Brita-Sophie—and again with your finger
feeling out the ruined date—.
Why does this discovery not grow stale?

Why do you pause just like the first time
so expectantly in this plot of elms,
which is damp and dark and never entered?

And what counter-urging lures you
to search for something in the sunny beds,
as though it were the name of a rose tree?

Why do you keep stopping? What do you hear?
And why do you finally see, as if lost,
Moths flickering around the tall phlox. (*New* 107, modified)

This too is a poem of fascination, but of a different tenor from, say, even the beginning of "Snake-Charming," which models indifference stumbling into bewitchment. Here there is an opacity to what draws the self, an opacity that remains and results in the poem's many questions.

"In a Foreign Park" is a poem of doubt.[44] Already the first three words seem to set up a hesitation between the "two paths"—one is reminded of the etymology of the German word for doubt, *Zweifel*, namely, "twofold" (modern German *zwiefältig*; this suggestion punningly anticipates "Falter" in the last line as well)—but in the poem, this hesitation itself turns out to be fleeting, or not finally relevant. Moreover, these opening lines are puzzling in other ways: the sentence "Sie führen keinen hin," which could be translated as "they take no one there," suggests that paths ordinarily "take" some people but not others, and it literalizes the metaphor by which we speak of paths as "taking" us places to begin with. The path itself is sentient, lost "in thought," as Rilke's word order has it (though we may naturalize the line by reassigning the phrase, on second thought,

44. Paul Claes's discussion of this poem (75–79) is especially good. See also Phelan 86–87.

to the addressee instead of the path). "In Gedanken" 'in thought' suggests that what is reached is elusive of direct approach, available only by accident, through preoccupation with something else or a relaxation of vigilant attention.

Ebbing purposefulness—or growing resistance—reduces *hinführen* (leading or taking) first to *lassen* (letting), then to *fehlgehen* (going astray) in line 3: in this strangely conscious garden, or this garden strangely like consciousness, the right track has all the marks of the wrong one at the moment when the person, rather than the park, enters the subject role: "it's as if you'd erred." But "left alone" (l. 5)—by whom? or what?—the poem's *you* finds himself suddenly "there," and (surprisingly, given the difficulty one had in finding the place) there "again": the word falls three times in three lines (ll. 5, 6, 7). The place exercises a compelled fascination to repeat—a drawing inward to the mystery of the gravestone—that is and is not at odds with the opening lines' gesture of deflection, since both moments are summed up in the question at the end of the first stanza: "Why does this discovery [dieses Finden] not grow stale?" The contradiction is present in the question itself. In a context like this one, "Finden" should not be sensibly repeatable: when we have "found" the mysterious quality of a gravestone inscription, then in subsequent encounters with it we would not speak of discovery—"this act of finding"—anymore. Rilke's line is about an experience that defies this rule. The stanza began with getting lost, and it ends with finding: the opening lines' topography of deflection and resistance may be what makes each return approach to the object a fresh discovery instead of a recognition of something familiar.

Freshness is an unexpected thing to associate with a ruined gravestone inscription; but the fascination with the name on the stone comes from the way it makes the observer present to himself as he stands facing into absence and death. Present time and present circumstance are thrown into relief against history, which was a counterworld fully as real and as infinite in extent as the present one, but is now vanished and present only *as* loss. The stone with its "ruined date" sets into later time a marker of the inexplicable, impossible conversion of being into non-being, of the named woman into a name alone, the name of an absence. The expression "feeling out" ("abfühlend" [l. 8]) gives the encounter the same kind of tentative uncertainty that characterized the finding of the place: both are *ein Finden*.

The gravestone occupies the psychological center of this poem (insofar as such hesitancy can have a center), but it gets only a third of the poem's eighteen lines. In lines 10–12 the site has changed, but both the hesitancy ("why do you pause") and the unfamiliarity of the familiar ("just like the first time") remain with the addressee; the comparison "just like" drops away arrestingly so that the very place where one stands is nevertheless said to be "never entered," as if the addressee himself (like the dead) had ceased to count as human. This word "niebetreten" also recalls the formulation of the opening lines, "Sie führen keinen hin": the paths "take no one there" (with that emphasis on "no one" rather than, say, on a simple negation of the verb).

Two items in this second stanza name the mood that prevails throughout the poem: "you hesitate" ("zögerst": Snow has "you pause") together with its modifier "expectantly" (ll. 10–11). The text draws hesitation very finely. A bare sense of expectation, shorn of any definite object, suffuses the poem, giving it a mild sense of puzzlement too atmospheric to promise any resolution. The poem concludes on a question without a question mark. Undecidedness and drifting susceptibility generate the alternating spaces of the "damp and dark" plot of elms (ll. 11–12) and the "sunny beds" (l. 14) that entice the addressee, but entice him only to further searching, and withhold moreover the definite object of his search ("something" [l. 14]). The phrase that should help to define this vague "something" only augments its indefiniteness: "as though it were the name of a rose tree." Rilke is thinking of gardens whose plants are tagged; this hypothetical name of a rose tree stands as an "opposite" (*Gegensatz*) to the name on the tombstone. But for all that, they are the *same* name: Paul Claes must be right to read the pronoun "it" in this line as a reference back to the name "Baroness Brita Sophie," since, as he notes, rose varieties do have names such as this (77–78); but the elapsed distance between the antecedent in lines 6–7 and the "it" in line 15 makes the reference easy to miss (and without it, line 15 is bewildering).[45] The plot becomes still thicker here in light of Rilke's letter of August 16, 1904, which he sent from the Borgeby-gård estate in Sweden (named in the poem's subtitle) to Lou Andreas-Salomé:

---

45. Compare variety names such as "Rosa Marchesa Boccella," "Rosa Lady Penzance," "Rosa Königin von Dänemark," and so on. Rilke would write in a prose poem years later, "Ô fleurs, . . . revenez-vous vers nous avec nos morts dans les veines?" 'O flowers, . . . do you return toward us with our dead in your veins?' (*SW* 2: 611): flowers and gravestones, the ephemeral and the lasting, insistently come together throughout Rilke's poetry as complementary or interchangeable expressions of the buried dead, whose not being there both flowers and tombstones paradoxically locate.

The days are long and quiet and go out slowly in long twilights. Then I walk back and forth underneath very large chestnut trees, underneath which is the space of a great hall, from one weather-worn gravestone, under a goldenchain tree, to another, around which phlox and poppy grow all mixed up together in tangles and fragrance. And on both stones is the same name, in Swedish: Brite Sophie Friherrinnan Hastfer. For Borgebygård has always belonged to women.[46]

In the experience that prompted Rilke's poem, there were *two* tombstones, both bearing one and the same name: an uncanny case of doubling. In the poem's version of events, however, the second tombstone has been suppressed (the motif of doubleness shows up only in the "two paths" of the poem's opening), leaving behind only the vague sense that there was "something" (l. 14) in the flower beds to draw one:

> And what counter-urging lures you
> to search for something in the sunny beds,
> as though it were the name of a rose tree?

It is hard enough to figure out what one name on a tombstone points to; but when one name appears on two stones—as if a single person could have two graves—then it could seem that the name *has* begun to work like the name of a species of rose (i.e., without regard for individuals). Reducing the second stone to the indefinite pronoun "something" both submerges its disturbing power and diffuses, or distributes, it into the sunny flower beds. This is another example of Rilke's sense that there is a kinship between grave markers and the flowers that grow full of the graves that lie beneath them.

The question "Why do you keep stopping?" continues the pattern of hesitation, and itself "stops" line 16 halfway, but it also could bring to mind the fact that the inscription on a tombstone demands just this, traditionally, of passersby: "Stay, traveler." The epitaph demands this because to read the inscription is to acknowledge the absence of someone who, but for that name on the stone, we might not have known had ever been present. But in the foreign park of consciousness, if that is where we are, we hesitate or "stop" between half-presences and inclinations that seem to belong equally to memory and to premonition. The object of these

46. *Briefwechsel* 179. Åström 21–25 gives photos of the two gravestones and translations of the full inscriptions.

intimations—the thing that is remembered or anticipated—remains inarticulate or unknown.

The grammatical suspension of the modifier "as if lost" in the second-to-last line balances the suspension of "in thought" in the second line ("in Gedanken"), which might have been taken to modify either "paths" or "you": here, the words "as if lost" hover undecidably between modifying "you" (l. 17) and modifying "moths" (l. 18):

> Und warum siehst du schließlich, wie verloren,
> die Falter flimmern um den hohen Phlox.

> And why do you finally see, as if lost,
> Moths flickering around the tall phlox.

It is typical of this poem to give us, as readers, the sensation of being even more lost by refusing to make it clear whether one is lost, or "as if lost," or not lost at all. The moths "flickering" around the tall phlox are figures of erratic motion; and if they are moths and not butterflies, they are out of their conventional place among the sunny flowers to begin with.[47] But I am certain that Rilke, who though no classicist loved word histories, is playing here with the etymology of *phlox*, Greek for "flame." The moths around the phlox are held fascinated by the linguistic, not the botanical. Like readers themselves, they circle the tall flower because of what its name—like the name of a rose tree, like the name on the tombstone—remembers and translates.[48] They are compelled, looking for something that is not there to be found, much though the name suggests it might be. If they found it, it would be death; but they will not find it. In these ways the moths are like the poem's *you* tracing the name on the tombstone in bewilderment.

The moths are "as if lost" because moths drawn to flame are doomed to die (they are "lost" in that fatal sense); then again, they are lost (that is, disoriented) because the flame they seek is not present, just a signifier that

47. Though, by contrast, a recollection of the Greek word *psuchē*—meaning "soul" but, personified as the beloved of Eros, represented as a butterfly (*OED* s.v. "psyche")—has prompted many an author to write butterflies into graveyards. Rilke's word *Falter* can mean either "moth" or "butterfly."

48. Their own name (*Falter*), too, punningly if unetymologically suggests that they are "those who fold" (*falten*), and recalls once more the twofoldness of the poem's two paths (as well as the letter's two identical gravestones).

the poem makes pull them, while giving no access to the signified thing. I remarked earlier that the phrase "as if lost" can equally well refer to the addressee instead of to the moths: in this case, the name "Baroness Brita-Sophie" (as much as the phlox) is what indicates death and disorients those whom it has drawn. But like the name "phlox" for the moths, the name of Death may fascinate, but it gives no access to what it designates, and the captive observer in the foreign park cannot solve its enigmatic mode of deferred signification.

The moths seem, as they "flicker" around the phlox (rather than the expected "flutter," *flattern*), already to be afire, given over to what will consume them.[49] But still the flame remains an "as if," not part of the scene described but latent in or behind the German and Greek words that feed it. If death haunts this poem, it is by being intimated but nowhere to be found in it.

Who is the target of the poem's address? It is a *you* of self-address (as the subtitle "Borgeby-Gård" biographically corroborates, commemorating Rilke's own encounter with tombstones and phlox at the Swedish estate of that name). The poem also effects an address to the reader: it projects her into a place and circumstance that she walks her way through in imagination, doing as she is told she does. As "Snake-Charming" and "Black Cat" also illustrated, second-person narrative sequences (in poems too) are well suited to unsettling scenes, since the reader feels simultaneously called to exert her imaginative powers and to submit to the scene imagined. This effect is pervasive in "In a Foreign Park," with its obscure sense that the addressee is anyway caught by something with a claim on herself.

The grip of uncertain expectation makes Rilke's poem recall the second moment of Ashbery's "At North Farm": "Will he give you the thing he has for you?" The motif of the gravestone, by contrast, recollects Mörike's "Think on It, O Soul!"—Rilke's poem is not a memento mori, but it is not free of that admonition either—and so also anticipates the poems I will come to in the next chapter, concerning epitaphs. What "In a Foreign Park" depicts is the inscribed gravestone as a final boundary to human certainty and so as an enthralling mystery. The confrontation with death, as also in Mörike's poem, pins the listener to a limit she will be able not to avoid or overcome but only to expect.

---

49. These connotations of *flimmern* also help to tilt the image toward moths instead of butterflies.

The poems in the next chapter show the perennial poetic response to the limit of death: relying on the continuance of poems beyond the poet's lifetime, they strive to connect death and life. Enlisting the implacable progress of time rather than defying or trying to escape it, self-consciously lasting poems borrow the fascination of the reader at the tombstone to surpass, in another sense, that ultimate boundary and give you, the reader, the thing they have for you.

3

The Continuance of Poems: Monument and Mouth

_____

> ... but to subsist in bones, and be but Pyramidically extant, is a fallacy in duration.
>
> —Sir Thomas Browne, *Hydriotaphia*

THIS CHAPTER takes up two ideas that, throughout the history of lyric poetry, have been closely intertwined: the hope that poems will continue to be read in the future, and the epitaphic commemoration of the mortal poet. Epitaphs by their nature aim to persist through time and to transmit, however concisely, some mark of a human being now lost. Lyric poems too are kept, and are handed on, and because lyric poets since the beginning have felt that they lodged their individuality in their poems, poets have hoped that they might be personally "kept alive" in their work as others read it. But the work itself, meditating on this hope, inevitably marks their mortality as surely as an epitaph does.[1] Where the continuance of readers and the cessation of the writer occupy the same ground, poetry's touch, and so poetic address, matter the most.

Neither commemoration of the dead writer nor bids for future readers need take the form of *you*-poems, however. In this chapter I will be concerned to develop the differences between the grammars in which the two ideas of continuance and cessation—immortality and epitaph—can find separate and common expression.[2] Before coming to modern poems on this theme by Rilke, Whitman, and Dickinson, I begin with a brief dis-

_____

1. See Schmitz-Emans, "Überleben im Text?"

2. Epitaphs claim continuance (they endure) but signal discontinuance (they mark someone's death). I emphasize the latter fact as an antithesis to "immortality"; but the ambiguity will become central to the discussion.

cussion of Horace's famous ode 3.30 and an obscure and beautiful Greek epitaph. Both of these two classical works allude to their being read, but both stop short of addressing their readers as *you*. They also set up a fundamental contrast: Horace's speaker is the living poet, while the *I* of the Greek epitaph speaks as the dead.

Horace's ode 3.30, the *locus classicus* for the claim that the literary work persists beyond the death of its author, crowns and concludes the poet's three book of odes, which were issued together in 23 BCE[3]:

> Exegi monumentum aere perennius
> regalique situ pyramidum altius,
> quod non imber edax, non Aquilo impotens
> possit diruere aut innumerabilis
> annorum series et fuga temporum.
> Non omnis moriar multaque pars mei
> vitabit Libitinam; usque ego postera
> crescam laude recens, dum Capitolium
> scandet cum tacita virgine pontifex;
> dicar, qua violens obstrepit Aufidus
> et qua pauper aquae Daunus agrestium
> regnavit populorum, ex humili potens
> princeps Aeolium carmen ad Italos
> deduxisse modos. Sume superbiam
> quaesitam meritis et mihi Delphica
> lauro cinge volens, Melpomene, comam. (92–93)

> I have finished a monument more lasting than bronze,
> higher than the royal structure of the pyramids,
> one that neither the biting rain nor the impotent north wind
> can destroy, nor the innumerable
> file of years and the flight of time.
> I shall not wholly die, and a great part of me
> will escape the death-goddess. I will grow on and on,
> fresh with the praise of posterity, as long as
> the pontifex climbs the Capitol with the silent vestal:
> I shall be said, where the violent Aufidus River sounds,
> and where Daunus once ruled a rustic people in a parched land,
> to be the one who, triumphant from humble beginnings,
> first wove Aeolian song into Latin measures.

---

3. Horace added a fourth book a decade later. The end of Ovid's *Metamorphoses* (15.871–79) represents the other great *locus* for the idea of personal survival through poetry. See also note 7 below; and see Curtius 476–77 and Woodman 156 n. 57 for references to the subsequent tradition.

> Melpomene, accept the glory
> won by your merits, and graciously crown
> my head with the Delphic laurel.

From the initial assertion that the poetic oeuvre itself will last, Horace moves in line 6 to the different assertion that he himself will not altogether die: "non omnis moriar." Kept fresh ("recens" [l. 8]) by the praise of later readers, he will grow ("crescam" [l. 8; l. 7 in the English]) as long as Rome lasts—which is to say, eternally, both because Rome is the Eternal City and because no poem, however ambitious, looks past the limits of its own language community.[4] (Poets do not write in order to live in translation.) Line 10 begins with the isolated verb "dicar," "I shall be said," which works first alone, as a continuation of the preceding lines' identification of the poet with his work; translators sometimes render the word as "I shall be spoken." But subsequently, line 14 (see ll. 12–13 in the English) supplies a complementary infinitive: I shall be said, namely, "to have brought" (or "spun" or "woven": *deduxisse*) Greek lyric forms into Latin measures. Both readings—"I shall be spoken" and "I shall be said to have woven"—are essential; Horace's fame for what he has achieved is itself woven into the future rehearsal, or reading aloud, of his poems (which are his surrogate self). Being spoken about is precious; but being *spoken* is what lets the dead poet continue to speak as if alive.

The monument, then, is only one of a string of disparate metaphors with which Horace proposes his own textual survival. There is also the curious "partial" escape from Libitina, the registrar of the dead;[5] plant-like growth; the being-uttered, like a phoneme or word; and his presumably lasting fête at the hands of the gods and Muses. This quick succession of alternate images is necessary to counter the problematic associations of the word *monumentum*, which designates a sepulcher as readily as it does any other edifice serving to remind.[6] The poem is meant to resist the

---

4. The appellation *urbs aeterna* dates from around Horace's time. See Commager 314 n. 8.

Poems written in a nonstandard dialect may hope (and say they hope) to reach readers beyond the circle of those who use the dialect; but in that sense their language community is the larger one (namely, speakers of the standard dialect).

5. This is David Ferry's phrase (330).

6. Woodman points out that "the two objects with which the *monumentum* is compared are both memorials to the dead: bronze plaques adorned the tombs of the dead in Italy, while the pyramids are of course the tombs of the Egyptian kings," and that the words *exegi monumentum* "bear a striking resemblance to inscriptions commonly found on Roman tombstones" (116).

associations with death that its own word "monument" sets up. And
what the poet will be remembered for, he claims, will be the transfer of
Aeolian song, *carmen* (Horace's models were the then six hundred–year-
old Greek works of the "Aeolian" poets Sappho and Alcaeus), to Latin
modos—the word means "measure" in many senses, but in connection
with song chiefly "melody" or "meter." The monument is finally a figure
for the conveying of music.[7]

The close association of monument and sound, though it comes to be
especially strong in the lyric tradition, is actually present early in the
Western history of inscription itself. Greek inscriptions (like all Greek
texts until the Middle Ages) were written entirely in majuscules and without any space between words or lines. Such texts had to be sounded out,
and their contents sometimes explicitly refer to this vocalization, which
was what "reading" always, reliably, was. The inscriptions were metrical
in composition. Here is an ancient Greek epitaph (of unknown date)
found south of the Black Sea, in what is now part of Turkey; it is a poem
of an art that we would call literary, and may stand also for the ways in
which such epitaphs take account of their future reading aloud. This six-
line epitaph is written in elegiac couplets (lines 1, 3, and 5 are dactylic
hexameter, lines 2, 4, and 6 hemiepes or "half-verses"). It begins with two
lines[8] that introduce the remaining four:

Σευῆρον πολύμητιν ἐπ(ε)ὶ [χ]άδε γαῖα θανόντα
    τόσσον ἀπὸ στήλης φθεγγόμενον παρέ[χ]ει·

Seuēron polumētin epei khade gaia thanonta,
    tosson apo stēlēs phtheggomenon parekhei:

Ever since the earth took in, by his dying, Sevēros of many counsels,
    it presents him saying this much from this gravestone:

What follows are four lines of first-person speech by the dead man. Already in these two introductory lines, though, there is an emphasis on

---

7. As it happens, both *monument* and *music* come from the same Indo-European root
men- (o-grade form *mon-*): the Muses, too, are the daughters of memory.

    Horace's claim to endure through verse was already traditional when he made it, trace-
able most prominently to Ennius, father of Roman poetry (fl. 200 BCE), and before him to the
Greeks Theognis (fl. 510 BCE) and Pindar (490 BCE). See, e.g., Ennius, *Varia* 18 ("volito vivos
per ora virum"), or Pindar's Pythian ode 6, lines 5–18. But "no poet before Horace . . . used
the metaphor of a tombstone to describe his poetry" (Woodman 152 n. 13).

8. With respect to the original layout (reproduced in Anderson, Cumont, and Grégoire
159), what we call lines are of course metrical, not typographic, entities.

Sevēros as someone with a voice worth listening to: the caesura in the first line follows and so emphasizes his epithet "polumētis" 'of many counsels.' *Mētis* is the faculty of advising, wise speech exercising influence over others; it also comes to mean poetic skill or craft (and its familiarity as an epithet of Odysseus in both the *Iliad* and the *Odyssey* cloaks Sevēros here in heroic language). With Sevēros having been taken in by the earth, his wisdom is now, accordingly, conveyed by stone (the caesura in line 2 falls after the word *stēlēs* 'gravestone'). The stone speaks of Sevēros, but in the subsequent lines, it speaks as he spoke, rendering his voice:

> Ζωὸν μὲν ζωοί με μέγ᾽ ἤναιον· αὐτὰρ ἐμοὶ νῦν
> μάρτυς ἀπο[φ]θιμένῳ καὶ λίθος ἐστὶν ὅδε,
> ὅς καὶ τεθνειῶτος ἐ[μ]ὴν ὄπα τήνδε φυλάξων
> ἀθάνατον ζωοῖς ἀντ᾽ ἐμέθεν προχέει.

> Zōon men zōoi me meg' ēinaion; autar emoi nun
> martus apophthimenōi kai lithos estin hode,
> hos kai tethneiōtos emēn opa tēnde phulaksōn
> athanaton zōois ant' emethen prokheei.

> When I lived the living praised me greatly; but now
> this stone is a witness to me dead.
> In place of me, a dead man, it guards this voice of mine and
> undyingly pours it forth to the living.[9]

In every line of these four, the caesura falls strongly after the word for the dead or the living: *zōoi* 'the living' (l. 3); *apophthimenōi* '[to me] dead' (l. 4); *tethneiōtos* '[on behalf of me] dead' (l. 5); and closing the frame, *zōois* 'to the living' (l. 6). The caesuras' effect is to emphasize these four words individually and the contrast they make between life and death, but also to make the living (lines 1 and 4) seem to contain the dead (lines 2 and 3). In addition, the words *zōon* '[when] living' (l. 3) and *athanaton* 'undyingly' (l. 6) are very emphatically placed at the beginning of their respective lines, framing the inscription with the contrast between the life now past and the deathlessness of the writing on the stone.

In the first clause of Sevēros's utterance—"when I lived the living praised me"—two things are important: the relations here are between the living (*zōoi*) and the living (*zōon*); and they are relations of praise, consti-

9. Anderson, Cumont, and Grégoire 3: 159; my translation. Lattimore includes the inscription (244), but silently omits the first two lines. I am indebted to Stephen Esposito for help with my discussion of this poem.

tuting the speaker's reputation. Praise, in turn, is a matter of speech: indeed, the root meaning of the verb in this line is "to speak [of]," and there could be good arguments for translating it that way here.[10] The end of the first line, with the words "but to me now" 'autar emoi nun,' marks an abrupt contrast. The emphasis shifts, namely, to the "witness" served by "this stone," the very one the reader is engaged in reading. "Witness" in Greek (*martus*) can suggest both visual proof and oral testimony: the stone stands as the visible sign of the dead man's having existed, and of the presence of his corpse, but the inscription on it also testifies to the good reputation of him who is dead, just as the living once praised him living.[11]

We would certainly be mistaken to think of the epitaph as a silent witness. As mentioned earlier, this Greek writing wholly anticipates vocalization, and this fact is not incidental to the text but, as the next lines make explicit, at the heart of its thought. Of the stone it is said:

> In place of me, a dead man, it guards this voice of mine and
> undyingly pours it forth to the living.

The grave marker comes in the place of the dead man, who can no longer present himself, and by the power of inscription it will "guard" his dead voice "immortally" (*athanaton*). The circumstances of reading put the point on the poem's word "this," as the passerby stands alone before the tomb and reads first the phrase "this stone" and then the phrase "this voice." Each of these two instances of the demonstrative "this" refers to the medium that makes its communication possible as that medium is present (supposedly) to both sender and receiver. That is, "this stone" is a felicitous expression only when written onto, and read off, a stone; and any use of the phrase "this (my) voice" presupposes that the *I* is audibly *speaking* these words and also that the recipient of the message is *hearing* the voice of the *I* as it enunciates them. The words "this my voice" always indicate the voice in whose grain they have, at that moment, their instantiated being. In a carved epitaph, therefore, the expression "this stone" (4) succeeds while "this voice" (5), to our customary way of thinking, does not. Any piece of *writing* that says "this voice" is perplexing; the fact that in this particular case the *I* presents himself as "now dead" just deepens or doubles that first conundrum.

10. The verb form *ēinaion* is both misspelled and nonmetrical, but it must be an imperfect of *aineō*.

11. The word *kai* in line 4 corroborates this parallel.

The way in which a gravestone does something at least analogous to the guarding of a voice is through the inscription chiseled into it, which in this case offers words composed in, as we say, the "voice" of the deceased: in his first-person idiom. The stone "defends" or guards his words, inscribed there upon itself, against forgetfulness. But this verb *phulattō*, to watch, guard, keep, or defend, can also have another meaning, namely, to watch for, lie in wait for, or simply "await" (Liddell and Scott). This secondary meaning plays a key role in the epitaph, since while the inscription is certainly claiming to keep the voice of the deceased, it also, as an inscription, lies in wait for its own vocal performance by a passerby, without which the marks on the stone do not become words at all and say nothing to anyone. In that sense the epitaph forever defends a voice that it also, ceaselessly, hopes to ambush.

We may wonder how the voice of the random passerby could be thought equivalent to the voice of the dead man, so possessively called "this voice of mine." The poignancy of mourning is the irreplaceable particularity of the lost person, which is the thought that lies behind the primary reading of *phulattō* here; when Tennyson writes, in "Break, Break, Break" (602; published 1842),

> But O for the touch of a vanished hand,
> And the sound of a voice that is still!

grief recalls the characteristic quality of the particular hand and voice that are missed most sorely. But the third and fourth lines of this Greek epitaph remind us that the Greeks cherished also an ancient Indo-European value they called *kleos,* which (like this text's words for "praise" and "witness") is rooted in the idea of "speaking about," but comes to mean "glory" or, for the less heroic, simply "good report." Such glory held immense significance in Indo-European societies, as did also, for that reason, the poet whose work created it. This central value of *kleos* was in every case an acoustic as well as a social quantity; in essence it is the sound of the human voice, repeating one's name in praise through countless generations; it is that which Achilles knowingly chose over the sweetness of being alive.[12]

I have said that everything in the epitaph anticipates the moment of its being read aloud. But poetry read aloud is not oral poetry: it is insepara-

12. *Iliad* 9: 410–16; Plato, *Symposium* 208c–d.

ble from writing. In reading aloud, the passerby makes the stone into a "witness"; putting his own voice at the service of the inscribed *I*, he confirms that the stone has successfully kept its voice. (He also knows that it will continue to lie in wait for that voice: *phulaksōn* is a future-tense form.) The reader's audible, metrical performance of the carved words makes the beautiful last line into truth, since "truth" in Greek is *a-lētheia*, "unforgettingness." The stone guards the voice against forgetfulness, and

> ἀθάνατον ζωοῖς ἀντ᾽ ἐμέθεν προχέει.
>
> athanaton zōois ant' emethen prokheei.
>
> on my behalf, undyingly pours it forth to the living.

The action of guarding, or keeping in, is inseparable from the complementary action of pouring out, and it is the office of the inscription to do both at the same time and by the same token. That token is the willing agency of the passerby, whose offered voice *becomes* the lost voice of the dead man in saying over the inscribed *I*-statement, while the same traveler simultaneously stands and hears that message as one of the living. A late Greek epitaph from Rome (third or fourth century CE) puts the matter similarly:

> Μή μου παρέλθῃς τὸ ἐπίγραμμα, ὁδοιπόρε,
> ἀλλὰ σταθεὶς ἄκουε καὶ μαθὼν ἄπι·
>
> Do not pass by my epitaph, wayfarer,
> but stand and listen, and when you have learned [it], go on.[13]

In our text, too, the wayfarer is to listen to the stone while he himself reads out what is written on it. Since the *I* of the epitaph, once the giver of good counsel and so the object of praise by the living, cannot now answer that praise, the stone pours forth his voice, as the inscription says, "on my behalf" or "in my place," *ant' emethen*.

The epitaph's final word in the Greek is the verb "pours forth," a bountiful image and—it may seem—a boldly figurative one, since stone does not pour. But "pour" also has other connotations in Greek that make it an apt and vivid closing gesture: the root verb *kheō* can mean, first, "to shed tears," which is what many Greek epitaphs, including the very oldest

13. Kaibel 646, cited in Lattimore 75.

ones, demand of their readers; but also, still more evocatively, it can mean "to pour a drink offering [khoē] on the tomb," as in the title of Aeschylus's play *The Libation-Bearers*.[14] Both weeping and offering are actions that the living might be expected to perform for the dead, but this text reverses the image, pouring from the stone expressly "to the living." This reversal is anything but a ghoulish attempt to freeze the living in their tracks, however.[15] Rather the epitaph relies on the voice of its reader, which commemorates the meeting but makes it beside the point to sort out the agency of each party in that commemoration. The poem's insistent repetition of words for life and death is structured as an embrace, with the word *tethneiōtos* ([of me] dead) removed from its governing preposition in line 6 and inserted a line earlier so that the four words for life (lines 3 and 6) will, when the epitaph is vocalized, contain and surround the two words for death (lines 4 and 5). This inscription, in other words, enacts a ceremony of meeting over, and in, the poem itself.[16] The ceremony is an acknowledgment (carried out by the rituals of reading) that the dead are not nonexistent; they are missing. Voice is both the marker of that loss as the reader sounds out the inscription and the locus of the contact by which the reader holds the dead as if present.

The Greeks knew another kind of funerary writing that observed more stringently the fact that inscriptions come not just on behalf of a person but literally in their place: what the wayfarer meets and hears is, in this version, no dead person's voice but the voice of the stone itself. The practice is related to an idea found in a celebrated passage of the *Phaedrus*. Plato there has Socrates object to writing on the grounds of its fixity: "The creatures [τα ἔκγονα, lit. 'the offspring'] of painting stand like living beings, but if you ask them something, they solemnly keep altogether silent. And it is the same with written words; you might think they speak as if they understood something, but if you ask them something, wanting to learn about their sayings, they always announce one and the same thing" (275d). In lamenting the once-and-for-all invariability of a written message, Socrates styles the inscription as an idiot interlocutor, or rather an automaton, giving the deceptive appearance of voice and presence but

14. See Benveniste's study of the Indo-European vocabulary for libations (*Indo-European* 476–80).

15. I allude to Paul de Man's much-cited argument, in "Autobiography as De-Facement," about reversal in Wordsworth's "Essay upon Epitaphs."

16. The verb for "speaking" in line 2, *phtheggomenos*, can also mean "extolling, celebrating one aloud" (Liddell and Scott).

actually devoid of a self. Socrates' complaint about writing is connected to the older assertions made on certain Greek votive and funerary inscriptions which use the first person to refer to the object on which they are inscribed. It is as though, in an age when writing was still felt as relatively new in Greece, the marks of writing were perceived as the object's own speech.[17] As Jesper Svenbro records:

> The base of a little bronze statue found on the Acropolis of Athens and dating from the end of the sixth century bears the following inscription. . . . "To whoever asks me, I reply with the same answer, namely that Andron, the son of Antiphanes, dedicated me as a tithe." The written text "replies with the same answer" to all those who question it. It is inflexible. Its message always reaches the one to whom it is addressed—the abstract reader—in the same unchanging form, as the inscription itself triumphantly proclaims. (28)

This "triumph" is pride at what the inscription has accomplished (and expected to accomplish) by force of its inalterability, which is to say, its fixity through time: transmission of one and the same answering utterance through—as things have turned out—twenty-five centuries. Both the votive inscription and Plato's *Phaedrus* emphasize the link between written letters and human voice and presence. The model of face-to-face human responsiveness lies behind these texts' shared interest in the way written words "always announce one and the same thing."

The writing is close to alive (Plato goes on to call writers the "parents" of their texts); but then it is even more arresting that these same first-person forms that Svenbro cites also occur often in early Greek *funerary* inscriptions, where what they inflexibly proclaim is death and absence. It is the monuments themselves, and not the deceased, who say *I* in these inscriptions: for example, "Eumares set me up as a monument"; or again, "I am the memorial of Glaukos." "Clearly," Svenbro remarks, such statements "are not transcriptions of something declared in an oral situation and then inscribed upon the object. . . . Assertions such as these are, in a sense, peculiar to writing, for writing makes it possible for inscribed objects to refer to themselves in the first person despite their being just objects, not living, thinking beings endowed with the power of speech" (30). But at the moment of vocalization for which such inscriptions aim, the author of the inscription would have disappeared just as surely as the dead

17. See Burzachechi; Svenbro passim; Thomas 63–65.

person being commemorated. A monument of this kind, too, waits for its *I* to be enacted by the presence of a foreseen reader, although the words belong to, and express their own deictic anchoring in, the funerary sign of death itself, where it is relevant that Greek *sēma* means at once "sign" and "tomb."[18]

The first-person funerary inscription ("I am the memorial of Glaukos") could be said to take the encounter of the wayfarer and the tombstone most literally. It is a linguistic fact that someone who is dead is inherently a "third person," an entity no longer participating in any discourse.[19] If the encounter of traveler and epitaph can be a metaphor for the encounter of a reader and a poem, then this acknowledgment in turn—the exclusion of the dead to third-person status, outside of linguistic exchange—yields the focus to the speaking *I* of the text itself, since, as Allen Grossman observes, "the speaker in the poem cannot go away, which is to say he cannot die" (259, §23.1). The speaking *I* is not, however, the proxy of the poet, but is the voice of the poem itself, like the voice of the gravestone which calls itself "I, a stone" and steps forth as the reader's partner in discourse.

W. S. Merwin's 1952 poem "Epitaph" adopts the motif of the first-person gravestone as a way to dampen, or silence, the buzz of "information" which modern society puts in our mouths when it comes to death:

> Death is not information.
> Stone that I am,
> He came into my quiet
> And I shall be still for him.

---

18. On *sign* and *tomb*, see Nagy. The tradition of epitaph poems is long. At its origins, see the epitaphs collected in book 7 of *The Greek* (or "Palatine") *Anthology*, vol. 2, which call out to the passerby (e.g., no. 342, κάτθανον, ἀλλὰ μένω σε 'I am dead, but await thee'; see also nos. 280–81), and Friedländer. For the tradition, see the entry and bibliography under "epitaph" in Preminger. The English poetic epitaph receives detailed scholarly treatment by Scodel; see also Lipking 138–91.

There are fascinating ways in which lyric poetry is epitaphic in a general sense. Some aspects of the topic occupy the following works: de Man's essay "Autobiography as De-Facement"; Fry, "The Absent Dead"; Hartman, *Wordsworth's Poetry* 3–30; Lipking, *The Life of the Poet* 138–91; Mills-Courts's deconstructionist *Poetry as Epitaph*; Segebrecht's "Steh, Leser, still!"; and not least T. S. Eliot's "Little Gidding" in *Four Quartets* (on which see also the discussion in Riquelme 59 and 232–33).

19. See Benveniste, "Relationships of Person in the Verb."

The poem becomes more moving when we recognize that "stone" here works as a figure for the printed poem itself: we can enlist, instead of suppressing or suspending, our commonsense assumption that this poem is not meant for actual inscription. The poem "contains" someone in its quiet. Its brief speaking is its mode of being still (as a poem it has no other means), and of being not for the reader (who might like more "information") but "still [even now] for him," for the dead man.

The epitaphic intentions of Rilke's 1922 *Sonnets to Orpheus* are more complex, as befits a fifty-five–poem cycle, but they are there, writ large, in the book's published dedication: "Written as a Grave-Monument for Wera Ouckama Knoop," a young dancer Rilke had known who had died at the age of nineteen. Wera Knoop is the Orphic poems' dead Eurydice, whose loss makes possible, in Rilke's conception, the sounding of the realms both of life and of death that Orpheus's song is. The *Sonnets* as a whole are a monument and an inscription, and as in our classical examples, the monument is a reverberant one (*sonnet*, as noted earlier, appropriately means "little sound").

Like traditional epitaphs, too, the *Sonnets to Orpheus* make frequent use of imperatives, occasionally in the plural *ihr*-form, more often in the singular *du*. Despite the title of the collection, very few of the sonnets are obviously addressed to Orpheus; in most of them it is unclear who is addressed and who is speaking. And yet the poems are intensely concerned with both speaking and being: like the archaic Greek inscriptions, this poetic edifice too affirms its own existence with the resounding final words of its final poem, "I am" (sonnet 2.29, *KA* 2: 272).[20] The context of these words shows Rilke's rethinking of poetry as monument, which takes a direction wholly different from the Greek examples and yet is reminiscent of their concern for acoustics, *kleos*, the voice of poetry spoken and heard. This final poem (sonnet 2.29) begins with a variant of the tombstone's conventional hailing: "Silent friend of many distances, feel. . . ." In place of the more frequent epitaphic call to a stranger, Rilke's poem anticipates a friend—but perhaps one who prefers to keep his distance, since a "friend of many distances" might be fond of those distances rather than, or as well as, *being* distant. (To make contact is not to abolish all separation.) I draw attention chiefly to the final lines:

---

20. The desire to be remembered (which is the desire really to *have been*, or just *to be*) is the "I am" of the monument. On this topic, and concerning literary memory and immortality, see Stephen Owen's eloquent study *Remembrances*.

Und wenn dich das Irdische vergaß,
zu der stillen Erde sag: Ich rinne.
Zu dem raschen Wasser sprich: Ich bin.

And if the earthly has forgotten you,
To the still earth say: I'm flowing.
To the rushing water speak: I am.

The peculiarity of these imperatives "say" and "speak" is that they do not
direct us to a future action, as speech-act theory would claim all imperatives do.[21] Read out and taken on by the willing reader, the appearances
of "I'm flowing" and "I am" in the final lines of this poem are themselves
the instances of those words intended by the imperatives "say" and
"speak"; they fulfill themselves in their own proposed utterance.

It is in one sense the "grave-monument" that says "I am," but it speaks
also on behalf of the absent Wera Knoop, it speaks as the testament of the
absent poet Rilke, and above all it speaks—it proposes and stages its own
vocal enunciation—by the power of its meeting with the present reader.
In the last two lines, the *I* occurs in and as a meeting, as an answering address; *I* discovers itself situationally, as the complement of whatever face
of the world is its *you*. The lines set forth continuity and change, Goethe's
Dauer and *Wechsel*, "I am" and "I'm flowing," as interchanging figure and
ground; *I* and *you* (or *I* and *not-I*) trade places responsively. The view most
neglected by scholarship would be that in which we, as readers, recognize ourselves as present and fundamentally implicated in the speech-
event that the poem is trying to be. The lines do not mean what they mean
until you have put yourself personally at the poem's disposal as the particular voice of the gravestone's "I am."

Another of Rilke's *Sonnets to Orpheus*, whose direct address appears in
two imperatives in the first line, explicitly rejects gravestones as a way to
memorialize absence, as if in echo of the Socratic complaint that inscriptions "always say one and the same thing." That invariability, the poem
implies, misrepresents the mutability and transience that gravestones
come to mark. The sonnet begins:

Errichtet keinen Denkstein. Lasst die Rose
nur jedes Jahr zu seinen Gunsten blühn.
Denn Orpheus ists. Seine Metamorphose
in dem und dem. Wir sollen uns nicht mühn

21. See, e.g., Campbell 10–11.

um andre Namen. Ein für alle Male
ists Orpheus, wenn es singt. Er kommt und geht.

(1.5, *KA* 2: 243)

Erect no gravestone. Only this:
Just let the rose bloom each year for his sake.
For it is Orpheus. His metamorphosis
in this one and in this. We should not look

for other names. Once and for all
it's Orpheus when it sings. He comes and goes.

In place of an enduring monument should come just the natural course of what would have happened anyway (the yearly, ephemeral blooming of the rose), with the difference that the verb "let" (and the phrase "for his sake") place the ordinary, uncaused event in a sphere of attention. Addressee, Orpheus, and rose join together with the invested force of a dedication and the simultaneous detachment of simply "allowing."

This is enough, and the gravestone is unnecessary, says the poem in line 3, because "it is Orpheus." The syntax here is ambiguous, and we can construe the "it" in this phrase in two different ways. First, the "it" that is Orpheus could be the unfolding of the rose itself—Orpheus is already there *as* the event that commemorates his loss. But at the same time, the pronoun "it" looks ahead to the phrase that comes next in the poem:

Denn Orpheus ists. Seine Metamorphose
in dem und dem.

For it is Orpheus. His metamorphosis
in this one and in this.

In other words, Orpheus *is* also his own metamorphoses. (Rilke conveys this hint by hiding Orpheus's name—along with the word "rose"—in the word "Metam-orphose.") In reading, we register his disappearance, just as the lines claim, as we move from "Orpheus" in the nominative to the possessive "his" (in the possessive, Orpheus as such is already gone), and on to "in dem und dem," "in this one and in this," whose dative forms in German show his transformation already accomplished.[22]

22. Translators often miss observing that the lines do *not* read "Seine Metamorphose / in das und das" 'His metamorphosis *into* this one and this.' But the poem goes on to restate the point firmly: "Even while his word surpasses being-here, / he's *there* already" (ll. 11–12). What we see is Orpheus's forms, not his moving between them.

The theme of voice enters this Orphic non-monument in the next stanza. Once again the dummy pronoun "it" plays an idiosyncratic role (in general, it functions in this poem as a marker for Orpheus's own elusiveness):

> Ein für alle Male
> ists Orpheus, wenn es singt.

> Once and for all
> it's Orpheus when it sings [i.e., when there's song].

"Es singt" seems to be an impersonal construction on the analogy of "it rains" or "it snows," with connotations that are likewise atmospheric. Orpheus is something temporally contingent (as the word "when" signals) and at the same time permanently valid ("once and for all"). The designation "Orpheus" names transitoriness—and the acoustic—*tout court*. In place of a monument, consequently, we have music, a substitution reinforced here by a pun: "ein für alle Male" means "once and for all," but "Male" could also be a variant plural of *das Mal*, "the memorial," the same word used in Rilke's dedication of the book as a grave-monument for Wera Knoop.

Rilke's Orphic *Grab-Mal*, like his "Archaic Torso of Apollo," brings together those arts—Apollinian stonework and Dionysian music—that Nietzsche's *Birth of Tragedy* had set asunder. The monument Rilke composes for his dead Eurydice reads "I'm flowing" as well as "I am"; like the archaic inscriptions on Greek tombs, it is a silent inscription (fixity) insistent on resounding (or flow). If writing—if the poem—is like an epitaph, its Rilkean auditory and vibrating form nevertheless casts it as an acoustic shimmer rather than an invariable edifice "always saying," like the Greek inscriptions, "one and the same thing."

In an exchange of letters with the critic Dieter Bassermann in 1926, Rilke considered the suggestion that he should record his own voice reading his poems on a phonograph record. He speaks eloquently of the ways in which such a recording could inscribe poetry for future readers more effectively than the printed word does alone, but then—on the verge of embracing this restoration of voice to the inscription, recording his own poetic memorial—Rilke backs away. Paradoxically, this act of supplying an intrinsic voice to the poems would, he argues, reduce their humanity.[23]

---

23. April 19, 1926, *Briefe* 2: 529–30. See Mehlman on the relation between inscription and the Orphic voice in Rilke's writings.

And by ensuring endless repetition in the place of ephemeral uniqueness, inscribing the voice would render poetry not less but more monumental—as Socrates would have agreed. If the admonition written on the grave-monument itself is "Erect no monument," in the acoustic realm this dictum is carried through by leaving the words silent. Instead, as voiceless writing they require, ever and again, the willing instrumentality of a reader who will put her own mortal voice at their service and so recall the mortality and transience that the stone on the grave (incongruously enough) means to present.

Written letters, which Plato criticizes for "always saying one and the same thing," and which, saying that thing, perdure even through generations of death and life, accomplish their marble and epitaphic task by dissolving on the tongue, dissolving into, as Rilke wrote in declining to record *his* voice, "uniqueness and unrecoverable transitoriness." Or as Shakespeare puts it to his young man:

> Your monument shall be my gentle verse,
> Which eyes not yet created shall o'er-read,
> And tongues to be your being shall rehearse,
> When all the breathers of this world are dead,
> You still shall live—such virtue hath my pen—
> Where breath most breathes, ev'n in the mouths of men.
>
> (sonnet 81)

The "immortality" of poetry is not in the monument but in the breath and voice of the reader. That means: in ourselves, now and here as we read these lines. It is easy, given the conventionality of the claim to have conquered time through verse, to overlook its breathtaking truth, and how that truth comes to be through our own willingness to look into it, to stop and reflect as the gravestone has required of us as passersby.

Of the poets who have reflected in their poems on the enigmatic encounter between their words and a reader after the poet's death, none has dwelt on the topic with such relish as Walt Whitman. Again and again his poems return to imagining a private intimacy with his addressed reader, and to imagining the world from the perspective of his own absence, which is epitaphic work. For Whitman, the idea of dying is an enigma, and his probing of it makes for some startling poems. Here, for instance, is his plainest reworking of the classical inscription "Stay, traveler"[24]:

24. "Messenger Leaves" group (1860), *Selected* 258.

TO YOU

> Stranger! if you, passing, meet me, and desire to speak to me,
>   why should you not speak to me?
> And why should I not speak to you?

Like the Greek epitaph, Whitman's poem posits a speaking *I*; the epitaphic genre (signaled by the poem's first four words and its two-line length) makes this *I* the conventional voice of the dead. But everything else—from the verb "meet" to the idea that speaker and reader can each address the other, or would want to—flouts the givens of the epitaphic context just established. To read an epitaph, even to read it aloud, is not actually to "speak to" the one commemorated, and while we may harbor the "desire" (l. 1) to converse again with our own loved dead, Whitman's poem explicitly addresses his "passing" reader as "Stranger!"—something else again. The cheerful carelessness of "why should you not speak to me?" adopts toward death and absence the same refusal to be embarrassed that Whitman characteristically displays toward the body and sexuality, which has the effect of suggesting that our common certainties about death are themselves no more than oppressive and dispensable social convention. Whitman's project of liberation, of returning the self to the self, messianically includes the suspension of what we know about the bounds of life. The verses hope to find readers who feel compelled, however fitfully, to wonder if what he says could somehow be true.

Whitman inspires, or wants to inspire, trust. Although he is not there, he comes close to you, pulling off layer after layer of your disbelief. What characterizes his explicitly epitaphic poems is the relentless attempt to "meet" his reader—to stop her in her tracks—but for her sake, not (since he will be dead) for his own. This investment in the needs of the reader, his care for her, is fundamental to many other poems, too, not just those in which he alludes to his own death or to epitaphic conventions. For example, in "Poem of You, Whoever You Are," the intimacy that appears is the same as the ground on which Whitman's poetic epitaphs are erected. Almost everything that marks Whitman's epitaphic texts is already here in this non-epitaphic poem, because for Whitman, sympathy—love—is almost everything:

> Whoever you are, now I place my hand upon you, that you be my poem,
> I whisper with my lips close to your ear,
> I have loved many women and men, but I love none better than you.

O I have been dilatory and dumb,
I should have made my way straight to you long ago,
I should have blabb'd nothing but you, I should have chanted nothing
    but you.
I will leave all and come and make the hymns of you,
None has understood you, but I understand you,
None has done justice to you, you have not done justice to yourself,
None but has found you imperfect, I only find no imperfection in you,
None but would subordinate you, I only am he who will never consent to
    subordinate you,
I only am he who places over you no master, owner, better, God, beyond
    what waits intrinsically in yourself. (*Selected* 132–34, ll. 4–15)

The indefinite "whoever" functions on the one hand as a message of acceptance; the speaker includes you regardless of who you are. On the other hand, the word "whoever" also freely admits that the speaker cannot know who his readers, his *you*, will be. But such obstacles, as he himself might say, avail not in the face of his sympathetic power. The declaration of physical contact—"now I place my hand upon you"—dramatically collapses the countless possibilities of "whoever you are" into the unique and certain immediacy of bodily presence, as it also turns acceptance into election, even consecration.

The lines that follow oppose, again and again, the insufficiencies of generality to the sufficiency of the exclusive, specific *you*. The speaker proposes to "leave all" and make "my way straight to you" as if he were the tireless messenger in Ashbery's "At North Farm." Generalities, as the poem presents them, have been insufficient to the self: none has understood us, or done justice to us, each has wished to subordinate us. This is a lonely misprision, because as human beings we always remain in part unknown to others. If, as we read Whitman's tender lines, something in us is inclined to give in to him, it is because this poet knows our deepest longing, which is to be seen, "made for," understood as a whole being and all the way to the bottom. He recognizes—and this already counts as his understanding us—that his readers *feel* misunderstood and misjudged, even by themselves ("You have not known what you are," he continues in line 23).

The poem anticipates the defenses ("mockeries") that its reader is sure to have in place against too-facile attempts at such solicitude:

The mockeries are not you,
Underneath them and within them I see you lurk,

I pursue you where none else has pursued you,
Silence, the desk, the flippant expression, the night, the accustom'd
    routine, if these conceal you from others or from yourself, they do not
    conceal you from me. . . . (ll. 27–30)

Finally, urging the reclamation of what has gone unacknowledged—
"Claim your own at any hazard!" (l. 39)—the "Poem of You, Whoever
You Are" promises that "what waits intrinsically in yourself" will be (al-
ways has been) enough:

The hopples fall from your ankles, you find an unfailing sufficiency,
Old or young, male or female, rude, low, rejected by the rest, whatever
    you are promulges itself,
Through birth, life, death, burial, the means are provided, nothing is
    scanted,
Through angers, losses, ambition, ignorance, ennui, what you are picks
    its way. (ll. 44–47)

This poem shows the basis of which Whitman's famous assertions of his
presence after his death are an inflection: his confidence first in the addressee, and then in the reality of his communion with her or him. Thinking—as he generally does in his poems—not of his contemporary readers
so much as of future, still unborn ones, Whitman is free to speak of es-
sentials, as, for example, of the "underneath" and "within" that each of
us is apt to conceal from the living. At the same time, he takes a guess as
to where his book is being read—people read poetry at night in their studies—and in line 30 he endeavors to find his reader just there: "Silence, the
desk, the flippant expression, the night, the accustom'd routine, if these
conceal you from others or from yourself, they do not conceal you from
me." My terms "guess" and "endeavor" impute an uncertainty to Whitman about accurately naming his reader's circumstances, but this line itself, and the whole poem, betray no hesitation. Like the figure, again, at
the opening of "At North Farm" (like all the agents, in the poems examined in the previous chapter, who hold the self in thrall), Whitman's
speaker cannot be warded off; he "will . . . know where to find you" far
better than you do yourself. His progress toward you is unimpeded by
lack of hearing or vision ("Silence . . . the night"), by physical objects ("the
desk"), by defensiveness ("the flippant expression") or dulling ("the accustom'd routine"). But his is a loving tenacity, discovering the you-ness

of you as a wonder, as a sufficiency that "picks its way" through obscurations uncompromised.

The relationship across time is reciprocal: if the reader is touched by the
absent poet, so also is the poet, thinking on his unknown reader, stirred
by the intuition of her presence. Her reading intelligence is palpable just
on the other side of each word the poet writes. Combined with this sympathy is Whitman's abiding sense of awe at the mysteriousness of this
near but wholly blind form of contact. It is a real fact, but it can only ever
be surmised. If "every poem [is] an epitaph," as T. S. Eliot writes in "Little Gidding," that is partly because poetry's contact through print is in all
salient ways identical to contact through a gravestone inscription. The
reader is utterly close to the poet in her word-by-word responsiveness to
his writing and, at the same time, irrevocably beyond his reach.

Those readers who are disinclined to find themselves addressed will refer Whitman's claims to a matrix of sociohistorical and psychological concerns, or will draw attention to the rhetorical strategies by which the poet
arrives at his assertions.[25] Such methods are necessary and illuminating;
still they inevitably omit the unprotected moment of reading, which in
Whitman's case means the factuality of the touch he so marvels at:

> And that my soul embraces you this hour, and we affect each other
>   without ever seeing each other, and never perhaps to see each
>   other, is every bit as wonderful:
>
> And that I can think such thoughts as these is just as wonderful,
> And that I can remind you, and you think them and know them to be true
>   is just as wonderful.[26]

In contrast to the previous poem, in these lines Whitman does not seek to
abolish distance. Admitting it, he wonders at it. The poet is plain, in other
words, about being known to us only as words on a page. This explicitness, far from diminishing his claims to a mutual interaction with his
reader, grounds those claims in the living fact of the reader's circumstances. Whitman steps out of time not by claiming an unchanged, Horatian continuance, but instead by discovering that the interlocking of the
moment of writing and the moment of reading ("this hour") is always ir-

25. Kerry Larson, *Whitman's Drama of Consensus*, is an example of such readings; see especially pt. 1, "A More Perfect Union: Whitman's 'Hymns of You'" (1–74). Railton proposes
attention to the erotic note in Whitman's *you*.

26. "Who Learns My Lesson Complete?" (1855), ll. 22–24, *Selected* 108.

revocably "live" in a way that time does not undo (not while the poems *are* read). Indeed it is by time, loss, and death that this real atemporal interlocking is made to happen.

Explicitly enlisting death in the poem's address generates a frisson, as in the conclusion to "Song of Myself":

> I bequeath myself to the dirt to grow from the grass I love,
> If you want me again look for me under your bootsoles.
>
> You will hardly know who I am or what I mean,
> But I shall be good health to you nevertheless,
> And filter and fibre your blood.
>
> Failing to fetch me at first keep encouraged,
> Missing me one place search another,
> I stop some where waiting for you[27]

The thought of this poem, as of all Whitman's poems about his care, in death, for the reader, is anchored in his full awareness that he would die *utterly*. As W. R. Johnson says of these lines, "He leaves us to struggle for ourselves, but not without the most gentle and selfless of benedictions" (190). We need not worry—nor did Whitman wish—that we might really "fetch" him, find him waiting, anywhere but in the committed moment of reading. The poems are an emblem of what generosity means, in other words, because they are left behind for some wayfarer to find alone.[28] The scene of our reading is one in which Walt Whitman has no part; it cannot matter to him, only to us.

All of these themes, and the insistent intimacy of the epitaph, come together again at the close of Whitman's book:

> So I pass—a little time vocal, visible, contrary,
> Afterward, a melodious echo, passionately bent for—(death making me
>   really undying,)
> The best of me then when no longer visible—for toward that
>   I have been incessantly preparing. ("*So Long!*" ll. 46–48)[29]

---

27. The first edition of 1855 omits any punctuation after the final word; ll. 1329–36, *Selected* 66.

28. See Lewis Hyde's chapter "A Draft of Whitman" (160–215) in his inspired book *The Gift*.

29. I cite the 1867 edition of this poem, which brings the concern for the addressee into sharper focus than the first, 1860 version; *Variorum* 2: 451–52.

We cannot gainsay Whitman's claim that he has been "incessantly prepar-
ing" toward his own absence: it is one of the central themes of his poetry.
The same words "so I pass" that mean "so I live" or "so I die" in the first
line serve in the light of the second line to describe the way that he now,
after his death, "passes" through the world as a body of poetry, "a melodious echo, passionately bent for" by readers.

The final lines of the poem "*So Long!*" and thus of Whitman's book perform a brazenly transgressive act not present in the poems examined hith-
erto. But we can see also how in another way everything about the new
claim—which is to *bodily* intimacy with the reader—was almost in place
in the earlier reflections on the real atemporal jointure of writer and
reader. The closing passage starts, for example, in terms very like those
of the speaker in "Poem of You, Whoever You Are," who promises to
"leave all and come" to you alone:

> My songs cease—I abandon them,
> From behind the screen where I hid, I advance personally, solely to you.
>
> (ll. 51–52)

As Tenney Nathanson observes, this passage "achieves its effect by de-
claring the distinction between word and body while depending on their
virtual equivalence" (152). That is, as Whitman's "songs cease," as he
abandons the poem or language, we as readers of the printed text would
expect to be left with nothing at all. Instead, the text turns out to have been
a "screen" for a real and physically present person.

It is a mark of how Whitman succeeds in nominating his *you*—since no
one would assert of *this* poem that we become its "utterer, saying the
words of the poem *in propria persona*"—that commentary on these lines
has not emphasized their temporal reference (even though the poem is
titled "*So Long!*").[30] "My songs cease" means "You are reading the end of
Leaves of Grass," but it must also mean, and equally, "I am writing the end
of *Leaves of Grass*." Suspended between those two widely separated times
of reference, the poem works at the seam where they nonetheless meet.
We do sometimes regard a lyric *I* as a sort of "screen" in front of the historical, embodied *I*. So there is a plain sense to Whitman's act of dropping,
finally, all pretense, all poetry, for the sake of frank openness. Obviously
it is within the poetry that this relinquishment occurs (but a reader who

---

30. Quotation from Vendler. See my introduction, p. 14.

congratulates herself on seeing through the trick has missed Whitman's point). It occurs also in tandem with another, different relinquishment, as the words "I advance personally, solely to you" abandon Whitman's own deictic coordinates, his own writerly sense of *here* and *now,* in favor of the *now* of the later reader. The implication is that the false or concealing screen now left behind is also Whitman's pastness, his presumed sequestration in a different time and place from *this* one of ours, here, now. Rather than, as is sometimes said, a fantastic egotism, Whitman's gesture partakes of utter generosity, the product of his imaginatively inhabiting so sustainedly—and having confidence in—a yet-to-be-realized world where his words, seemingly fresh, will be "passionately bent for" but without the threat that he will be there to know that. Circulation is unimpaired only when the ego is subtracted, as death subtracts it ("The best of me then when no longer visible"), and Whitman is nothing if not the poet of circulation.

"*So Long!*" concludes like this:

> Camerado! This is no book,
> Who touches this, touches a man,
> (Is it night? Are we here alone?),
> It is I you hold, and who holds you,
> I spring from the pages into your arms—decease calls me forth.
> . . . .
> Dear friend, whoever you are, here, take this kiss,
> I give it especially to you—Do not forget me,
> I feel like one who has done his work—I progress on,—(long enough
>   have I dallied with Life,)
> The unknown sphere, more real than I dream'd, more direct,
>   darts awakening rays about me—*So long!*
> Remember my words—I love you—I depart from materials,
> I am as one disembodied, triumphant, dead. (ll. 53–57; 64–69)

What makes this writing epitaphic is also what makes it strange and powerful: it takes the writer's nonexistence not just as its subject but as its occasion. It speaks of Whitman's "decease" not as future (which it was for him) but as factual (which it would be for his later readers). This concession distinguishes his thought entirely from Horace's and allows him to work his unequaled metonymy: "Camerado! This is no book, / Who touches this, touches a man."[31] The lines do what they do only because

31. Hollis (154–203) discusses Whitman the "metonymic poet," and suggests with respect

this *is* a book, for us (Whitman, writing this, had no printed book before him: that thrilling word "this" had least force at the moment when he wrote it, because it had not yet acquired its referent in the world). "The Book is really not for you," Whitman writes in the unpublished 1861 introduction, "and has not done its office," "unless such meditations come" as may convince you into sympathy—which means convince you that his presence is as literal and as real as your own (267). When one happens to exist is not significant here: the presently living exist no more finally nor fully than the formerly living, just at an arbitrarily different time. The fact is hard to keep in focus. But once seen, it converts Whitman's rhetorically constructed presence back into something that points, as directly as he could make it point, at his own literal being. The lines "This is no book, / Who touches this, touches a man" are a transubstantiation.

Whitman's undertaking to write not from his bodily location at the time of writing but rather from the disembodied "location" he anticipates having from the perspective of his later readers actually reintroduces his body (his "being-there"). This poet's turn to the epitaphic turns out to be the necessarily entailed obverse of his more widely noted emphasis on corporeality ("in the best poems re-appears the body").[32] Sharon Cameron underlines the rigorous honesty of Whitman's perception in her discussion of "Crossing Brooklyn Ferry": "'It avails not, time nor place—distance avails not' is no fanciful assertion based on the speaker's desire to importune other worlds into the shape of this one; it is rather a glimmering of the truth that real connection is atemporal, impalpable, unembodied" (225).

Having advanced "personally solely to you" and having found this—found everything—to be (the word falls four times) "enough," Whitman then bids explicit, and moving, farewell:

> *So long!*
> Remember my words—I love you—I depart from materials,
> I am as one disembodied, triumphant, dead.

If "I depart from materials" refers to the time of Whitman's writing, or to the time of his death, it refers to history long past; by contrast, it is from

---

to the lines just quoted that when metonymy appears this suddenly, "in our surprise we may react as to a metaphor" (203). (Hollis is also a highly readable critic on Whitman's *you*. See especially "Audience Involvement, 1855–1860" 88–123.)

32. "Poem of The Sayers of The Words of The Earth" (1856), *Selected* 161.

our perspective, not his, that Whitman is "dead" (it is the last word in his book). As the sentence moves from "I depart" to "I am," then, it seems to move from what linguistics calls coding time, the moment of utterance or (in this case) inscription, to receiving time.[33] But Whitman's work in concluding *Leaves of Grass* has been to make the end of his book coincide with the end of his life, as the text becomes his body. This means that his departure from materials occurs at the instant of reading, as well as in his 1860 separation from these words by their being first written and then printed, and as well as in his death in 1891. The final lines *are* "triumphant," in a way, for they bring together, in one movement, the really existing (and therefore now factually dead) writer, the "disembodied" textual self of the forever-speaking *I*, the loved reader, and the work—the now completed *monumentum*—through which this extratemporal meeting-in-departure can never stop occurring.

I close this chapter with four short poems by another poet; these exemplify a different grammar from the other works discussed in this book, since they are poems without a *you*, poems that in effect leave behind second-person address in favor of an oblique allusion to the reader's presence. I mentioned in the introduction that such allusions ("this book," "my song," "my papers, yellowed with their age," and so on) lie adjacent to the topic of lyric address in formal (grammatical) terms, but overlap with it in the way they implicate the later reader in the fact of the poem's continuance. These poems too are, in their own way, epitaphic; but in sharp contrast to Whitman's tenacity, every metaphor in these four varied poems emphasizes the reader's mediated separation from and independence from the writer. Form—the discretion of alluding to the reader, not addressing her—accords in this way with content.

In 1872, Emily Dickinson included the following poem in a letter to her "little cousins" Louise and Frances Norcross:

> A word left careless on a page
> May consecrate an eye,

33. I invoke the linguistic terms "coding time" and "receiving time" here as an economical way to discuss the complexities of time-deixis in poetry. (See Levinson, *Pragmatics* 73–79, for a lucid presentation of the need for these terms and of their usage.) In the case of literature, one must doubt the adequacy of the terms—particularly of "receiving time," since the "receiving" of poetry is likely to happen later, away from the text, as a line releases itself in the mind; but the terminology may serve heuristically. On deixis generally, see the indispensable work by Fillmore. See Nathanson 315 on the last line's "as."

When folded in perpetual seam
The wrinkled author lie.[34]

Horace may stand for (though he did not invent) the idea of the poet as a forceful figure trying to shape an unruly posterity to an approximation of his desired reading. Dickinson turns that Horatian idea on its head: as the opposition between "careless" and the high solemnity of "consecrate" indicates, the writer's act is negligent, even inadvertent. The *I* (or "eye") that may be consecrated is not the "great part" of the author himself that Horace hoped he had lodged in his lasting poems, but instead, unexpectedly, the *I* of the reader. Dickinson does not try to explain the alchemy by which the carelessness of a word "left" on a page (the three indefinite articles in lines 1–2 reinforce the sense of random chance involved) may come to exert an ultimate claim—a religious one—on its putatively casual reader. Like the hailing of the chance passerby at the tombstone, the poem seems to be about a way in which the author's detachment, at death, from all author-ity over her works paradoxically becomes the root of their power to hold the reader steady.[35]

Lines 3 and 4 of "A word left careless" evoke the author's deadness in one of those metaphors that are instantly recognizable as Dickinsonian. The author "folded in perpetual seam" belongs physically to the "page" on which her words, careless or otherwise, appear. (Even "wrinkled" could apply to paper as well as to the corpse.) It is an unfamiliar way of thinking about death, since something folded in a seam is not absent, just lost to view. The second surprise is the thought that being merely lost to view could be nonetheless an irrevocable state, "perpetual" (l. 3). That word conveys the conclusiveness of death, but at the same time, defying the usual notion of death as cessation, it suggests something that does *not* cease but continues uninterruptedly. (The way "perpetual" revises familiar temporal ideas about death [death is stopping] is analogous to the way "folded" and "seam" revise familiar spatial ones [death is absence].) The effect of both words, together with the image of the "wrinkled author" lying somewhere—as if the *body* were the lasting thing—is to imply a near-

34. *Poems,* Franklin ed. 2: 1094 (F 1268); *Complete,* Johnson ed. 3: 878 (variant of J 1261). The letter's date is uncertain (Dickinson, *Letters* 499; letter 379).

35. Grossman (§40.2) suggests that haunting poems are the ones that, like Dickinson's, renounce their authors as living persons: "The availability of the text as an occasion of the bodily self-discovery by the reader depends on the severity with which the poet in history has severed him*self* from the poem, has given away his voice, and passed into fictional explicitness, speaking" (342).

ness of the dead writer to the text, or to the reader, or simply to the living, that may nevertheless be (as in fact it is) an absolute divorce.

Something consecrated is set apart from the merely earthly; it is sanctified or (in the case of a person) initiated into a higher order, which is why I spoke earlier of the claims of the poem on its reader's eye as "ultimate" ones. The word can also be used in two other senses which, though both are a little slant to Dickinson's syntax and context in this poem, may influence the line's meaning: we speak of things or customs consecrated by time—made venerable, if not actually sacred—and this first usage is relevant here because it may be the lapse of time that has given the poem so much more power than its "careless" origins would have suggested. Second, to consecrate is to devote or dedicate something to a solemn purpose, and as I will argue, especially in the next chapter, the reader may indeed feel her Eye and *I* enlisted in and answerable to the moment of poetic reception. Such works remind us of what would get left out if we investigated poetic address by using a purely grammatical definition of it (the pronoun *you*). Although Dickinson's poem offers not a single deictic form that linguistics would recognize as implicating the text's reader, it surely savors the small vertigo by which it may seem to speak at one moment of the poet's own reading experiences with poets dead before her, at the next moment of ours as we read her work.

Like many of Dickinson's poems, this one appears in variant forms, and I have been unorthodox in presenting the poem first in the form it took as part of a letter. Readers of Dickinson will know the poem better in the different form it takes in her own penciled worksheet, probably from the same year (1872); and this more widely known version alters the metaphor for poetry's endurance so discomfitingly that we must take it as a new poem on the same subject:

> A Word dropped careless on a Page
> May stimulate an Eye
> When folded in perpetual seam
> The Wrinkled Maker lie
>
> Infection in the sentence breeds
> We may inhale Despair
> At distances of Centuries
> From the Malaria - [36]

36. *Poems*, Franklin ed. 2: 1093 (F 1268); *Complete*, Johnson ed. 3: 878 (J 1261). In saying

The variant words in the first stanza already alter the poem noticeably: "left," "consecrate," and "author" have become "dropped," "stimulate," and "Maker." "Dropped" in line 1 bespeaks inadvertence even more than did the word "left" in the first version, and it makes the "Word" more physical. "Stimulate," on the one hand a banally physiological idea compared to "consecrate," on the other hand gestures beyond itself, ambiguously so (stimulate to what?), and so prepares for the second stanza's turn to morbidity. With "Maker" (l. 4) Dickinson plays off the Latin root of "Infection" (l. 5), *fectum* 'made,' and draws attention to the apparent contradiction between the writer's divine authority as "Maker," intending her text in every point and nuance, and the way in which words ungovernably "drop" from the worktable of invention and "breed" effects quite on their own.

In the newly added second stanza, disease, recalling the Wrinkled Maker unhygienically "folded in" the papery "seam" of existence, breeds "in" the sentence (l. 5). That sense of enclosure is emphasized by the prefix in "Infection" (l. 5) and "inhale" (l. 6) as well. The word "inhale" makes the pathogen inhere in the reader ("we" [l. 6]), as virulently as it did in the text. The phrase "distances of Centuries" imagines time as if it were extent in space, so that inhaling (the body's nearest exchange with what is outside it) becomes a magic bridge between separate eras. Like Shakespeare and like Rilke, Dickinson imagines reading as a matter of the breath as well as of the eye, as if "Despair" were the name of a kind of air. But for these other writers, to put poetry in the mouth is to associate it with breath as the sign of organic life and with expressive speech; both poets are thinking of exhalation. Dickinson thinks instead of the orifice's vulnerability, of our helplessness before the power of what we read and take in.

This helplessness then becomes the true correlate of the ungovernable "carelessness" of the writer's activity: neither sender nor receiver is finally in control of language's effects. The "Malaria" from which we are centuries removed may not have been the same thing as the "Despair" we now inhale. These two words rhyme through the detour of calque translation—*malaria* means "bad air," which *does* rhyme with "Despair" —more than through the direct sensoriness of assonance. The pathogen

that this version "alters" the metaphor, I do not mean to imply that this variant was written later than the other (the chronology is unclear). I use words like "alter," "new," "first version," and so on as a convenient way of referring to the order in which I myself present the variants.

may have bred, with similar indirection, in the written sentence rather than in the author's life. It is as if Dickinson took literally Horace's claim that in his poems he would "grow on and on" after death, like an infectious agent, still with the result that the written poem may intrude life-changingly into the life of the passerby who stops and reads. If "stimulate" does not interrupt the reader's progress through life as forcefully as "consecrate" did in the alternate version of Dickinson's poem, nevertheless the centuries-old infection from which "we may inhale Despair" does so unequivocally.[37]

Epitaphic poems are preeminently written poems, poems whose writtenness is one of their themes. As such they are poems of the eye (even when, like the Greek epitaph, they also count on voicing: as I noted earlier, poetry read aloud is anything but oral poetry). The motif of optical "stimulation" connects "A Word dropped careless" with an earlier work of Dickinson's which treats the idea of poetry's continuance less disquietingly. In "The Poets light but Lamps" (1865), poems are styled as oil lamps, spreading light rather than disease. The most important difference from "A Word dropped careless" is that here the transmission that is poetic art is purposeful, and also useful. But the poet's mortality figures in this text too, and the consequent emphasis on the mediatedness of poetic "survival" is even clearer than in the previous poem:

> The Poets light but Lamps -
> Themselves - go out -
> The Wicks they stimulate
> If vital Light
>
> Inhere as do the Suns -
> Each Age a Lens
> Disseminating their
> Circumference - [38]

The first two lines seem to posit more than a reciprocity between author and work, as if the writing of the poem actually entailed the extinguishing of the author. Once again we may hear a rejoinder to the boast of the

---

37. Compare Mallarmé's sonnet "Le tombeau de Charles Baudelaire" (1895), where the dead poet is "un poison tutélaire / Toujours à respirer si nous en périssons" 'a tutelary poison / Always to breathe in though we perish of it.'

38. *Poems*, Franklin ed. 2: 855 (F 930; J 883). Compare the end of Whitman's "*So Long!*" See Ong, "*Maranatha*" 232–35 and Ricoeur 137 on the ways in which "to read a book is to consider its author as already dead" (Ricoeur).

Horatian tradition "I shall not altogether die," a rejoinder that accounts for the word "but" in Dickinson's first line: not the poet survives, just the lamp she lit. But the apparently smaller claim is hardly less magical than its classical precedent, since "The Wicks they stimulate," the speaker tells us, will then "Inhere as do the Suns - ." The image of the poets who "stimulate" wicks (as the poem in turn may later "stimulate an Eye") suggests that a poem is something preexisting, like language, not made so much as it is found and ignited. But the parenthetical phrase "If vital Light," which evidently refers to the wicks, makes "Wicks" and "Light" interchangeable, or shows, perhaps, how a wick once lit seems to be all light (disappearing behind or becoming its flame). The description of the light as "Vital" recovers something of the rejected Horatian conceit: perhaps the *poet* is not alive in her works, but the works are felt to be living nonetheless (or may be so felt, "if" the wicks or the light are sufficiently "vital"). Such lamps, the poem goes on, "Inhere as do the Suns": they are made to "stick" (the etymological meaning of "inhere") so deeply that they become not just intrinsic constituents of the cosmos but comparable to the source of all life and energy. Dickinson's claim for poetry—of course she could be thinking of earlier poets, but how not to recall herself?—begins modestly, but by this fifth line it far surpasses Horace in its grand sweep.[39]

Before reading the last three lines I want to back up and propose a second, alternate reading of the poem so far. It looks very different if we parse the syntax in another way. What if "go out" meant "go out of," as when we speak of "going out the door"? Then lines 2–5 could assert of the Poets, "Themselves go out the Wicks they stimulate," with the added proviso, "If vital Light Inhere as do the Suns."[40] Suddenly, with this reading, the poem *does* say that poets themselves, if not contained within their poems, emerge out of them nonetheless: those texts continue to "say" their authors (Horace's "dicar") from age to age. The condition, "If vital Light // Inhere as do the Suns," makes a better comparison than the first reading, which made "Wicks" the subject of "Inhere." The light is literally "vital" if it is the essence of the poet, and the question that the word "if" leaves open is whether this vitality *can* stick fast as the uncreated energies of nature ("the suns") do. In either case, "inhere" opposes "go out"

39. Cf. F 533 (J 569): "I reckon - When I count at all - / First - Poets - Then the Sun - ."

40. I thank Eliza Richards for suggesting this reading to me. Dickinson's manuscript shows her characteristic dash after "stimulate" very low on the line, like a comma (Dickinson, *Manuscript* 2: 1065). Johnson's edition includes the mark as a dash, while Franklin's edition omits it without explanation.

(whether that means "be extinguished" or "exit"). "Inhere" also contrasts with the later word "Disseminating" (l. 7), which, however, is meant to culminate, not counter, the inhering.

The last three lines have their own riches:

> Each Age a Lens
> Disseminating their
> Circumference -

"Their" refers in our first reading to the plural subject of the verb "inhere," which was "Wicks" (a metaphor for poems): successive ages spread abroad (amplify and project) the circle of light shed by a poem. In our second reading, where "inhere" is a subjunctive singular form, "their" must instead refer to "The Poets" ("Themselves"): each age sows, like a seed, the unknowable mind of the poet. This second paraphrase draws on Dickinson's fondness for using the word "Circumference" to indicate "the boundary of human knowledge" (Benfey 84), whether that be death, God, or as here, another person's mind. Each age is a "Lens," which brings to mind among other things the lens of the (reading) eye. The seeming contradiction latent in the word *disseminate* is that while certain kinds of lenses may indeed scatter the light of a flame, others—like the eye's lens—concentrate it; this concentration accords with the etymological basis of *dissemination,* namely, "seed." Poems and poets are carried in ever-widening rings as they are read and handed on from age to age. At the same time, for each reader, the poem (and whatever part of the poet "inheres" in her poem) is a germ, a tiny vessel packed with an intensity of potential significances made not less but more focused by the process Dickinson calls dissemination.[41]

Like "A Word dropped careless on a Page," this poem does not address its reader, nor does it speak overtly about its own survival. It must occur to the reader on his own—or fail to—that by the fact of this his present reading in a different "Age," the poem is showing its aphoristic statements to be true of itself as well. Dickinson hints at this immediacy by a pun, which cannot be fit into any syntactical sense but floats free like a fragmentary, subliminal message (and is similarly hard to get out of one's head once one has seen it): "Inhere" also says "in here," inhering in this my poem as you, reader, are now receiving it.

41. "Disseminating" also echoes the word "seam" in "A Word dropped careless," infolding the "Wrinkled Maker" herself into the made poem on the page.

The written poem is an object in the visual field; a delimited thing, it can indicate itself *as* a thing in a way that a stretch of spoken language cannot do (the joke on "in here" illustrates this capacity). It is also, very fundamentally, a *made* thing.[42] Horace marks this fact with his ode's proud first word, "Exegi" 'I have completed,' and with the metaphor of spinning or weaving later in the text. Dickinson, in a third poem about poetry's life beyond the poet, sees the madeness of poetry—as if in inversion of the outward-spreading "dissemination" of "The poets light but Lamps"—as a tremendous compression, and transformation, of the visual ("Suns" again). The poem concerns the making of things that outlast (and perhaps exceed) their makers. This poem again explicitly shows us the poet's death along with the poem's continuance, though as in "A Word dropped careless," the terms mingle. (Here the writer is vaguely mummified by the transfer of her bodily "decay" to another term in the poem.) But in this work, the mediating term that conveys the poem's own lasting power can become instead an open door in time:

> Essential Oils - are wrung -
> The Attar from the Rose
> Be not expressed by Suns - alone -
> It is the gift of Screws -
>
> The General Rose - decay -
> But this - in Lady's Drawer
> Make Summer - When the Lady lie
> In Ceaseless Rosemary - [43]

I want first to suggest that "Essential Oils" is Dickinson's specific response to Shakespeare's sonnet 5. That sonnet runs:

> Those hours that with gentle work did frame
> The lovely gaze where every eye doth dwell
> Will play the tyrants to the very same,
> And that unfair which fairly doth excel;
> For never-resting time leads summer on
> To hideous winter and confounds him there,
> Sap checked with frost and lusty leaves quite gone,
> Beauty o'ersnowed and bareness every where.

42. See Barbara Herrnstein Smith's excellent *Poetic Closure* on the ways poems work to close in on themselves, and on how we recognize something as "closed" at all.

43. Poem F 772 (J 675), *Poems*, Franklin ed. 2: 728–29 (ca. 1863), cited in variant B.

> Then were not summer's distillation left
> A liquid prisoner pent in walls of glass,
> Beauty's effect with beauty were bereft,
> Nor it nor no remembrance what it was.
> But flowers distilled, though they with winter meet,
> Leese but their show; their substance still lives sweet.[44]

Shakespeare's thought pertains most closely to the second half of Dickinson's poem, though that most memorable line about summer's distillation, "A liquid prisoner pent in walls of glass" (l. 10), could have stimulated the imagery of torture in the later poet's words "wrung" and "Screws." Both poets' images concern the austere containment of much in little, but where Shakespeare's "prisoner pent" asks for release (or "dissemination"), Dickinson's "wrung" and "Screws" drive painfully inward, emphasizing concentration, and cost. Moreover, in the closely connected sonnet 6 and in *A Midsummer Night's Dream*, Shakespeare associates "the rose distilled" with marriage and procreation; Dickinson may be retorting with a pun on "sons" in her line 3.

"Never-resting time" and the transience of life are the background of Dickinson's poem and the foreground of Shakespeare's first two quatrains, but the concern of both texts is the manufacture of essence, "Beauty's effect," lest the end of life be "Nor it nor no remembrance what it was." "Ceaseless Rosemary," in Dickinson's text, corresponds to "perpetual seam" in "A Word dropped careless"; it is the adjacency in which poets lie folded (literally "im-plic-ated") as a secondary effect of the remembrance accorded to their works. Shakespeare's word "remembrance" has not one but two analogues in "Essential Oils." First, as in Shakespeare's sonnet itself, it corresponds to the "Attar" of flowers distilled. But also—by a detour through the language of flowers in, for example, Shakespeare's plays ("There's rosemary, that's for remembrance" [*Hamlet* 4.5.175])—the word "remembrance" stands for death itself. By this doubling (and because "Rosemary" includes the word "Rose"), Dickinson disrupts a simple summer/winter opposition. In her poem, it remains true that roses in general ("The General Rose") decay while attar "still lives sweet" (and I take it Shakespeare's "still" is thinking of distilling here, too), but the "Lady" lying "in Ceaseless Rosemary" inhabits,

---

44. "Leese" means *lose*. "Flowers distilled" appear elsewhere in Shakespeare specifically as roses; see sonnet 54 and, differently, the opening to *A Midsummer Night's Dream* (1.1. 74–78).

even in death, some pocket of things that keeps her from being likewise "o'ersnowed" or bare of leaves.

The comparison with Rilke's sonnet 1.5, quoted in part earlier ("Erect no gravestone"), throws into relief each poet's characteristic thought in their mingling of permanence and impermanence in the image of the rose. For Rilke, the decaying of "The General Rose" is part of Orpheus's constancy, even part of commemoration, so that the rose itself becomes a token of remembrance. Both poems concern at once the effort to memorialize (analogous to writing) and the later reception or acknowledgment of the tokens of memory (analogous to reading).

A closer look at Dickinson's poem will make it clearer what is "pent" in her poem that gives it this extraordinary confidence in remembrance.

> Essential Oils - are wrung -
> The Attar from the Rose
> Be not expressed by Suns - alone -
> It is the gift of Screws -
>
> The General Rose - decay -
> But this - in Lady's Drawer
> Make Summer - When the Lady lie
> In Ceaseless Rosemary -

A first reading of the text will find a poem about the precious Attar of Roses, a rare perfume produced (the poem observes) not by nature but by the application of force and artifice to nature. The prize won by this violence is an essence, something that outlasts what nature can produce on her own (the "General Rose"), and outlasts even "the Lady," the immediate beneficiary (or, generalizing slightly, the agent) of the wringing process itself. This product, not "expressed" by "Suns," nevertheless seems charged with their luminary force as it "makes Summer"—calls back, and indoors, not only the original roses but somehow the full season and summer world of their bloom—even after long confinement "in Lady's Drawer."

Quickly an experienced reader will be likely to abstract this first reading to a second, which, reading "Rose" and "Attar" as figures, finds a poem about the human endeavor to distill something precious out of experience, the costs and rewards of that effort, and the implications of success.

The argument I want to make builds on these two readings; it cannot dispense with an interpretation of Dickinson's poem along the lines I have so briefly sketched, but only aims to add something to it. In each of those two readings, the literal and the figurative, the word "this" (l. 6) was taken as anaphoric, referring to "the gift of Screws" or (what is essentially the same thing) to "Attar."[45] Though it may have taken a first-time reader a moment's thought to determine that antecedent for the word "this," once it is proposed, the referent "Attar" seems well supported by the poem's sustained contrast between roses on the one hand and their essential oil ("Attar") on the other. (That contrast is what accounts for the adversative "But this - ").

But the second reading, the figurative one which takes the poem as a metaphor for a view of human life, can also prompt in its turn a different way of reading the word "this." As it happens, this alternative is stimulated by, rather than contradicting, my first suggestion that the word refers to "Attar." Namely, the word "this" could be read as not in the first place anaphoric ("pointing backward" to an antecedent) nor cataphoric ("pointing forward" to a later word), but—in the coinage of M. A. K. Halliday—"homophoric," a word pointing to itself. The word "this" could designate, in other words, "this poem."[46]

We could suppose the plausibility of such a reading because we know that poets are naturally preoccupied with poetry, and because we know that for this reason images of distillation, extraction, or compression (not to mention a host of associated others), throughout literary history, are readily interpretable as figures for the poet's own work. In this case, moreover, the "Lady" stands in nicely for Dickinson herself. And most vividly of all, the image of this "gift" lying in "Lady's Drawer" after her death brings to mind, all in a rush, the historical facts of Dickinson's own poetic legacy: in Dickinson's room, the week after her death, her sister

45. Confusingly, classical rhetoric calls anaphora the repetition of an initial word. But since the root sense is "carrying back," that is, pointing to an antecedent, linguistics has designated anaphora and its pair cataphora (pointing forward in the text) as terms for the kind of intratextual referring that words such as pronouns do. See Quirk 347, §6.15.

46. Halliday's term is cited and discussed in Widdowson, *Stylistics* 65–66. Literary critics have tended to speak in such cases of "self-referentiality." In this instance I would prefer the linguistic term "token-reflexivity," to make it clear that I think of Dickinson's "this" not as referring to poetry in general (although someone might plausibly argue for such a reading), but to the specific utterance of which the word "this" is a part: this poem. My reading is not even interested in other instantiations of the poem "Essential Oils"—other places where the "same" poem might exist in print—but rather intends exactly the unique page that one is reading at that moment. This is true token-reflexivity. (On token-reflexivity and the type/token distinction, see Lyons 13–18, §1.4.)

Lavinia "found," as she wrote, "a box (locked) containing 7 hundred wonderful poems, carefully copied" and sewn into fascicles.[47]

> The General Rose - decay -
> But this - in Lady's Drawer
> Make Summer - When the Lady lie
> In Ceaseless Rosemary -

This dramatic image brings out a crucial aspect of the token-reflexive (or "self-referential") reading of the word "this" as it dovetails with the anaphoric reference to "Attar." Insofar as it suggests the labor and even agony of poetic creation ("the gift of Screws"), "this" names the poem *as written*, the poem as it appeared under Dickinson's own pen (at "coding time"). But associating the image of "Lady's Drawer" with Dickinson's box of poems moves us closer to yet another way of reading altogether. How is it, to come to the point, that "this" can "Make Summer"? The poem can give of itself only in the reading; if "this" is said to "Make Summer," the word "this" must to that extent proleptically indicate receiving time. Seen from this angle, the poem becomes a "gift" (l. 4) expressly meant for a reader who will come "When the Lady lie / In Ceaseless Rosemary" (ll. 7–8).

This ability of the word "this" to pivot, even within its homophoric reading, pointing now to the poem as it is being written and now to the poem as it is being read, entails another dimension to the deictic behavior of the word, and another consequence for ourselves as readers. That is, as a reference to the utterance itself at two possible, widely separated moments, the word "this" behaves something like a *temporal* deictic (such as "now"). More exactly, its functions as a token-reflexive discourse deictic ("this utterance") and as a spatial deictic ("this written or printed poem visible before me or you") both take on a temporal quality, as the orientation to the speaker (which is, in normal discourse, the default assumption) gives way—in light of the words "when Lady lie / In Ceaseless Rosemary"—to an orientation to the receiver, the reader who may come across this poem when Dickinson is dead.[48]

---

47. Cited in introduction to *Poems*, Franklin ed. 7.
48. Levinson (*Pragmatics* 73–74) gives examples of how the deictic center may be similarly projected onto the addressee, and so into receiving time, in letter writing and the pre-recording of broadcasts: "This programme was recorded last Wednesday, April 1st, to be relayed today." In this example, the sender of the message indicates its temporal projection

The giving way, the shifting of deictic reference from Dickinson at her writing desk to ourselves as we read the poem here, in our circumstances, and perhaps back and forth again, is the temporal oscillation of the word "this" and with it, of the whole poem. And it is by this swinging door that the poem offers an intimacy with the unrepresentably private moment of its composition, which is to say an intimacy with its writer.

The indirection of Dickinson's "this," by virtue of its subtlety, even surprise (we may need several readings to become aware of this temporal dimension of the deictic at all), may make it a more effective means of intimate contact for many readers than would be the overt hailing of a readerly *you*.

It is the task of reading the poem in this way to understand its own character as expressive "Attar": Of what sort of rose, in this light, is the poem the "Essential Oil"? What sequence of "Suns" and "Screws" has concentrated in its narrow bounds the power to "Make Summer"? And most consequential for the reader is to discover what is meant by "Make Summer": What does this image stand for when we read the poem self-referentially? We can make hypotheses, in general terms, about how to interpret the "Rose" figuratively; and if we take the "Screws" to be a wringing of language (as the word "expressed" also hints), we can identify some of Dickinson's own preferred screws as this poem itself shows their work.[49] But the meaning of "Make Summer" is falsified as soon as we undertake an answer in third-person terms; for even in this poem without a *you*, it is a second-person stance of responsiveness and personal engagement that the work asks of its reader.

The poem seeks a reader's presence; that is, it wants a reader who will make its "this" her own, who will recognize its deixis as indicating the page held open by her hands and no others, precisely this moment of her reading. The door of "this," which opens one way onto the moment of Dickinson's composition, has found its other side, its other opening, with this your act of reading. The willingness to read this way is a commitment, since it would seem to follow that if "this" is the very place the

---

forward by referring to his own present time in the past tense, because reception is anticipated later. Significantly, Dickinson's trademark uninflected verb forms (e.g., "But this - in Lady's Drawer / *Make* Summer") suspend the possibility of such tense-marking in her poem. The resulting ambiguity helps to concentrate the double deixis of her poem in the single word "this."

49. Cristanne Miller examines some of these linguistic deformations in her reading of this poem (2-5).

poem means, then no other place could be meant: the poem can have, in this sense, only one target, and it has found it in you. Seeing this fact is as much as seeing that you have full responsibility for reading the poem, for receiving everything it has to impart as a message and a "gift" (l. 4); it has—can have—no other reader, no better reader nor any as good as you in this moment.

It is in undergoing and taking on this obligation—an exigent one—that one may, at the same time, feel Summer made. To adopt this stance as a reader (one may do so provisionally, but only if one then forgets the provisionality) engages one with the poem with a wholeness of one's own capacities and attention that enables the poem to offer itself fully, and in most solemn confidence. If this is epitaphic reading, it is that because the author's disappearance is folded into the poem itself, and because the act of reading is depended on as if it were (as it really is) not less than everything, as it was too for the *I* of the Greek epitaph. The gift and the requirement are given together, as a single thing. This demanding generosity of the writing dead—a special case of the epitaphic poem—is the topic of the next chapter, a coda on poetry's touch.

4

Hand-Writing and Readerly Intimacy

It is not difficult to imagine a . . . model of literary history and criticism in which writing is deliberately taken as a gift to others . . . or as an exercise in generosity, and where this feature is energetically foregrounded. In such a reading the theme of communication (reaching out to those known and those unknown alike) interlaces in paradoxical and sweet ways with the theme of love.

—Virgil Nemoianu

This hour I tell things in confidence,
I might not tell everybody but I will tell you.

—Walt Whitman, "Song of Myself"

THIS FINAL CHAPTER, like the foregoing one, works at describing certain ways in which literature presses for a close relation with those into whose hands it may fall. These readings emphasize the lapse of time in a poem's historical existence. This inquiry could therefore be seen as a kind of literary history. But it is not a familiar kind: when we include our own act of reading in the consideration of a text's life, taking our own experience as our example of how texts come to and exert influence on later readers, our account of these matters will prove not strictly rational, shot through with affective interest. To feel this interest is to begin to acknowledge the claims made on us as individuals by our engagement with poems. Criticism which serves poorly that level of personal engagement misses something essential. This chapter turns, accordingly, to poems that express a dependence on the later reader, seeking her answering pressure. They are works suggesting a readerly reach through history, a gesture of touch everywhere attended, but nowhere held fast, by the play of time.

One of the strongest testaments—in more than one sense of that word—to the unsettling power of ambiguous address remains Keats's late poem or fragment "This living hand":

> This living hand, now warm and capable
> Of earnest grasping, would, if it were cold
> And in the icy silence of the tomb,
> So haunt thy days and chill thy dreaming nights
> That thou would wish thine own heart dry of blood
> So in my veins red life might stream again,
> And thou be conscience-calm'd—see, here it is—
> I hold it towards you. (384)

Overwhelmingly, this writing wishes to reach someone. To ask who that someone is would be natural, perhaps inevitable; but in another sense, it would be to dodge the extended hand. Earlier Keats criticism proposed to discover Keats's fiancée Fanny Brawne in this addressee (and he did write accusing letters to her); later conjecture took the lines to be material for a play (and they are melodramatic). But to hold that the force of this poem's *you* is a spectacle only, or that it expended itself wholly on some third person in the past, is to block the strange spell that must grip a reader who accedes to the hailing of the poem and so becomes the intended interlocutor of the dead. Since the poem is and will always be mysterious, "third-person" critical stances may be a reaction against its haunting power, may be a critic's willful impoverishment ensuring his or her immunity to the effect of literature.[1]

Keats spins these lines over the oral/written dichotomy mentioned in my introduction as foundational to the modern lyric. The poem starts with an obliquely self-referential gesture: "this hand" is, while not the same as "this poem," its immediate metonym for the writer, and with these words the text underscores its own status as a written thing. Con-

---

1. For the history of speculations about the poem's composition, see Bate 626. These alternative possibilities are fruitfully discussed in Lipking's excellent *Life of the Poet* 180–84 and by Hopkins. See also Bahti.

versely, the poem's last lines abruptly flout this fact by using language that belongs to a face-to-face, oral situation of utterance ("see, here it is—").[2] The poem exploits and sharpens its paradox also in another, still stronger way: it founds its power—its animate "reach," we might say— on the trust that poems, as inanimate artifacts, may outlive their authors.

"This living hand" is the hand Keats saw before him as he wrote the handwritten poem, as the deictics "this" and "now" confirm. It is the agent of his expression, "warm and capable" of earnestly grasping, among other things, his pen. Against the sense of himself as there, as real and capable of exerting an effect on the world, Keats develops a counterfactual, imaginary antithesis. The verb "would" splits his first lines in the middle, doubling the familiar and alive with its own self strange and dead. The lines foreshadow the features of the uncanny that Freud delineated in 1919: the strangeness of what was before familiar, the uncertainty as to whether a thing is alive or inanimate, and the disruption of identity through doubling. When at length the poem breaks off the increasingly intricate grammar of this long subjunctive scenario, and we emerge abruptly into "—see, here it is— / I hold it towards you," then how can we describe what has happened? I want to argue that the first answer must be sought in the field of pronoun reference, what linguists call, in such cases, anaphora.[3] We must ask, that is, what do these instances of "it" refer back to?

It would seem natural to arrive at an answer by bracketing that long hypothetical middle altogether. The poem started with the words "This living hand," and surely it's the same hand that is presented at the end of the poem. Reasonably, in other words, we could identify the key elements of the poem's syntax as follows:

> This living hand, now warm [etc.]
> . . . .
> . . . . . . —see, here it is—
> I hold it towards you.

But what is striking about this skeletal version of the poem's syntax is that it so obviously fails to show the skeleton in the poem. The chilling effect

2. This description, like some that follow, simplifies certain intricacies which could be more accurately detailed in the terminology of pragmatics, but the cost of that rigor is rebarbative language.

3. See note 45 in chapter 3 for my use of the term *anaphora*.

clearly depends on having what is omitted here, namely the hypothetical subjunctives, present.

Must we reason, then, that when the poem breaks into "see, here it is— I hold it towards you," the anaphoric pronouns refer to the earlier "it" of line 2 ("if it were cold"), to the fictional dead hand? Unlikely, since then we'd be faced with the logical and syntactic incoherence of the poet claiming he holds toward us the merely hypothetical hand he has imagined would be (but is not) in the tomb.

We are, in other words, caught in an anaphoric muddle. The reader is left (possibly without noticing the fact) with a cloudy sense of whether it is the living hand or the dead one that the poem tries to hold toward us; and if the poem does succeed in haunting us, we can find the origin of that haunting in our uncertainty (carefully prepared by the poem's grammar) as to whether the crucial shape in the poem is living or dead.

I mentioned that this text is written under the aegis of the age-old promise that poems may still be read when their authors are gone. Keats's poem, we might say, goes further: it is written in a way that incorporates the death of its writer. The force of the poem depends on the way time is figured into it. The long conditional scenario in the middle of the poem— "would, if it were cold / . . . / So haunt"—is motivated not only by fantasy, but also by the thought of mortality, which was never far from John Keats's mind, given his doubtful tubercular prognosis. In writing a poem, the thought of death is the thought of, in Shakespeare's words, the "eyes not yet created" that will "o'erread" this text, later (as if reading an epitaph) when the writer is gone.[4] At this time of later reading, the grammar of Keats's poem will be at odds with fact: the living hand will be dead and the imagined one (the one in the tomb) true.

The agency of this inversion of the poem is the poet's own empirical death. The truth of the living hand gave way to the truth of the cold, dead one upon Keats's death in 1821. It is, in other words, history that makes the indicative into a falsehood and the subjunctive true. But this infolding of temporality, although it is at the very heart of the poem, is not something its writer could bring about, nor is it something for which the reader is responsible either. Rather Keats's relation to his own mortality in writing this poem is best characterized by saying that he relied on it. Writing with his living hand, he relied on his own death, his own ab-

4. Sonnet 81. Horace's ode 1.28 includes the "conscience calm'd" topos. Stewart's short discussion of Keats's poem (161) is densely insightful.

sence; and so the poem at every point counts on being turned inside out by time.

Although it is a grammatically subjunctive hand that lies in the icy silence of the tomb, nevertheless the possibility of presenting this dead hand in actuality—the possibility, in other words, that the "it" of

> —see, here it is—
> I hold it towards you

could be holding out as much the dead hand as the living one—this possibility is realized by the reader who recognizes how time has turned Keats's imagined death into prosaic fact, and how the poem's intention reaches, impossibly, through this same dimension, out of poetry into reality, "through" death into actual being. Keats is dead and gone, but his poem knows that, and this is the source of its unquiet power.

The change from "thou" to "you" has baffled critics.[5] But it is another element of the poem's gradual revelation that the living reader is implicated: where *thou* is poetical, *you* was for Keats the address to a contemporary, "outside" of literature—as a glance at his letters makes clear. (This observation also argues against the proposal that the lines were composed for a play.)

The astonishing force of this Keats poem is its intense "addressivity": it is about the possibility of haunting someone after the poet dies, haunting by means of a hand which is extended in the very medium of the poem. To haunt by means of a poem, one must have readers.[6] What this poem requires, in any way of looking at it, is an other, a *you* to haunt. It demands the presence of a reader as a poem has seldom demanded it. And it is of much less concern who that reader is than that a reader be there, becoming absorbed in reading, suspending his or her empirical life (as Jonathan Culler says in remarking on this poem) to perform the transfusion—at least in imaginative terms—that the poem predicts, giving life to Keats in the act of reading, and being haunted.[7]

5. An exception is Macksey 854, 881.

6. True, the reader of this poem must be stricken by conscience, but who among the living is not thus stricken in the presence of the dead (why him, why not me?) (I owe this point to David Ferry.)

7. Bennett argues that the poem's logic strictly entails that "the reader must have died" (12), which presupposition he finds central to (English) Romanticism generally. His description of how readers handle this presupposition in the Keats poem is unconvincing at key junctures (e.g., to refuse the logic is to become a "non-audience," which in turn means that "for this poem at least, the audience has died" [12]).

Thrillingly exact for "This living hand," by contrast, is Georges Poulet's description of lit-

Jonathan Culler brought Keats's poem to the notice of a comparatist readership by including it at the end of his 1977 essay "Apostrophe," revised in *The Pursuit of Signs*. The essay, which understands apostrophe as address to nonhearing things and forces, duly observes that Keats's poem "eschews apostrophe for direct address" [153]). But the context has generated lingering confusion about how much this poem shares "the time of the apostrophic *now*" (153) or other features of apostrophes to inanimate or abstract beings, which Culler sees as invocatory attempts to interrupt time or to recapture a lost presence.[8] "This living hand," writes Culler, though it addresses a human listener and so is not apostrophic, works as though it were: "This poem, whose deictics—'This living hand, now warm . . . ,' 'see, here it is'—give it the special temporality of apostrophic lyrics, is a daring and successful example of the attempt to produce in fiction an event by replacing a temporal presence and absence with an apostrophic presence and absence" (153–54). The strain of pressing reader address into service as the crowning example in a discussion of apostrophe is evident, though, if we reflect how much more radical Keats's "temporality" is than what apostrophe displays. What gives his poem its chill is not its insistence on the "*now* . . . of writing," "beyond the movement of temporality" (152), but its incorporation of the immediate presence, by definition, of any written text to its reader. Temporality is not "neutralized" but rather enlisted; this poem, in contrast to what Culler claims for apostrophe, depends for its effect wholly on the real-world passage of time. "The poem is under way," as Paul Celan wrote, and "the writer stays with it."[9] It is the *now* of *reading*—and in equal measure the "here"—that Keats exploits by yoking them to the time and scene of writing. And this, his poem's central accomplishment, is not shared with poetic apostrophes nor approached by them. One critic misidentifies both "the first and last lines" of Keats's poem as showing "the deictic movements of the present writing," "a 'present' that is clearly fictional in the manner of Culler's 'apostrophic *now*.'"[10] But the hand *was* warm and ca-

---

erary reading generally: "A literary work, insofar as that insufflation of life caused by reading is at work in it, becomes for its part—at the expense of the reader whose own life it annuls—a sort of human being, which is to say a thought conscious of itself and constituting itself as the subject of its objects" (285).

8. See the critiques in Engler and in Findlay.

9. "Das Gedicht ist . . . unterwegs. Wer es schreibt, bleibt ihm mitgegeben." ("Der Meridian" 198).

10. Macksey 854. Macksey goes on to claim that "This living hand" represents "direct address that 'becomes' apostrophic . . . through the prolepsis of the 'if' clause." Since Macksey does clearly take the reader to be the poem's addressee, this sentence defies understanding.

pable while writing—line 1 is no fiction—and the final lines appeal more emphatically to the time of reading, which is not fictional either.

As a way of generalizing the kind of readerly stance I have been trying to describe in Keats's poem, I turn to an essay titled "On the Interlocutor" ("O sobesednike"), published in 1913 by the Russian poet Osip Mandelstam. "At a critical moment," writes Mandelstam, "a seafarer throws into the ocean waves a sealed bottle, containing his name and an account of his fate. Many years later, wandering along the dunes, I find it in the sand, read the message, learn the date of the event and the last will of one now lost. I had the right to do so. I did not open someone else's mail. The message sealed in the bottle was addressed to the one who would find it. I found it. That means I really am its secret addressee" (234–35). This message in a bottle provides Mandelstam with his governing metaphor for the way poetry is "sent" and "received." Here the question of "answer" may seem foreclosed: the tides have made the bottle's path from its origin to our beach unknowable, and in any case the date of the message assures us the writer is dead and gone. There is neither means to answer nor anyone to answer to, much less anyone *expecting* answer; the message is in this sense gratuitous, extra; it leaves us free.

And yet the curious sense that by the act of finding, one has really become the "secret addressee" of this message—this sense does hold us somehow. Mandelstam goes on to describe the feeling of receiving a poem that is mindful, like the message in a bottle, of its eventual and unknown reader: "Reading this poem . . . I experience the same feeling as I would if such a bottle had come into my hands. The ocean in all its great element has come to its aid, has helped it fulfill its destiny; and that feeling of providence grips the finder" (235). The word "providence" captures the double feeling: on the one hand, it is the unlooked-for event, something that is not made to happen but just comes; it exerts no claim and exacts no return. On the other hand, "providence" means the sudden thought of vast and unseen patterns—intentions—at work behind the seeming accidents of precisely your life. It is an overwhelming feeling of

---

I can only think that he has confused apostrophe with prosopopoeia (the figure of making the dead speak), a trope that Culler, citing de Man, also introduced into his discussion of Keats. This part of Macksey's confusion could originate with de Man, since de Man too twice muddles apostrophe and prosopopoeia ("prosopopoeia, the fiction of . . . apostrophe" ["Autobiography" 75; see also 78]). For classical definitions and examples, see Lausberg § 762–65 and § 826–29 (377–79 and 411–13). See also Kneale, who claims that Culler misidentifies apostrophe to begin with.

"intendedness" that, as Mandelstam says, "grips" one. It is the sense that the ocean has helped the poem to fulfill its "destiny." Mandelstam's word here is "prednaznacheniye," which suggests something like "earmarking": the poem has incessantly sought its true addressee, the one for whom it is meant, and in finding and reading it, you are discovered as (made into) that one. "I would like to know," writes Mandelstam, "who among those chancing to read [such a] poem . . . will not start with that joyful and uncanny shiver one experiences when one is unexpectedly hailed by name" (235). The poem chooses you, the poem's *you* becomes your name, and the poem singles you out by calling it. Then the quite reasonable thought that, really, anyone at all could have found the message, that it was after all addressed to no one—this thought is set aside, forgotten, or even no longer true. Once you have found the message, there will be no other addressee. In this way you become answerable for it.

Remarkably, then, the sense of unimaginable distance in the intervening oceans of time and space is at the same time, without losing any of that distance, a feeling of unexpected nearness. When such a message comes into your hands, the abysses separating you from its sender dramatically intensify the feeling of a "providential" closeness to him (in Mandelstam's unsentimental sense of that word).

Mandelstam's metaphor can serve as a *point d'appui* for my argument, which aims to bring out this sense in which certain poems seek an interlocutor (the *sobesednik* of Mandelstam's title); and criticism, in this case, must work to imagine the act of reading that could acknowledge such claims and so give answer to the poem. This line of inquiry also begins, of its own accord, to touch upon the tricky question of what we now call readerly "answerability," through this "providential grip" of the message encountered by chance and engaged with as necessity.

> I open eye and ear, I extend my hand and feel in the same
> moment inseparably: You and I, I and You.
> —Friedrich Heinrich Jacobi

> I feel through every leaf the pressure of your hand, which I
>   return.
> And thus upon our journey link'd together let us go.
> —Walt Whitman, "Inscription"

The figure of the offered hand appears again in a posthumously published fragment of Rilke's,[11] written in 1925, a year before his death:

> Aber versuchtest du dies: Hand in der Hand mir zu sein
> wie im Weinglas der Wein Wein ist.
> Versuchtest du dies.

Edward Snow's translation reflects something of the idiosyncrasy of the German:

> But if you'd try this: to be hand in my hand
> as in the wineglass the wine is wine.
> If you'd try this.

This poem is about contact; it's about the relation between *I* and *you*, which is to say about the attempt to get *I* and *you* right—right in their relation to each other, first; and so each right in itself. As a poem, it is about wanting someone to be present to the poem, and about someone wanting to be present to it: about the endeavor to find the second person who will, in answering, find the poem's first person.

All this does not make the text a metapoetic commentary—a poem about poetry—so much as something closer: it is an attempt at nearness and an offer. As we ourselves become interested in the poem, we may begin to feel—not altogether rationally, but compellingly—that we are also implicated in it.

This poem opens with the word "but," an adversative, which at once presupposes (simultaneously sets up and reveals) some antecedent scenario or some foregoing alternative to which the poem opposes itself. The shape of this implied context—what must "have preceded" this opening of the poem—may be pieced together as the converse of what the text itself presents.[12]

11. To my knowledge there exists no critical commentary on these lines. *KA* 2: 397; *Uncollected* 233.

The obvious rendition "hand in hand to be mine" is avoided because "Hand in der Hand mir" is not a German idiom but Rilke's coinage, and also because the original pointedly evades rhyme. Snow's "hand in my hand" is not literal, though, and I depart from it where my discussion requires.

12. In linguistic terms, there is an uncertain boundary here between conventional implicature (the fixed function of contrast in the word "aber") and conversational implicature (the specific contour and character of that adversativity in a given utterance). On implicature (a concept developed by H. P. Grice), see Levinson, *Pragmatics* chap. 3, esp. 127–28.

If we imagine the first-time reader pausing at the caesura (punctuated here with a colon), we can inquire once again what would be at stake in that reader's tentatively, even fleetingly, putting on the poem's *you*.

> But if you'd try this:

Up to here the line can work at a very general level: since it is a question of *versuchen*, of attempting something, we could surmise that here being *you* is about having not reached some goal, having already attempted without success, or having sought without finding.

Being addressed by this poem's second-person pronoun thus means accepting the implication that one feels, personally, a history of endeavor and failure, or uncompleted search. Some of the pull of this line—"But if you'd try this"—is the sense that one could really get it, that the sought-for thing (whatever it might be) is within reach. But at the same time, the repetition of this phrase to end the fragment has a tinge of wistfulness. It is uncertain whether the addressee will ever make the attempt. So while it would be missing the mark to call this particular freestanding conditional ("if you'd try") a wish contrary to fact—it need not be really counterfactual, say, in the manner of a perfect subjunctive—the poem is accompanied by the thought that what it proposes will not necessarily be taken up. This thought, in turn, accords with the original implicature of "If you'd try this," the presupposition of a history of failures or misfires.

It is in this tone and against this background that the poem proposes something. Once again the poem offers its addressee the poet's hand, but here it is a gesture at once more intimate and milder than Keats's graphic and disquieting reach:

> But if you'd try this: to be hand in my hand
> as in the wineglass the wine is wine.
> If you'd try this.

Strictly speaking, it may be misplacing the emphasis to say a hand is offered here, since the first line attributes the agency unmistakably to the addressee. In this respect the line reflects the peculiar pragmatics of written address generally, where—in contrast to oral communication—it lies with the reader or addressee, not with the "sender," to set the communicative transaction going. That is to say, the line is true to the reading situation. Yet the reader is also faced with a pragmatic impasse similar to that on which the Keats poem was centered: in Rilke's poem, the reader is invited to hold hands, but invited by a written text. But if the reader does not falter at the impasse; if, in the privacy of a reading moment, the desire for contact seems to matter more than the literal absurdity of it; then you may attempt to discover for yourself (even if it is finally for yourself alone) what motions of the mind or heart might count as taking up the offered hand of the dead.

The invitation is elaborated in the poem's second line; but it is a line apt to be misread, in a way that brings into relief the unexpected turn of thought in Rilke's simile. It would be easy to alter the line unconsciously to "wie im Weinglas der Wein ist." It was just here that the seemingly indefatigable Rilke translator J. B. Leishman nodded, so publishing this misreading forth into libraries everywhere: "as in the wineglass the wine" (341). In this rendition Leishman, as if correcting the original to "Wie in dem Weinglas der Wein," further ignores the striking way Rilke's addition of the (grammatically superfluous) verb "ist" deliberately derails just that easy meter and rhyme.

If this were how the poem went, it would do some of the things that Rilke's poem does, but not all. This hypothetical, simpler version of the poem would invite repose and offer supporting encirclement, mapping the wine resting in the wineglass's embrace onto the image of your hand resting in the hand of the poem's speaker. The repetition of the same word "Hand" in line 1 would modulate directly into the echoing, but significantly differing, pair "Wein"–"Weinglas." And so on.

But Rilke's lines read otherwise, in ways I hope the false variant just considered will help to make apparent:

> Hand in der Hand mir zu sein
> wie im Weinglas der Wein Wein ist.

> to be hand in my hand
> as in the wineglass the wine is wine.

Added here is the metrically obtrusive repetition of the word "Wein." The addition fundamentally changes the grammar of the simile: instead of a predicate of location (der Wein ist im Weinglas), Rilke has a predicate of identity, or tautology (der Wein ist Wein). The location ("im Weinglas") only designates a site for this tautology. The phrase emphasizes first how *in* such a clasp of hands each hand becomes more itself, experiences itself as what it is. I take the poem to be claiming that the same is true not just of lover and beloved but also of reader and writer, even reader and poem.[13] The poem, made by and offered in the poet's hand, develops into itself in your hands as it breathes (as wine does, as poetic meter does). The poem realizes itself in the reading.

In "Hand in der Hand," the two instances of "Hand" represent two separate entities meeting: the second "Hand" is not the same as the first. But they are two entities of one kind. "Wein," by contrast, is not a countable noun. In a sense, the different syntax of the two images reflects and presents this difference: two clasped hands inherently retain a "prepositional" relationship with each other, but wine—even two wines poured together—is wine.

The thought of the poem's second line—"as in the wineglass the wine is wine"—is remarkable (and Rilkean) in the *Aufeinanderbezogenheit*, the interrelatedness, interdependence, mutual constitution of identity that it expresses. The wine is known as wine by being found in the wineglass, as at the same time the wineglass is a wineglass because of the wine it contains. Human beings are not human in and of themselves, but become what they are by saying *you*, which is to say by way of the second-person claims they make and acknowledge. I am, in the end, completely myself only in and because of my relation to you.[14] This is Rilke's Communion.

But those who find themselves in relation may also lose themselves there. This we can see when we take the step of mapping this image of "wine as wine in the wineglass" back onto—here Snow's translation cannot accompany us so well—the phrase "Hand in der Hand." For the two distinctive roles, the individual players, are masked in the phrase "Hand in der Hand"; one cannot determine, so to speak, which hand belongs to the *I*, which to the *you*. It's as if the invitation were to an intimacy whereby the concepts "my" and "your" would drop away from the phrase "my hand in your hand," leaving just some hand in some hand: a kind of loving bewilderment of forgotten identity. This is the resolution sought, as

13. Compare Grossman § 40 Scholium A: "The meaning of speaking (of which poems are instances) is secured as a consequence of the will (the *will*-ingness) of the hearer to construct, and assent to, the non-present personhood of the speaker. In speaking we are in one another's hands" (340).

14. Martin Buber's 1923 book *I and Thou*, together with his 1929 essay "Dialogue" (*Zwiesprache*), bring indispensable insight to this topic. Similarly, Gadamer's *Truth and Method* touches repeatedly on points germane to my argument. Kepnes (27), writing on Buber, expresses dismay that Gadamer nowhere cites Buber as the source of his ideas. But the complaint is fallacious, since the I-you relation is not a concept and need not come from study.

well, in George Herbert's poem "Clasping of Hands" (157), where, after eighteen lines of address to God which track the instability of the categories "mine" and "thine" in the experience of prayer, the poet finds the clasp of hands in not making this knowledge of which is which:

> O be mine still! still make me thine!
> Or rather make no Thine and Mine!

In the case of Rilke's poem, the bewilderment is extraordinary because of the asymmetricality, or even radical disjunction, of the roles it forgets: reader and writer, living and dead. The poem's opening "but" clause, with its entailment of a certain specific history (a history of fruitless search) on the part of the *you*, selects its addressee in a way that might lay the groundwork for the kind of trust that such forgetting as this exacts. It is trust: in the touch of hand and hand, one hand does not know the other (it is not "knowledge"). Intimacy in touch is partly the quality of awareness that the other is *what* one does not know, is the boundary to any hope of certainty.[15]

The attempt (*Versuch*) is therefore an uncertain one; but if you as reader of the writer's poem can forget which is which, who is who, and just rest "Hand in der Hand," one clasped with the other, knowing no more than that one is clasped with the other, then—the poem promises—you will find this is like wine being wine:

> wie im Weinglas der Wein Wein ist.

But as we sit with the text before us, no hand actually appears; and more than that, Rilke is gone: the caring and fellowship offered here are no one's, only intermittent vestiges of a dead man's capacity for feeling. If the hand that any poem extends to us is both living and dead, is it wise to lay ourselves open to the poem's address, to invest ourselves in the call of this "no one"?

The experience of intimate engagement with a *you* poem always occurs in such double vision: one responds to the address, and finds no one calling; you answer to the fellow human emotion that really does seek answer, but in the end you remain alone, answering. This being left alone is what Rilke's poem enacts, as the companionship of the first line (hand in

---

15. I borrow this opposition between knowledge and more intimate kinds of experience ("nearness") from Benfey's thoughtful *Emily Dickinson and the Problem of Others*.

hand) falls away, leaving the singular identity of the second (wine is wine); where "mir" ("to me"; Snow's "my") promised meeting, it withdraws, and what is held within the wineglass is finally one thing, in the right place, and just itself.

It could sound like failure. But discerning in the poem even the trace, the hollow form of the poet's living hand, we may find that this matters. We find ourselves accountable to the gesture that we have stumbled across in this way. The poem really does impart something; it becomes a space for the virtual transformation of the reader—the wineglass within which wine may, despite everything, find itself to be wine. In return for this gift, the poem's urgent claim is that we hold to it, that we press toward our own answerability as we read. Perhaps, though our obligation has been awakened by receiving something from the hand of a historically real other, the obligation comes not directly from accepting what is offered so much as from that other moment, the moment of knowing— as we must—that we are still alone, reading.

Detained by a poem, one finds with growing seriousness of attention that the poem meets and responds to just that quality of one's attention; one finds it still capable at the level of one's own most searching capabilities. The decisive moment occurs when you unexpectedly get something from the poem that is not locatable within any of the poem's parts, but that emerges from the many parts working all at once and has as well crucially to do with your own reading presence, your investment of an attention that you experience as yours. You see something that cannot be said. This place where reader and text touch is like the unnameable point of contact between two of Rodin's sculpted bodies, as Rilke saw it: "A hand which makes contact with the shoulder or thigh of another no longer belongs wholly to the body from which it came. Out of it and the object that it touches or grasps there comes into being a new thing, one thing more, which has no name and belongs to no one; and then it is a matter of *this* thing, which has its own boundaries."[16] Since you cannot "pass it on," at that point, the buck (so to speak) stops with you. You can't tell anyone else what you have seen, not whole, not the way you got it. It is, just as Whitman says, "in confidence" that something has been vouchsafed to you.[17]

The crucial fact is that for all you know, no one else has ever seen what

16. "Rodin. Erster Teil," *KA* 4: 422.
17. "Song of Myself" (1855), ll. 386–87 (§ 19 in later editions), *Selected* 30.

you have seen. And no matter how inclined one is to check one's reading experiences against others', or to defer to some more expert reader than oneself, these possibilities are closed. For all one can know, this gift that is the poem may be going unopened through the world like a sealed letter. The thought is accompanied by the loneliness of understanding that you who receive this message cannot share it either: the true privacy of reading.

What is at stake, again, is our ability to acknowledge the claims made on us by the works of art with which we engage. These are the claims of the aesthetic. In the acknowledgment (the "admission") of one's untutored awe or gratitude lies, as I see it, the closest and easiest to overlook of that gamut of ways in which texts matter across time.

No writer has testified more tenderly to the force of these claims than the great postwar poet Paul Celan when he wrote as Osip Mandelstam's unknown reader. Celan dedicated (in both senses) a volume of his own poetry to Mandelstam (*Die Niemandsrose* [1963]) and translated the Russian poet's work into German. But he expresses his closeness to Mandelstam most clearly in one of his few speeches, in which, however, the Russian poet is never explicitly named.[18] In this text Celan cites Mandelstam's essay "On the Interlocutor" without citing him, sending out the message of—specifically—the message in a bottle just as if it were his own (which it then must have become). This act is also the concern of the message itself, namely, the meeting of two people ("conversers," *sobesedniki*) over, through, and in the message, which becomes in this way time's corridor:

> Das Gedicht kann, da es ja eine Erscheinungsform der Sprache und damit seinem Wesen nach dialogisch ist, eine Flaschenpost sein, aufgegeben in dem—gewiss nicht immer hoffnungsstarken—Glauben, sie könnte irgendwo und irgendwann an Land gespült werden, an Herzland vielleicht. Gedichte sind auch in dieser Weise unterwegs: sie halten auf etwas zu. ("Ansprache" 186)

> A poem, since it is an instance of language, hence in its essence dialogic, may be a letter in a bottle thrown out to sea in the—surely not always strongly hopeful—belief that it may sometime wash up somewhere, perhaps on a shoreline of the heart. In this way, too, poems are under way: they are headed toward something.[19]

18. The subtlest meditation on *Die Niemandsrose* and on Celan's relationship to Mandelstam is Broda's *Dans la main de personne.*

19. Some phrases in the translation here are borrowed from Waldrop (Celan, *Collected*

Celan did not know Mandelstam, who had died twenty years before in transit to Siberian exile. Reaching through time, the work reaches through the writer's own death and so always appears as a gift held in his absent hand, a thing offered by someone not there. By the graces of that contract we hold with the texts we call literary, when Celan reaches in faithfulness back to Mandelstam, he likewise reaches through Mandelstam, not only in gratitude but also "out of" gratitude, out to unknown others.

The assertion that the bottle cast out to sea is not merely "under way" but heading for something ("Gedichte . . . halten auf etwas zu") represents for the poet a kind of trust in (to use Mandelstam's word once again) providence; or, we could say, it represents the incorporation, backwards into the bottle's path, of the astonished perspective of its eventual receiver. It is with respect to its finding that the bottle can be said to have been "heading for" something, for—as Celan puts it—a shoreline of the heart, for a "reality," for you:

> Gedichte . . . halten auf etwas zu.
>   Worauf? Auf etwas Offenstehendes, Besetzbares, auf ein ansprechbares Du vielleicht, auf eine ansprechbare Wirklichkeit.
>   Um solche Wirklichkeiten geht es, so denke ich, dem Gedicht.
>
> Poems . . . are headed toward something.
>   Toward what? Toward something open, inhabitable, an addressable *you* perhaps, an addressable reality.
>   Such realities are, I think, at stake in a poem.

Thinking of poetry as a means of real contact in this way is, again, not a rhetorical effect. It is the experience of someone who "carries his existence into language," as Celan concludes his speech; and this means, in equal part but wholly dark to each other, separated by the written language with which they touch, both poet and reader.

Invoking this means of contact calls up Celan's own reflection on the proximity of the human hand to the poem it writes, or holds in order to read. In stressing the fundamental importance of "craft" to the poet's work, Celan here restores the hand latent in the German word for craft, *Handwerk*:

> Handwerk—das ist Sache der Hände. Und diese Hände wiederum gehören nur *einem* Menschen, d.h. einem einmaligen und sterblichen

---

Prose). Subsequent quotations from Celan are (except as noted) Waldrop's translation, with small modifications.

Seelewesen, das mit seiner Stimme und seiner Stummheit einen Weg sucht.
Nur wahre Hände schreiben wahre Gedichte. Ich sehe keinen prinzi-
piellen Unterschied zwischen Händedruck und Gedicht. ("Brief")

Craft means handiwork, a matter of hands. And these hands in turn belong to just one person, that is, to a unique and mortal soul searching for a
way with its voice and its dumbness.
Only real hands write real poems. I cannot see any basic difference between a pressing of hands and a poem.[20]

Celan brings the abstraction of *Handwerk*, craft, into etymological focus
as *Hand-Werk*, the work of hands, which means the two hands of one human being, a being tentative, partly mute, and finally mortal. The writing
of real poems, it is said, requires real hands; and these real hands, seeking
a way, accompany the poem, indeed *are* the poem to such an extent that
Celan finds the poem to be a "Händedruck." This word *Händedruck* is
extraordinary, partly by virtue of its apparent ordinariness: it is, first, the
common word for "handshake" (though less breezy than that American
word; Eliot writes somewhere of "a shake of the hand," which would be
a better equivalent). A handshake greets, but it also seals and affirms; it
verifies something, or testifies to it. In this sense the *Händedruck* may be
the guarantor of the hands' *Wahrheit*, their "truthfulness," their "reality."
But this reality must be found on both sides, as Mandelstam agreed, in
words that press upon Celan's thought here: "Only a reality can call into
life another reality" (240). If only real hands write real poems, only real
hands can receive them, or can return the pressure of the poet's writing
hand. The translation "handshake" in the passage just cited was rejected
partly for reasons of tone, partly because if Celan dismantles the word
"Handwerk" in this same passage, then we must be alert, also, to the com-
ponents of "Händedruck," namely, "hands" (*die Hände*) and "pressure"
(*der Druck*). And we must see, also, how the sentence's willed superpo-
sition of *Händedruck* and poem pulls forth the other meaning of *Druck*,
which is "printing." The sense in which a handshake (*Händedruck*) is an
impressing (*Eindruck*), or an expression (*Ausdruck*) by hand, may under-
gird the sense in which a poem is not just a printing (*Druck*) of something
handwritten but also an impression of the writing hand, and the hand's

20. Compare, from William Stafford's poem "Writing":

> Or by a hand like someone's you put your
> hand: nothing felt but the truth when
> they touch, and unspoken questions.

expressive pressure. With this word, then, that joins together the touch of hands and the unguided drift of the printed page through the contingencies of time and space, Celan brings together the two metaphors for the private reading of poetry which have occupied us in this passage. The *Flaschenpost,* the letter in a bottle, is a matter of vast distance, great uncertainty, and perhaps reaches of time necessarily entailing the death— the absence from the world—of the writer who sought human contact in this way. If in any communication, even face-to-face, there is always the possibility that our intended message will not receive the proper uptake from our interlocutor, then the message in a bottle raises that uncertainty to its highest power.

A clasp of hands would seem altogether different. This is communication in which two bodies touch, in which misgivings about response may evaporate. As Celan says, it is (or can be) a matter of *presence,* of reality; two human beings sharing, with their pronouns *I* and *you,* the same ontological space. But here we find ourselves again in the territory of the uncanny, where people incalculably distant, even dead, may appear immediately present; where the fixity of the printed word can stir, and reach, and call; where the strange and the familiar come together in one shape. "Poems are also gifts," as Celan puts it, "—gifts to the attentive"; but they can give of themselves precisely because they are not timeless but are the vessels of time's lapse, as that lapse is felt.[21] They are the registers of those same losses that make them more worth keeping. "The poem," writes Celan, "admittedly makes a bid to have no end. It tries to reach through time—through it, not around it."[22] The consciousness of our own reading's historical singularity (it will not come again, nor come to others as it does to us, now) is the thought that may move us, sometimes, to take responsibility for being the poem's reader:

> But if you'd try this: to be hand in my hand
> as in the wineglass the wine is wine.
> If you'd try this.

Astonishingly, someone made this thing; and at the heart of such a speaking gift lies, palpably, the maker's wish that it be received by someone. It is you who are that "indefinite" but utterly particular recipient.

21. "Gedichte, das sind auch Geschenke—Geschenke an die Aufmerksamen" ("Brief").

22. "Gewiss, [das Gedicht] erhebt einen Unendlichkeitsanspruch, es sucht, durch die Zeit hindurchzugreifen—durch sie hindurch, nicht über sie hinweg" ("Ansprache"; my translation).

Any feeling of obligation here will be your feeling, not a burden imposed by another. If, trusting, you make the attempt, and reach to take the offered hand, it is of yourself you become aware, open, obliged, held as if coincident with yourself in the poem's hollow form

wie im Weinglas der Wein Wein ist.

Nay, if you read this line, remember not
The hand that writ it

—Shakespeare, sonnet 71

With slow readings of two poems I have attempted to tease out some implications of the more general thought that our condition is to be mostly in the dark about how to situate the poems we read, as we are with other things that lodge in our affections. It is futile to try to enumerate the imaginative positionings a reader can take up with respect to a poem's elements—say, for our purposes here, with respect to its pronouns *I, you,* or the third person—because the array is infinite, illimitably nuanced, and only in part conscious, like the ways we relate to other people. Poems cast wholly in the first or third person may draw us to an imaginative participation as vivid as what a *you*-poem can elicit. Address can recall me to my own presence—to myself, as it were, seen from the point of view of the poem—and so foreground acts and styles of reception. Or it can suspend the border between poetry and reality to give place, if not to their coincidence, then to a mutual self-reference of poetic fiction and readerly fact.

In a much-cited poem Emily Dickinson writes, "This is my letter to the World / That never wrote to Me - ."[23] Here, too, as in "Essential Oils," Dickinson's "this" points to the body of her poetry, or to the very poem that says "this." It is a mode of access to the reader, since the demonstrative refers with equal force to the poem beneath the poet's pen circa 1862 and to the instantiation of it that I, now, hold to read. Such is the line of the poem's own thought, as the poet writes that her

23. *Poems,* Franklin ed. 1: 527–28 (F 519; J 441).

> Message is committed
> To Hands I cannot see -

As Virginia Jackson movingly writes, "Reading Emily Dickinson here and now, ours are the unseen hands most deeply 'committed' " (98). That commitment is like our willingness to bear the self-reflexive force of "this." The poem gestures to the page you hold open ("*this* is my letter"): yours are the hands that the poet knows of—or rather trusts in—but "cannot see." It is not evident, given her oeuvre, that Dickinson was other than serious about the "letter to the World." If it seems pressing that this degree of caring about something be, in some way, met, then we cannot justifiably assume that another has discharged the responsibility that Dickinson's work gives into the hands of its reader. Not finding a way to ensure my superfluity in this respect, I must—and what could sound like egoism is grievously humbling, an experience of utmost inadequacy—come to the text as if my presence mattered to it.

Literary reception is generally a matter of what Mandelstam calls the ocean, the complex social forces that convey poems like Dickinson's to other writers and to a collective readership. But now and then a reader will stumble into a reception both personal and immediate, a sudden understanding of himself or herself as exactly the poem's "secret addressee." To take on a work in this way means to discover that something has "made" you, as Gadamer writes, into "the person to whom the text was originally addressed" (*Truth* 333); such a reception—privately, fleetingly—lets factual knowledge go dark; and in the reluctant moment you find, disbelieving, the elision of history in the poet's unseeing nearness to your own reading hands.

Bibliography

Althusser, Louis. "Ideology and Ideological State Apparatuses (Notes towards an Investigation)." *Essays on Ideology.* 1970. London: Verso, 1984. 1–60.

Altieri, Charles. "Life after Difference: The Positions of the Interpreter and the Positionings of the Interpreted." *Canons and Consequences: Reflections on the Ethical Force of Imaginative Ideals.* Evanston: Northwestern University Press, 1990. 291–317.

Anderson, J. G. C., Franz Cumont, and Henri Grégoire, eds. *Studia Pontica.* Vol. 3, *Recueil des inscriptions grecques et latines du Pont et de l'Arménie.* Brussels: Lamertin, 1910.

Anderson, Stephen R., and Edward L. Keenan. "Deixis." *Language Typology and Syntactic Description.* Vol. 3, *Grammatical Categories and the Lexicon.* Ed. Timothy Shopen. Cambridge: Cambridge University Press, 1985. 259–308.

Ashbery, John. "At North Farm." *A Wave.* 1984. Reprinted in *Three Books.* New York: Penguin, 1993. 139.

Åström, Paul, ed. *Rainer Maria Rilke: Briefe an Ernst Norlind.* Partille, Sweden: Paul Åströms Förlag, 1986.

Auden, W. H. *Collected Poems.* Ed. Edward Mendelson. New York: Vintage, 1991.

Auerbach, Erich. "Dante's Addresses to the Reader." *Romance Philology* 7 (1954): 268–78.

Austin, Timothy R. *Poetic Voices: Discourse Linguistics and the Poetic Text.* Tuscaloosa: University of Alabama Press, 1994.

Bahti, Timothy. "Ambiguity and Indeterminacy: The Juncture." *Comparative Literature* 38 (1986): 218–23.

Bar-Hillel, Yehoshua. "Indexical Expressions." *Mind* 63 (1954): 359–79.

Bate, Walter Jackson. *John Keats.* Cambridge: Harvard University Press, 1963.

Benfey, Christopher. *Emily Dickinson and the Problem of Others.* Amherst: University of Massachusetts Press, 1984.

Benn, Gottfried. *Probleme der Lyrik*. Wiesbaden: Limes, 1951.

Benn, Gottfried, and Alexander Lernet-Holenia. *Monologische Kunst — ?* Wiesbaden: Limes, 1953.

Bennett, Andrew. *Keats, Narrative, and Audience: The Posthumous Life of Writing*. Cambridge: Cambridge University Press, 1994.

Benveniste, Émile. *Indo-European Language and Society*. Trans. Elizabeth Palmer. Miami: University of Miami Press, 1973.

——. "Relationships of Person in the Verb." *Problems in General Linguistics*. Trans. Mary Elizabeth Meek. Coral Gables: University of Miami Press, 1971. 195–204.

Berendt, Hans. *Rainer Maria Rilkes Neue Gedichte: Versuch einer Deutung*. Bonn: Bouvier, 1957.

Berlant, Lauren. "Intimacy: A Special Issue." *Critical Inquiry* 24 (1998): 281–88.

Bernstein, Charles, ed. *Close Listening: Poetry and the Performed Word*. New York: Oxford University Press, 1998.

Berry, Francis. *Poetry and the Physical Voice*. London: Routledge, 1962.

Bishop, Elizabeth. *The Complete Poems: 1927–1979*. New York: Farrar, 1983.

Blanchot, Maurice. *L'espace littéraire*. Paris: Gallimard, 1955.

Bradley, Brigitte. *Rainer Maria Rilkes "Der neuen Gedichte anderer Teil."* Bern: Francke, 1976.

Broda, Martine. *Dans la main de personne: essai sur Paul Celan*. Paris: Editions du Cerf, 1986.

Brown, Bernard. "The 'Briefwechsel in Gedichten mit Erika Mitterer': Monologue, Dialogue, or Duet?" *Rilke und der Wandel in der Sensibilität*. Ed. Herbert Herzmann and Hugh Ridley. Essen: Verlag Die Blaue Eule, 1990. 107–20.

Brown, Penelope, and Stephen C. Levinson. *Politeness: Some Universals in Language Usage*. Cambridge: Cambridge University Press, 1987.

Brown, Roger, and Albert Gilman. "The Pronouns of Power and Solidarity." *Style in Language*. Ed. Thomas A. Sebeok. Cambridge: MIT Press, 1960. 253–76.

Buber, Martin. *Ich und Du*. 1923. Heidelberg: Lambert Schneider, 1983.

——. *Zwiesprache*. 1929. Berlin: Schocken, 1932.

Burdorf, Dieter. *Einführung in die Gedichtanalyse*. Stuttgart: Metzler, 1995.

Burzachechi, Mario. "Oggetti parlanti nelle epigrafi greche." *Epigraphica* 24 (1962): 3–54.

Cameron, Sharon. *Lyric Time: Dickinson and the Limits of Genre*. Baltimore: Johns Hopkins University Press, 1979.

Campbell, B. G. "Toward a Workable Taxonomy of Illocutionary Forces, and Its Implication to Works of Imaginative Literature." *Language and Style* 8.1 (1975): 3–20.

Catullus. *The Poems*. Ed. Kenneth Quinn. 2nd ed. London: Macmillan, 1973.

Cavafy, Constantine [Kabaphes, K. P.]. *Poiēmata en olō*. Athens: Monternoi Kairoi, 1998.

Celan, Paul. "Ansprache anlässlich der Entgegennahme des Literaturpreises der Freien Hansestadt Bremen." *GW*, 3: 185–86.

——. "Brief an Hans Bender." *GW*, 3: 177–78.

——. *Collected Prose*, trans. Rosmarie Waldrop. Riverdale-on-Hudson, N.Y.: Sheep Meadow Press, 1986.

——. *Gesammelte Werke in 5 Bänden*. Ed. Beda Allemann and Stefan Reichert. Frankfurt: Suhrkamp, 1983. Cited as *GW*.

———. "Der Meridian." *GW*, 3: 187–202.

Claes, Paul. *Raadsels van Rilke: Een nieuwe lezing van de Neue Gedichte.* Amsterdam: De Bezige Bij, 1996.

Clark, Herbert. *Arenas of Language Use.* Chicago: University of Chicago Press, 1992.

———. *Using Language.* Cambridge: Cambridge University Press, 1996.

Clark, Herbert, and Thomas B. Carlson. "Hearers and Speech Acts." *Language* 58 (1982): 332–73.

Clymer, Lorna. "Graved in Tropes: The Figural Logic of Epitaphs and Elegies in Blair, Gray, Cowper, and Wordsworth." *ELH* 62 (1995): 347–86.

Commager, Steele. *The Odes of Horace: A Critical Study.* Bloomington: Indiana University Press, 1962.

Costello, Bonnie. "John Ashbery and the Idea of the Reader." *Contemporary Literature* 23 (1982): 493–514.

Coulmas, Florian. *Über Schrift.* Frankfurt: Suhrkamp, 1982.

Culler, Jonathan. "Apostrophe." *The Pursuit of Signs.* Ithaca: Cornell University Press, 1981. 135–54.

———. "Changes in the Study of the Lyric." Hošek and Parker 38–54.

———. *Literary Theory: A Very Short Introduction.* New York: Oxford University Press, 1997.

———. "The Modern Lyric: Generic Continuity and Critical Practice." *The Comparative Perspective on Literature.* Ed. Clayton Koelb and Susan Noakes. Ithaca: Cornell University Press, 1988. 284–99.

———. "Poetics of the Lyric." *Structuralist Poetics.* Ithaca: Cornell University Press, 1975. 161–88.

———. "Reading Lyric." *Yale French Studies* 69 (1989): 98–106.

Curtius, Ernst Robert. *European Literature and the Latin Middle Ages.* Trans. Willard R. Trask. New York: Harper, 1953.

de Man, Paul. "Anthropomorphism and Trope in the Lyric." *The Rhetoric of Romanticism.* New York: Columbia University Press, 1984. 239–62.

———. "Autobiography as De-Facement." *The Rhetoric of Romanticism.* New York: Columbia University Press, 1984. 67–81.

———. "Lyrical Voice in Contemporary Theory: Riffaterre and Jauss." Hošek and Parker 55–72.

Derrida, Jacques. *Of Grammatology.* 1967. Trans. Gayatri Chakravorty Spivak. Baltimore: Johns Hopkins University Press, 1976.

Destro, Alberto. "Dialogstrukturen in Rilkes Lyrik." *"Stets wird die Wahrheit hadern mit dem Schönen": Festschrift für Manfred Windfuhr zum 60. Geburtstag.* Ed. Gertrude Cepl-Kaufmann. Cologne: Böhlau, 1990. 357–65.

Detienne, Marcel, and Giorgio Camassa. *Les savoirs de l'écriture: en Grèce ancienne.* [Villeneuve-d'Ascq, France]: Presses Universitaires de Lille, 1988.

Devlin, D. D. *Wordsworth and the Poetry of Epitaphs.* Totowa, N.J.: Barnes & Noble, 1981.

Dickinson, Emily. *The Complete Poems of Emily Dickinson.* Ed. Thomas H. Johnson. Boston: Little, 1960.

———. *The Letters of Emily Dickinson.* Ed. Thomas H. Johnson. 3 vols. Harvard University Press, 1965.

——. *The Manuscript Books of Emily Dickinson*. Ed. R. W. Franklin. 2 vols. Cambridge: Harvard University Press, 1981.

——. *The Poems of Emily Dickinson*. Ed. Thomas H. Johnson. 3 vols. Cambridge: Harvard University Press, 1979.

——. *The Poems of Emily Dickinson: Variorum Edition*. Ed. R. W. Franklin. 3 vols. Cambridge: Harvard University Press, 1998.

Diehl, Patrick S. *The Medieval European Religious Lyric: An Ars Poetica*. Berkeley: University of California Press, 1985.

Diels, Hermann. *Die Fragmente der Vorsokratiker*. 4th ed. 3 vols. Berlin: Weidmannsche Buchhandlung, 1922.

Doane, A. N., and Carol Braun Pasternack, eds. *Vox intexta: Orality and Textuality in the Middle Ages*. Madison: University of Wisconsin Press, 1991.

Donnelly, Daria. "The Power to Die: Emily Dickinson's Letters of Consolation." *Epistolary Selves: Letters and Letter Writers, 1600–1945*. Ed. Rebecca Earle. Aldershot, Eng.: Ashgate, 1999. 134–51.

Dubrow, Heather. "'Incertainties Now Crown Themselves Assur'd': The Politics of Plotting Shakespeare's Sonnets." *Shakespeare's Sonnets: Critical Essays*. Ed. James Schiffer. New York: Garland, 1999. 113–33.

——. "Shakespeare's Undramatic Monologues: Toward a Reading of the Sonnets." *Shakespeare Quarterly* 32 (1981): 55–68.

Dupont, Florence. *The Invention of Literature: From Greek Intoxication to the Latin Book*. Trans. Janet Lloyd. Baltimore: Johns Hopkins University Press, 1999.

Dupriez, Bernard. "Apostrophe." *A Dictionary of Literary Devices*. Trans. Albert W. Halsall. Toronto: University of Toronto Press, 1991. 58–60.

Easthope, Anthony. *Poetry as Discourse*. London: Methuen, 1983.

Ehlich, Konrad. "Text und sprachliches Handeln: Die Entstehung von Texten aus dem Bedürfnis nach Überlieferung." *Schrift und Gedächtnis: Beiträge zur Archäologie der literarischen Kommunikation*. Ed. Aleida Assmann, Jan Assmann, and Christof Hardmeier. Munich: Fink, 1983. 24–43.

Eliot, T. S. *Collected Poems, 1909–1962*. London: Faber, 1963.

——. *Four Quartets*. 1943. San Diego: Harcourt, 1971.

——. "The Three Voices of Poetry." *On Poetry and Poets*. London: Faber and Faber, 1957. 89–102.

Engler, Balz. "Deictics and the Status of Poetic Texts." *The Structure of Texts*. Ed. Udo Fries. Tübingen: Narr, 1987. 65–73.

Fabb, Nigel. *Linguistics and Literature: Language in the Verbal Arts of the World*. Oxford: Blackwell, 1997.

Ferry, Anne. *The Title to the Poem*. Stanford: Stanford University Press, 1996.

Ferry, David, trans. *The Odes of Horace*. New York: Noonday-Farrar, 1997.

Fillmore, Charles J. *Lectures on Deixis*. Stanford: CSLI Publications, 1997.

Findlay, L. M. "Culler and Byron on Apostrophe and Lyric Time." *Studies in Romanticism* 24 (1985): 335–53.

Fitzgerald, William. *Catullan Provocations: Lyric Poetry and the Drama of Position*. Berkeley: University of California Press, 1995.

Fludernik, Monika, ed. *Second-Person Narrative*. Special issue, *Style* 28.3 (1994).

——. "Second-Person Narrative: A Bibliography." *Style* 28.4 (1994): 525–48.

Fordyce, C. J. *Catullus: A Commentary*. Oxford: Oxford University Press, 1961.

Fowler, Alastair. *Kinds of Literature: An Introduction to the Theory of Genres*. Cambridge: Harvard University Press, 1982.

Freud, Sigmund. "The Uncanny." 1919. *The Standard Edition of the Complete Psychological Works of Sigmund Freud*. Ed. James Strachey. Vol. 17. London: Hogarth, 1953–74. 219–52.

Friedländer, Paul. *Epigrammata: Greek Inscriptions in Verse*. Berkeley: University of California Press, 1948.

Fry, Paul. "The Absent Dead: Wordsworth, Byron, and the Epitaph." *A Defense of Poetry*. Stanford: Stanford University Press, 1995. 159–80.

——. *The Poet's Calling in the English Ode*. New Haven: Yale University Press, 1980.

Frye, Northrop. *Anatomy of Criticism*. Princeton: Princeton University Press, 1957.

——. "Approaching the Lyric." Hošek and Parker 31–37.

Furrow, Melissa. "Listening Reader and Impotent Speaker: The Role of Deixis in Literature." *Language and Style* 21 (1988): 365–78.

Gadamer, Hans-Georg. *Truth and Method [Wahrheit und Methode]*. 1960. Trans. Joel Weinsheimer and Donald Marshall. 2nd ed. New York: Crossroad, 1989.

——. "Wer bin ich und wer bist Du?" *Über Paul Celan*. Ed. Dietlind Meinecke. Frankfurt: Suhrkamp, 1970. 258–64.

Genette, Gérard. *Paratexts: Thresholds of Interpretation*. Trans. Jane E. Lewin. Cambridge: Cambridge University Press, 1997.

George, Stefan. *Werke*. 4th ed. 2 vols. Stuttgart: Klett-Cotta, 1984.

Goffman, Erving. "Footing." *Forms of Talk*. Philadelphia: University of Pennsylvania Press, 1981. 124–59.

Goody, Jack. *The Logic of Writing and the Organization of Society*. New York: Cambridge University Press, 1986.

Grabher, Gudrun M. *Das lyrische Du: Du-Vergessenheit und Möglichkeiten der Du-Bestimmung in der amerikanischen Dichtung*. Heidelberg: Winter, 1989.

The Greek Anthology. Loeb Classical Library. Cambridge: Harvard University Press, 1958.

Green, Georgia M. *Pragmatics and Natural Language Understanding*. Hillsdale, N.J.: Lawrence Erlbaum, 1989.

Greene, Thomas M. *The Light in Troy: Imitation and Discovery in Renaissance Poetry*. New Haven: Yale University Press, 1982.

——. "Poetry as Invocation." *New Literary History* 24 (1993): 195–517.

Grice, H. P. "Logic and Conversation." *Syntax and Semantics: Speech Acts*. Ed. P. Cole and J. Morgan. Vol. 3. New York: Academic Press, 1975. 41–58.

Griffiths, Eric. *The Printed Voice of Victorian Poetry*. Oxford: Clarendon-Oxford University Press, 1989.

Groddeck, Wolfram, ed. *Duineser Elegien, Die Sonette an Orpheus: Nach den Erstdrücken von 1923 kritisch herausgegeben*. By Rainer Maria Rilke. Stuttgart: Reclam, 1997.

Grossman, Allen. "Summa Lyrica: A Primer of the Commonplaces in Speculative Poetics." *The Sighted Singer*. Baltimore: Johns Hopkins University Press, 1992. 205–383.

Hall, Donald. *Claims for Poetry*. Ann Arbor: University of Michigan Press, 1982.

Hamburger, Käte. *The Logic of Literature*. 1973. Trans. Marilyn J. Rose. 2nd ed. Bloomington: Indiana University Press, 1993.

——. *Die Logik der Dichtung.* 3rd ed. Frankfurt: Klett-Cotta, 1980.

Hanks, William F. *Referential Practice: Language and Lived Space among the Maya.* Chicago: University of Chicago Press, 1990.

Hartman, Geoffrey. *Wordsworth's Poetry, 1787–1814.* Cambridge: Harvard University Press, 1971.

Havelock, Eric. *The Muse Learns to Write: Reflections on Orality and Literacy from Antiquity to the Present.* New Haven: Yale University Press, 1986.

——. *Preface to Plato.* Cambridge: Harvard University Press, 1963.

Heidegger, Martin. "Language." *Poetry, Language, Thought.* Ed. Albert Hofstadter. New York: Harper, 1971. 187–210.

Herbert, George. *The Works of George Herbert.* Ed. F. E. Hutchinson. Oxford University Press, 1941.

Herman, Vimala. "Deictic Projection and Conceptual Blending in Epistolarity." *Poetics Today* 20.3 (1999): 523–41.

Heselhaus, Clemens. "Else Lasker-Schülers literarisches Traumspiel." *Deutsche Lyrik der Moderne.* Düsseldorf: Bagel, 1961. 213–28.

Holden, Jonathan. "The Abuse of the Second-Person Pronoun." *The Rhetoric of the Contemporary Lyric.* Bloomington: Indiana University Press, 1980. 38–56.

Hölderlin, Friedrich. *Gedichte.* Ed. Jochen Schmidt. Frankfurt: Insel, 1984.

Hollander, John. "Poetic Imperatives." *Melodious Guile: Fictive Pattern in Poetic Language.* New Haven: Yale University Press, 1988. 64–84.

Hollis, C. Carroll. *Language and Style in "Leaves of Grass."* Baton Rouge: Louisiana State University Press, 1983.

Holloway, Vance R. "El tú en la poesía de Antonio Machado." *Explicación de textos literarios—Hispanic Press* 16.2 (1987–88): 70–84.

Hopkins, Brooke. "Keats and the Uncanny: 'This living hand.' " *Kenyon Review* 11.4 (1989): 28–40.

Horace. *The Odes.* Ed. Kenneth Quinn. London: Macmillan, 1980.

Hošek, Chaviva, and Patricia Parker, eds. *Lyric Poetry: Beyond New Criticism.* Ithaca: Cornell University Press, 1985.

Hötzer, Ulrich. "Mörike: 'Denk' es, o Seele!'" *Germanistik in Forschung und Lehre.* Ed. Rudolf Henss and Hugo Moser. Berlin: Erich Schmidt, 1965. 157–68.

Houston, G[ertrude] Craig, trans. *Where Silence Reigns: Selected Prose by Rainer Maria Rilke.* New York: New Directions, 1978.

Hughes, Merritt Y., ed. *John Milton: Complete Poems and Major Prose.* New York: Odyssey, 1957.

Hyde, Lewis. *The Gift: Imagination and the Erotic Life of Property.* New York: Vintage-Random, 1983.

Iser, Wolfgang. *Die Appellstruktur der Texte: Unbestimmtheit als Wirkungsbedingung literarischer Prosa.* Constance: Konstanz University Press, 1971.

Jackson, Virginia. "Dickinson's Figure of Address." *Dickinson and Audience.* Ed. Martin Orzeck and Robert Weisbuch. Ann Arbor: University of Michigan Press, 1996. 77–103.

Jakobson, Roman. "Concluding Statement: Linguistics and Poetics." *Style in Language.* Ed. Thomas A. Sebeok. Cambridge: MIT Press, 1960. 350–77.

Joffe, Natalie F. "Milk." *Funk & Wagnall's Standard Dictionary of Folklore, Mythology, and Legend.* Ed. Maria Leach. San Francisco: Harper, 1972. 725.

Johnson, Barbara. "Apostrophe, Animation, and Abortion." *A World of Difference*. Baltimore: Johns Hopkins University Press, 1987. 184–99.

Johnson, W. R. *The Idea of Lyric: Lyric Modes in Ancient and Modern Poetry*. Berkeley: University of California Press, 1982.

Kacandes, Irene. "Are You in the Text? The 'Literary Performative' in Postmodernist Fiction." *Text and Performance Quarterly* 13 (1993): 1–15.

——. "Narrative Apostrophe: Case Studies in Second Person Fiction." Ph.D. diss. Harvard University, 1990.

——. "Narrative Apostrophe: Reading, Rhetoric, and Resistance in Michel Butor's *La modification* and Julio Cortázar's 'Graffiti.'" *Style* 28 (1994): 329–49.

Kafka, Franz. "Beim Bau der chinesischen Mauer." *Ein Landarzt und andere Prosa*. Ed. Michael Müller. Stuttgart: Reclam, 1995. 65–79.

——. "Eine kaiserliche Botschaft." *Ein Landarzt und andere Prosa*. Ed. Michael Müller. Stuttgart: Reclam, 1995. 29–30.

——. *The Transformation and Other Stories*, trans. Malcolm Pasley. New York: Penguin, 1992.

Kaibel, Georg. *Epigrammata Graeca*. Berlin: G. Reimer, 1878.

Kaiser, Gerhard. *Geschichte der deutschen Lyrik von Heine bis zur Gegenwart*. 3 vols. Frankfurt: Suhrkamp, 1991.

Kasher, Asa, and Naomi Kasher. "Speech Acts, Contexts, and Valuable Ambiguities." *Pragmatics of Language and Literature*. Ed. Teun van Dijk. New York: American Elsevier, 1976. 77–81.

Keats, John. *Complete Poems*. Ed. Jack Stillinger. Cambridge: Harvard University Press, 1982.

Keeley, Edmund, and Philip Sherrard, eds. *C. P. Cavafy: Collected Poems*. 2nd ed. Princeton: Princeton University Press, 1992.

Keeley, Edmund. *Cavafy's Alexandria: Study of a Myth in Progress*. Cambridge: Harvard University Press, 1976.

Kepnes, Steven. *The Text as Thou: Martin Buber's Dialogical Hermeneutics and Narrative Theology*. Bloomington: Indiana University Press, 1992.

Kinnell, Galway. *Selected Poems*. Boston: Houghton, 1982.

Kneale, J. Douglas. *Romantic Aversions: Aftermaths of Classicism in Wordsworth and Coleridge*. Montreal: McGill-Queen's University Press, 1999.

——. "Romantic Aversions: Apostrophe Reconsidered." *ELH* 58 (1991): 141–65.

Koch, Kenneth. *New Addresses: Poems*. New York: Knopf, 2000.

Komar, Kathleen. *Transcending Angels: Rainer Maria Rilke's "Duino Elegies."* Lincoln: University of Nebraska Press, 1987.

Kußler, Rainer. *Deutsche Lyrik als fremde Lyrik*. Munich: Hueber, 1981.

Lamping, Dieter. *Das lyrische Gedicht: Definitionen zu Theorie und Geschichte der Gattung*. Göttingen: Vandenhoeck, 1989.

Langbaum, Robert. *The Poetry of Experience: The Dramatic Monologue in Modern Literary Tradition*. 3rd ed. Chicago: University of Chicago Press, 1985.

Langen, August. *Dialogisches Spiel: Formen und Wandlungen des Wechselgesangs in der deutschen Dichtung, 1600–1900*. Heidelberg: Winter, 1966.

Larson, Kerry. *Whitman's Drama of Consensus*. Chicago: University of Chicago Press, 1988.

Lasker-Schüler, Else. *Sämtliche Gedichte*. Munich: Kösel, 1966.

——. *Your Diamond Dreams Cut Open My Arteries: Poems by Else Lasker-Schüler,* trans. Robert P. Newton. Chapel Hill: University of North Carolina Press, 1982.

Latta, Bernd. "Zu Catulls Carmen 1." *Museum Helveticum* 29 (1972): 201–13.

Lattimore, Richmond. *Themes in Greek and Latin Epitaphs.* Urbana: University of Illinois Press, 1962.

Lausberg, Heinrich. *Handbuch der literarischen Rhetorik.* 2 vols. Vol. 1. Munich: Hueber, 1960.

Leishman, J. B., trans. *Poems, 1906 to 1926.* By Rainer Maria Rilke. New York: New Directions, 1957.

Leisi, Ernst. *Rilkes Sonette an Orpheus: Interpretation, Kommentar, Glossar.* Tübingen: Narr, 1987.

Levenston, E. A. *The Stuff of Literature: Physical Aspects of Texts and Their Relation to Literary Meaning.* Albany: State University of New York Press, 1992.

Leverenz, David. " 'I' and 'You' in the American Renaissance." *Manhood and the American Renaissance.* Ithaca: Cornell University Press, 1989. 9–41.

Levinas, Emmanuel. *Totality and Infinity.* Trans. Alphonso Lingis. Dordrecht: Kluwer Academic Publishers, 1991.

Levinson, Stephen C. *Pragmatics.* Cambridge: Cambridge University Press, 1983.

——. "Putting Linguistics on a Proper Footing: Explorations in Goffman's Concepts of Participation." *Erving Goffman: Exploring the Interaction Order.* Ed. Paul Drew and Anthony Wootton. Boston: Northeastern University Press, 1988. 161–227.

Liddell and Scott. *An Intermediate Greek-English Lexicon.* New York: Oxford University Press, 1889.

Lindley, David. *Lyric.* New York: Methuen, 1985.

Lipking, Lawrence. *The Life of the Poet: Beginning and Ending Poetic Careers.* Chicago: University of Chicago Press, 1981.

Lockemann, Fritz. "Gedanken über das lyrische Du." *Volk Sprache Dichtung: Festschrift für Kurt Wagner.* Ed. Karl Bischoff and Lutz Röhrich. Giessen: Schmitz, 1960. 79–106.

Lyons, John. *Semantics.* 2 vols. Cambridge: Cambridge University Press, 1977.

Machor, James L., ed. *Readers in History: Nineteenth-Century American Literature and the Contexts of Response.* Baltimore: Johns Hopkins University Press, 1993.

Macksey, Richard. "Keats and the Poetics of Extremity." *MLN* 99 (1984): 845–84.

Macovski, Michael Steven. *Dialogue and Literature: Apostrophe, Auditors, and the Collapse of Romantic Discourse.* New York: Oxford University Press, 1994.

Mandelstam, Osip. "O sobesednike." *Sobranie Sochinenii v trekh tomakh.* Ed. G. P. Struve and B. A. Filipoff. 2nd ed. Vol. 2. New York: Inter-Language Literary Associates, 1971. 233–40.

Marks, Herbert. "The Counter-intelligence of Robert Frost." *Yale Review* 71 (1982): 554–78.

Marotti, Arthur F. *Manuscript, Print, and the English Renaissance Lyric.* Ithaca: Cornell University Press, 1995.

Martin, Christopher. *Policy in Love: Lyric and Public in Ovid, Petrarch, and Shakespeare.* Pittsburgh: Duquesne University Press, 1994.

Martin, Robert K., ed. *The Continuing Presence of Walt Whitman: The Life after the Life.* Iowa City: University of Iowa Press, 1992.

Masel, Caroline. "The Tutelary *You*: A Reading of the Act of Address in Stevens, Yeats, and Eliot." *New Comparison* 9 (1990): 158–69.

Mason, Eudo C. *Rilke, Europe, and the English-Speaking World*. Cambridge: Cambridge University Press, 1961.

McCarthy, Thomas J. *Relationships of Sympathy: The Writer and the Reader in British Romanticism*. Nineteenth Century Series. Aldershot, Eng.: Scolar Press, 1997.

Mehlman, Jeffrey. "Orphée scripteur: Blanchot, Rilke, Derrida." *Poétique* 20 (1974): 458–82.

Merwin, W. S. "Epitaph." *A Mask for Janus*. 1952. Reprinted in *The First Four Books of Poems*. New York: Atheneum, 1975. 35.

Mill, John Stuart. "What Is Poetry?" 1833. *Essays on Poetry by John Stuart Mill*. Ed. F. Parvin Sharpless. Columbia: University of South Carolina Press, 1976. 3–22.

Miller, Cristanne. *Emily Dickinson: A Poet's Grammar*. Cambridge: Harvard University Press, 1987.

Mills-Courts, Karen. *Poetry as Epitaph: Representation and Poetic Language*. Baton Rouge: Louisiana State University Press, 1990.

Milton, John. *The Works of John Milton*. Ed. Frank Allen Patterson et al. Vol. 1. New York: Columbia University Press, 1931.

Mörike, Eduard. "Denk' es, o Seele!" *Werke in drei Bänden*. Ed. Gisela Spiekerkötter. Zurich: Stauffacher, 1965. 1: 272.

Morse, Benjamin. "Rainer Maria Rilke und Martin Buber." *Alles Lebendige meinet den Menschen: Gedenkbuch für Max Niehans*. Ed. Irmgard Buck and Georg K. Schauer. Bern: Francke, 1972. 102–28.

Müller, Wolfgang. *Rainer Maria Rilkes "Neue Gedichte": Vielfältigkeit eines Gedichttypus*. Meisenheim am Glan: Hain, 1971.

Nagy, Gregory. "Sêma and Nóēsis: The Hero's Tomb and the 'Reading' of Symbols in Homer and Hesiod." *Greek Mythology and Poetics*. Ithaca: Cornell University Press, 1990. 202–22.

Nathanson, Tenney. *Whitman's Presence: Body, Voice, and Writing in Leaves of Grass*. New York: New York University Press, 1992.

Nemoianu, Virgil. "Literary History: Some Roads Not (Yet) Taken." *MLQ* 54.1 (1993): 31–40.

Novalis [Friedrich von Hardenberg]. *Werke in einem Band*. Munich: Hanser, 1981.

Nussbaum, Martha C. *Love's Knowledge: Essays on Philosophy and Literature*. New York: Oxford University Press, 1990.

Nystrand, Martin. *The Structure of Written Communication: Studies in Reciprocity between Writers and Readers*. Orlando: Academic Press, 1987.

Ong, Walter J. "*Maranatha*: Death and Life in the Text of the Book." *Interfaces of the Word*. Ithaca: Cornell University Press, 1977. 230–71.

——. *Orality and Literacy: The Technologizing of the Word*. London: Routledge, 1982.

Oppert, Kurt. "Das Dinggedicht." *Deutsche Vierteljahrsschrift für Literaturwissenschaft und Geistesgeschichte* 4 (1926): 747–83.

Ovid. *Metamorphosen*. Ed. Moritz Haupt and Otto Korn. 2 vols. Dublin: Weidmann, 1966.

Owen, Stephen. *Mi-Lou: Poetry and the Labyrinth of Desire*. Cambridge: Harvard University Press, 1989.

——. *Remembrances: The Experience of the Past in Classical Chinese Literature.* Cambridge: Harvard University Press, 1986.

Paz, Octavio. "The Few and the Many." Trans. Helen Lane. *The Other Voice: Essays on Modern Poetry.* San Diego: Harcourt, 1990. 77–98.

Phelan, Anthony. *Rilke: Neue Gedichte.* London: Grant & Cutler, 1992.

Plath, Sylvia. "You're." *Ariel.* 1965. New York: Harper, 1999. 60.

Plato. "Phaedrus." *Platonis Opera.* Ed. John Burnet. Vol. 2. Oxford: Clarendon-Oxford University Press, 1901. 227–79.

Poulet, Georges. *La conscience critique.* Paris: Corti, 1971.

Preminger, Alex, et al., eds. *The New Princeton Encyclopedia of Poetry and Poetics.* Princeton: Princeton University Press, 1993.

Quinn, Kenneth. *Catullus: An Interpretation.* New York: Harper, 1973.

Quirk, Randolph, et al. *A Comprehensive Grammar of the English Language.* London: Longman, 1985.

Rader, Ralph. "The Dramatic Monologue and Related Forms." *Critical Inquiry* 3 (1976): 131–51.

Railton, Stephen. " 'As If I Were with You': The Performance of Whitman's Poetry." *The Cambridge Companion to Walt Whitman.* Ed. Ezra Greenspan. New York: Cambridge University Press, 1995. 7–26.

Ricoeur, Paul. "What Is a Text? Explanation and Interpretation." *Mythic-Symbolic Language and Philosophical Anthropology.* Ed. David M. Rasmussen. The Hague: Martinus Nijhoff, 1971. 135–50.

Riffaterre, Michael. "Prosopopeia." *Yale French Studies* 69 (1989): 107–23.

Rilke, Rainer Maria. *Briefe.* Ed. Karl Altheim. 2 vols. Frankfurt: Insel, 1950.

——. *Briefe an Gräfin Sizzo.* Ed. Ingeborg Schnack. Frankfurt: Insel, 1977.

——. *Kommentierte Ausgabe in vier Bänden.* Ed. Manfred Engel, Ulrich Fülleborn, Horst Nalewski, and August Stahl. Frankfurt: Insel, 1996. Cited as *KA.*

——. *New Poems: A Revised Bilingual Edition,* trans. Edward Snow. San Francisco: North Point-Farrar, 2001.

——. *New Poems [1907],* trans. Edward Snow. San Francisco: North Point, 1984.

——. *New Poems: The Other Part [1908],* trans. Edward Snow. San Francisco: North Point, 1987.

——. *Sämtliche Werke in sechs Bänden,* ed. Ernst Zinn. Frankfurt: Insel, 1955–66. Cited as *SW.*

——. *Uncollected Poems,* trans. Edward Snow. New York: North Point-Farrar, 1996.

Rilke, Rainer Maria, and Lou Andreas-Salomé. *Rainer Maria Rilke–Lou Andreas-Salomé Briefwechsel.* Ed. Ernst Pfeiffer. Frankfurt: Insel, 1989.

Riquelme, John Paul. *Harmony of Dissonances: T. S. Eliot, Romanticism, and Imagination.* Baltimore: Johns Hopkins University Press, 1991.

Rosenthal, Olivia. "Présences du lecteur dans la poésie lyrique du XVIe siècle." *Poétique* 105 (1996): 71–85.

Ryan, Judith. "Monologische Lyrik: Paul Celans Antwort auf Gottfried Benn." *Basis* 2 (1971): 260–82.

——. *Rilke, Modernism, and Poetic Tradition.* Cambridge: Cambridge University Press, 1999.

Ryan, Lawrence. "*Neue Gedichte*—New Poems." *A Companion to the Works of Rainer Maria Rilke.* Ed. Erika A. Metzger and Michael M. Metzger. Rochester, N.Y.: Camden House-Boydell, 2001. 128–53.

Scarry, Elaine. *On Beauty and Being Just.* Princeton: Princeton University Press, 1999.

Schaeffer, Jean-Marie. *Qu'est-ce qu'un genre littéraire?* Paris: Seuil, 1989.

Schindler, Walter. *Voice and Crisis: Invocation in Milton's Poetry.* Hamden, Conn.: Archon, 1984.

Schlaffer, Heinz. "Die Aneignung von Gedichten." *Poetica* 27 (1995): 1–2, 38–57.

Schmitz-Emans, Monika. *Schrift und Abwesenheit: Historische Paradigmen zu einer Poetik der Entzifferung und des Schreibens.* Munich: Fink, 1995.

——. "Überleben im Text? Zu einem Grundmotiv literarischen Schreibens und einigen Formen seiner Reflexion im poetischen Medium." *Colloquia Germanica* 26.2 (1993): 135–61.

Schnack, Ingeborg. *Rainer Maria Rilke: Chronik seines Lebens und seines Werkes.* 2 vols. Frankfurt: Insel, 1975.

Scodel, Joshua. *The English Poetic Epitaph: Commemoration and Conflict from Jonson to Wordsworth.* Ithaca: Cornell University Press, 1991.

Segal, Charles. *Orpheus: The Myth of the Poet.* Baltimore: Johns Hopkins University Press, 1989.

Segebrecht, Wulf. " 'Steh, Leser, still!' Prolegomena zu einer situationsbezogenen Poetik der Lyrik, entwickelt am Beispiel von poetischen Grabschriften und Grabschriftenvorschlägen in Leichencarmina des 17. und 18. Jahrhunderts." *Deutsche Vierteljahrsschrift für Literaturwissenschaft und Geistesgeschichte* 52 (1978): 430–68.

Sell, Roger D. *Literature as Communication.* Amsterdam: Benjamins, 2000.

Shakespeare, William. *Shakespeare's Sonnets.* Ed. Stephen Booth. New Haven: Yale University Press, 1977.

Shapiro, Marianne, and Michael Shapiro. "Dialogism and the Addressee in Lyric Poetry." *University of Toronto Quarterly* 61 (1992): 392–413.

Smith, Barbara Herrnstein. *On the Margins of Discourse: The Relation of Literature to Language.* Chicago: University of Chicago Press, 1978.

——. *Poetic Closure: A Study of How Poems End.* Chicago: University of Chicago Press, 1968.

Sorg, Bernhard. *Das lyrische Ich.* Tübingen: Niemeyer, 1984.

Sperber, Dan, and Deirdre Wilson. *Relevance: Communication and Cognition.* Cambridge: Harvard University Press, 1986.

Spitzer, Leo. "The Addresses to the Reader in the *Commedia.*" *Leo Spitzer: Representative Essays.* Ed. Herbert Lindenberger, Alban K. Forcione, and Madeline Sutherland. Stanford: Stanford University Press, 1988. 178–203.

——. "American Advertising Explained as Popular Art." *Leo Spitzer: Representative Essays.* Ed. Herbert Lindenberger, Alban K. Forcione, and Madeline Sutherland. Stanford: Stanford University Press, 1988. 327–56.

Steiner, George. " 'Critic' / 'Reader.' " *George Steiner: A Reader.* New York: Oxford University Press, 1984. 67–98.

——. *Real Presences.* Chicago: University of Chicago Press, 1989.

Stevens, Wallace. *Wallace Stevens: Collected Works.* Ed. Frank Kermode and Joan Richardson. New York: Library of America, 1997.

Stewart, Susan. *Poetry and the Fate of the Senses.* Chicago: University of Chicago Press, 2002.

Svenbro, Jesper. *Phrasikleia: An Anthropology of Reading in Ancient Greece.* Trans. Janet Lloyd. Ithaca: Cornell University Press, 1993.

Tedlock, Dennis. *The Spoken Word and the Work of Interpretation.* Philadelphia: University of Pennsylvania Press, 1983.

Tennyson, Alfred. *The Poems of Tennyson.* Ed. Christopher Ricks. London: Longmans, 1969.

Theobaldy, Jürgen. "Irgend etwas." *Zweiter Klasse: Gedichte.* Berlin: Rotbuch, 1976. 44.

Thomas, Rosalind. *Literacy and Orality in Ancient Greece.* Cambridge: Cambridge University Press, 1992.

Trotter, David. *The Making of the Reader.* New York: St. Martin's, 1984.

Tucker, Herbert F. "Dramatic Monologue and the Overhearing of Lyric." Hošek and Parker 226–43.

Vendler, Helen. *The Given and the Made: Strategies of Poetic Redefinition.* Cambridge: Harvard University Press, 1995.

Wallmann, Jürgen P. "'Ein alter Tibetteppich' (Die Interpretation)." *Neue Deutsche Hefte* 102 (1964): 63–69.

Waters, William. "Answerable Aesthetics: Reading 'You' in Rilke." *Comparative Literature* 48 (1996): 128–49.

——. "Poetic Address and Intimate Reading: The Offered Hand." *Literary Imagination* 2 (2000): 188–220.

Wheeler, Lesley. *The Poetics of Enclosure: American Women Poets from Dickinson to Dove.* Knoxville: University of Tennessee Press, 2002.

Whitman, Walt. *Leaves of Grass: A Textual Variorum of the Printed Poems.* Ed. Sculley Bradley et al. 3 vols. New York: New York University Press, 1980.

——. *Selected Poems, 1855–1892.* Ed. Gary Schmidgall. New York: St. Martin's Press, 1999.

Widdowson, H. G. *Practical Stylistics: An Approach to Poetry.* Oxford: Oxford University Press, 1992.

——. *Stylistics and the Teaching of Literature.* London: Longman, 1975.

Williams, Gordon, ed. *Carmina Liber 3: The Third Book of Horace's "Odes."* Oxford: Clarendon-Oxford University Press, 1969.

Williams, William Carlos. *Collected Poems.* Ed. A. Walton Litz and Christopher Mac-Gowan. 2 vols. Vol. 1, *1901–1939.* New York: New Directions, 1986.

Wolff, Joachim. *Rilkes Grabschrift.* Heidelberg: Stiehm, 1983.

Wolfson, Susan J. *The Questioning Presence: Wordsworth, Keats, and the Interrogative Mode in Romantic Poetry.* Ithaca: Cornell University Press, 1986.

Woodman, Tony. "*Exegi monumentum*: Horace, *Odes* 3.30." *Quality and Pleasure in Latin Poetry.* Ed. Tony Woodman and David West. Cambridge: Cambridge University Press, 1974. 115–28.

Woodman, Tony, and Jonathan Powell, eds. *Author and Audience in Latin Literature.* Cambridge: Cambridge University Press, 1992.

York, R. A. *The Poem as Utterance.* New York: Methuen, 1986.

Zimmermann, Éléonore M. "Un héritage romantique dévoyé: l'apostrophe dans 'Le lac,' 'Tristesse d'Olympio' et 'La Chevelure.' *French Forum* 13 (1988): 205–15.

Zumthor, Paul. *La lettre et la voix: de la "littérature" médiévale.* Paris: Seuil, 1987.

——. *La poésie et la voix dans la civilisation médiévale.* Paris: Seuil, 1987.

——. "Spoken Language and Oral Poetry in the Middle Ages." *Style* 19 (1985): 191–98.

——. "The Text and the Voice." *New Literary History* 16 (1984–85): 67–92.

Index